# Praise for the "Kids Love" Gui

*On-Air Personality Comments (Television Interviews)*

*"The great thing about these books is that your whole family actually lives these adventures"* – **(WKRC-TV**, Cincinnati)

*"Very helpful to lots of families when the kids say, I'm bored...and I don't want to go to same places again!"* – **(WISH-TV**, Indianapolis)

*"Dividing the state into many sections, the book has something for everyone...everywhere."* – **(WLVT-TV**, Pennsylvania)

*"These authors know first-hand that it's important to find hands-on activities that engage your children..."* **(WBNS-TV**, Columbus)

*"You spent more than 1000 hours doing this research for us, that's really great – we just have to pick up the book and it's done..."*
**(WTVR-TV**, Richmond)

*"A family that's a great source for travel ideas..."*
**(WBRA-TV**, Roanoke)

*"What a great idea...this book needed to be done a long time ago!"*
**(WKYT-TV**, Lexington)

*"A fabulous idea...places to travel that your kids will enjoy"*
**(WOOD-TV**, Grand Rapids)

*"The Zavatskys call it a dream come true, running their own business while keeping the family together. Their goal, encourage other parents to create special family travel memories."* - **(WLVT-TV,** Pennsylvania)

*"It's a wonderful book, and as someone who has been to a lot of these places...you hit it right on the money!"* – **(WKRC-TV**, Cincinnati)

# Praise for the "Kids Love" Guidebook travel series
*Customer Comments (actual letters on file)*

*"I wanted to tell you how helpful all your books have been to my family of 6. I rarely find books that cater to families with kids. I have your Indiana, Ohio, Kentucky, Michigan, and Pennsylvania books. I don't want to miss any of the new books that come out. Keep up the great ideas. The books are fantastic. I have shown them to tons of my friends. They love them, too."* – H.M.

*"I bought the Ohio and Indiana books yesterday and what a blessing these are for us!!! We love taking our grandsons on Grammie & Papaw trips thru the year and these books are making it soooo much easier to plan. The info is complete and full of ideas. Even the layout of the book is easy to follow...I just wanted to thank you for all your work in developing these books for us..."* – G.K

*"I have purchased your book. My grandchildren and I have gone to many of the places listed in your book. They mark them off as we visit them. We are looking forward to seeing many more. It is their favorite thing to look at book when they come over and find new places to explore. Thank you for publishing this book!"* - B.A.

*"At a retail price of under $15.00, any of the books would be well worth buying even for a one-time only vacation trip. Until now, when the opportunity arose for a day or weekend trip with the kids I was often at a loss to pick a destination that I could be sure was convenient, educational, child-friendly, and above all, fun. Now I have a new problem: How in the world will we ever be able to see and do all the great ideas listed in this book? I'd better get started planning our next trip right away. At least I won't have to worry about where we're going or what to do when we get there!"* – VA Homeschool Newsletter

*"My family and I used this book this summer to explore Ohio! We lived here nearly our entire life and yet over half the book we never knew existed. These people really know what kids love! Highly recommended for all parents, grandparents, etc."* – Barnes and Noble website reviewer

# A Family Travel Guide to Exploring "Kid-Tested" Places in Michigan...Year Round!

George & Michele Zavatsky

# Dedicated to the Families
# of Michigan

For the latest major updates corresponding to the pages in this book visit our website:

## www.KidsLoveTravel.com

❑ *REMEMBER: Museum exhibits change frequently. Check the site's website before you visit to note any changes. Also, HOURS and ADMISSIONS are subject to change at the owner's discretion. If you are tight on time or money, check the attraction's website or call before you visit.*

❑ *INTERNET PRECAUTION: All websites mentioned in KIDS LOVE MICHIGAN have been checked for appropriate content. However, due to the fast-changing nature of the Internet, we strongly urge parents to preview any recommended sites and to always supervise their children when on-line.*

ISBN-13: 978-0-9726854-8-1
ISBN-10: 0-9726854-8-0

KIDS ♥ MICHIGAN ™ Kids Love Publications

# TABLE OF CONTENTS

# State Map
## (With Major Routes and Cities Marked)

# Chapter Area Map

# CITY INDEX (Listed by City & Area)

# CITY INDEX (Listed by City & Area)

Cities appearing in *italics* occur
only in the Seasonal Chapter

# Acknowledgements

We are most thankful to be blessed with our parents, Barbara (Darrall) Callahan & George and Catherine Zavatsky who help us every way they can – researching, proofing and babysitting. More importantly, they are great sounding boards and offer unconditional support. So many places around Michigan remind us of family vacations years ago…

We also want to express our thanks to the many Convention & Visitor Bureaus' staff for providing the attention to detail that helps to complete a project. We felt very welcome during our travels in Michigan and would be proud to call it home!

Our own kids, Jenny and Daniel, were delightful and fun children during our trips across the state. What a joy it is to be their parents…we couldn't do it without them as our "kid-testers"!

We both sincerely thank each other – our partnership has created an even greater business/personal "marriage" with lots of exciting moments, laughs, and new adventures in life woven throughout. Above all, we praise the Lord for His so many blessings through the last few years.

We think Michigan is a wonderful, friendly area of the country with more activities than you could imagine. Our sincere wish is that this book will help everyone "fall in love" with Michigan.

In a Hundred Years…
It will not matter, The size of my bank account…
The kind of house that I lived in, the kind of car that I drove…
But what will matter is…
That the world may be different
Because I was important in the life of a child.

-   *author unknown*

# HOW TO USE THIS BOOK

If you are excited about discovering Michigan, this is the book for you and your family! We've spent over a thousand hours doing all the scouting, collecting and compiling (*and most often visiting!*) so that you could spend less time searching and more time having fun.

*Here are a few hints to make your adventures run smoothly:*

❑ Consider the **child's age** before deciding to take a visit.

❑ Know **directions** and parking. Call ahead (or visit the company's website) if you have questions *and* bring this book. Also, don't forget your camera! *(please honor rules regarding use).*

❑ **Estimate the duration** of the trip. Bring small surprises (favorite juice boxes) travel books, and toys.

❑ Call ahead for **reservations** or details, if necessary.

❑ Most listings are **closed major holidays** unless noted.

❑ Make a **family "treasure chest"**. Decorate a big box or use an old popcorn tin. Store memorabilia from a fun outing, journals, pictures, brochures and souvenirs. Once a year, look through the "treasure chest" and reminisce. "Kids Love Travel Memories!" is an excellent travel journal & scrapbook that your family can create. *(See the order form in back of this book).*

❑ Plan **picnics** along the way. Many state history sites and state parks are scattered throughout Michigan. Allow time for a rural /scenic route to take advantage of these free picnic facilities.

❑ Some activities, especially tours, require **groups** of 10 or more. To participate, you may either ask to be part of another tour group or get a group together yourself (neighbors, friends, organizations). If you arrange a group outing, most places offer discounts.

❑ For the latest **updates** corresponding to the pages in this book, visit our website: **www.KidsLoveTravel.com.**

❑ Each chapter represents an area of the state. Each listing is further identified by city, zip code, and place/event name. Our popular **Activity Index** in the back of the book **lists places by Activity Heading** (i.e. State History, Tours, Outdoors, Museums, etc.).

# MISSION STATEMENT

At first glance, you may think that this is a book that just lists hundreds of places to travel. While it is true that we've invested thousands of hours of exhaustive research (*and drove over 3000 miles in Michigan*) to prepare this travel resource...just listing places to travel is <u>not</u> the mission statement of these projects.

As children, Michele and I were able to travel extensively throughout the United States. We consider these family times some of the greatest memories we cherish today. We, quite frankly, felt that most children had this opportunity to travel with their family as we did. However, as we became adults and started our own family, we found that this wasn't necessarily the case. We continually heard friends express several concerns when deciding how to spend "quality" and "quantity" family time. 1) What to do? 2) Where to do it? 3) How much will it cost? 4) How do I know that my kids will enjoy it?

Interestingly enough, as we compare our experiences with our families when we were kids, many of our fondest memories were not made at an expensive attraction, but rather when it was least expected.

It is our belief and mission statement that if you as a family will study and <u>use</u> the contained information <u>to create family memories,</u> these memories will grow a stronger, tighter family. Our ultimate mission statement is, that your children will develop a love and a passion for quality family experiences that they can pass to another generation of family travelers.

We thank you for purchasing this book, and we hope to see you on the road (*and hear your travel stories!*) God bless your journeys and happy exploring!

*George, Michele, Jenny and Daniel*

# General State Agency & Recreation Information

Call *(or visit the websites)* for the services of interest. Request to be added to their mailing lists.

- ❑ DNR Parks & Recreation - (517) 373-9900 or (800) 44-PARKS or **www.michigan.gov/dnr**
- ❑ Fisheries Division - (517) 373-1280
- ❑ Fishing Hotline - (800) 275-3474
- ❑ Skiing, **www.ultimateskiguide.com**
- ❑ Snowmobiling, Skiing and Cross-Country Skiing - (888) 78-GREAT, **www.michigan.org**
- ❑ Michigan Festivals and Events Association - **www.mfea.org**.
- ❑ Michigan Association of Recreational Vehicles and Campgrounds, MARVAC - (800) 422-6478, **www.MARVAC.org**
- ❑ Michigan Association of Private Campground Owners (MAPCO) - **www.michcampgrounds.com**
- ❑ Oakland County Parks - (248) 858-0306
- ❑ West Michigan Tourist Association - Grand Rapids (800) 442-2084 or **www.wmta.org**
- ❑ Travel Michigan - (888) 784-7328 or **http://travel.michigan.org**
- ❑ MSU Sports (517) 355-1610, **www.msuspartans.com**
- ❑ U of M Sports (734) 647-2583 or **www.umich.edu**
- ❑ **CE** - Blue Water Area – Port Huron – along Rte. 25 on the St. Clair River. CVB info: **www.bluewater.org** or (800) 852-4242.
- ❑ **CE** - Genessee County Parks (810) 736-7100 or (800) 648-PARK.
- ❑ **CE** - Saginaw County Parks (989) 790-5280 or **www.saginawcounty.com/parks/**
- ❑ **CW** - Muskegon County Parks (231) 744-3580
- ❑ **CW** - Newaygo County Parks, (269) 689-7383.
- ❑ **NE** - Mackinaw Area Visitors Bureau (800) 666-0160 or **www.mackinawcity.com**
- ❑ **SE** - Detroit CVB (800) Detroit or **www.visitdetroit.com**
- ❑ **SE** - Greater Lansing CVB (888) 2-LANSING or **www.lansing.org**
- ❑ **SE** - Huron-Clinton Metroparks (800) 47-PARKS, **www.metroparks.com**
- ❑ **SE** - Ingham County Parks (888) 517-1086
- ❑ **SE** - Washtenaw County Parks, (734) 426-8211.
- ❑ **SW** - Kalamazoo Area county Parks (269) 383-8776
- ❑ **SW** - St. Joseph County Parks (269) 467-5519.

*Check out these businesses / services in your area for tour ideas:*

## AIRPORTS

All children love to visit the airport! Why not take a tour and understand all the jobs it takes to run an airport? Tour the terminal, baggage claim, gates and security / currency exchange. Maybe you'll even get to board a plane.

## ANIMAL SHELTERS

Great for the would-be pet owner. Not only will you see many cats and dogs available for adoption, but a guide will show you the clinic and explain the needs of a pet. Be prepared to have the children "fall in love" with one of the animals while they are there!

## BANKS

Take a "behind the scenes" look at automated teller machines, bank vaults and drive-thru window chutes. You may want to take this tour and then open a savings account for your child.

## CITY HALLS

Halls of Fame, City Council Chambers & Meeting Room, Mayor's Office and famous statues.

## ELECTRIC COMPANY / POWER PLANTS

Modern science has created many ways to generate electricity today, but what really goes on with the "flip of a switch". Because coal can be dirty, wear old, comfortable clothes. Coal furnaces heat water, which produces steam, that propels turbines, that drives generators, that make electricity.

## FIRE STATIONS

Many Open Houses in October, Fire Prevention Month. Take a look into the life of the firefighters servicing your area and try on their gear. See where they hang out, sleep and eat. Hop aboard a real-life fire engine truck and learn fire safety too.

## HOSPITALS

Some Children's Hospitals offer pre-surgery and general tours.

## NEWSPAPERS

You'll be amazed at all the new technology. See monster printers and robotics. See samples in the layout department and maybe try to put together your own page. After seeing a newspaper made, most companies give you a free copy (dated that day) as your souvenir. National Newspaper Week is in October.

# RESTAURANTS

### PIZZA HUT & PAPA JOHN'S

❑  Participating locations

Telephone the store manager. Best days are Monday, Tuesday and Wednesday mid-afternoon. Minimum of 10 people. Small charge per person. All children love pizza – especially when they can create their own! As the children tour the kitchen, they learn how to make a pizza, bake it, and then eat it. The admission charge generally includes lots of creatively made pizzas, beverage and coloring book.

### KRISPY KREME DONUTS

❑  Participating locations

Get an "inside look" and learn the techniques that make these donuts some of our favorites! Watch the dough being made in "giant" mixers, being formed into donuts and taking a "trip" through the fryer. Seeing them being iced and topped with colorful sprinkles is always a favorite with the kids. Contact your local store manager. They prefer Monday or Tuesday. Free.

## SUPERMARKETS

Kids are fascinated to go behind the scenes of the same store where Mom and Dad shop. Usually you will see them grind meat, walk into large freezer rooms, watch cakes and bread bake and receive free samples along the way. Maybe you'll even get to pet a live lobster!

## TV / RADIO STATIONS

Studios, newsrooms, Fox kids clubs. Why do weathermen never wear blue clothes on TV? What makes a "DJ's" voice sound so deep and smooth?

## WATER TREATMENT PLANTS

A giant science experiment! You can watch seven stages of water treatment. The favorite is usually the wall of bright buttons flashing as workers monitor the different processes.

## U.S. MAIN POST OFFICES

Did you know Ben Franklin was the first Postmaster General (over 200 years ago)? Most interesting is the high-speed automated mail processing equipment. Learn how to address envelopes so they will be sent quicker (there are secrets). To make your tour more interesting, have your children write a letter to themselves and address it with colorful markers. Mail it earlier that day and they will stay interested trying to locate their letter in all the high-speed machinery.

# Chapter 1
## *Central East Area*

# Our Favorites...

\* Crossroads Village & Huckleberry RR - Flint

\* Frankenmuth Shop Tours - Frankenmuth

\* H.H. Dow Historical Museum - Midland

\* Edison Depot Museum - Port Huron

\* Huron Lightship - Port Huron

*A Lighthouse Ship? Hear the great stories!*

# SANILAC PETROGLYPHS HISTORIC STATE PARK

(M-53 to Bay City - Forestville Road Exit - East to Germania Road South), **Bad Axe** 48413

❑   Phone: (517) 373-3559, **Web: www.michigan.gov/hal**
❑   Hours: Wednesday-Sunday 11:30am-4:30pm (early June - late August).
❑   Admission: FREE.
❑   Tours: Guided tours (45 minutes)

Take a 1-mile, self-guided walking trail through the forest along the Cass River. Stop at the 19th Century logging camp or 100+ year old white pine tree. The main reason you probably came though is the petroglyphs. In the late 1800's, forest fires revealed chiseled sandstone etchings by Native Americans of an ancient woodland people dating back 300 - 1000 years ago. Look for figures like a hunter / archer or animals and birds.

# BAY CITY STATE RECREATION AREA

3582 State Park Drive (I-75 exit 168 east to Euclid Avenue)

**Bay City** 48706

❑   Phone: (989) 684-3020
      **Web: www.michigandnr.com/parksandtrails/parklist.asp**
❑   Admission: $4.00 per vehicle

Lots of camping (tent and cabins) plus a swimming beach free from sharp zebra mussels found in the area, make this an attraction. Also find boating, fishing, trails, winter sports. Another highlight is the Saginaw Bay Visitors Center which focuses on the importance of wetlands to the bay. It's open Tuesday - Sunday, Noon - 5:00pm. A great spot for birding, you'll also learn from the 15 minute video presentation, boardwalks and observation trails.

# BAY COUNTY HISTORICAL MUSEUM

**Bay City** - *321 Washington Avenue (I-75, take exit 162A to Downtown), 48708. Web: www.bchsmuseum.org. Phone: (989) 893-5733. Hours: Monday-Friday 10:00am-5:00pm, Saturday & Sunday Noon-4:00pm. Miscellaneous: Every Saturday at 2:00pm,* *a trolley leaves from the Museum for a 75-minute tour.* Visitors will experience maritime history from the geological formation of the Great Lakes and the Saginaw River to the completion of the area's first lighthouse. Exhibits focus on the shipbuilding and lumbering industries. Visitors will enter a re-creation of the tug wheelhouse, experience what the docks were like, and view an interactive shipwreck exhibit. A series of seven period rooms compares and contrasts life in the 1880s to the early 1930s. Visitors will see recreated rooms of the era and also see how consumerism helped to develop the "modern" home. You can also learn about Native Americans and the fur trade and early Bay County settlers. Many industries such as agriculture, lumbering and manufacturing will highlight the recent history section of the gallery.

### DELTA COLLEGE PLANETARIUM & LEARNING CENTER

**Bay City** - *100 Center Avenue, 48708. Phone: (989) 667-2260* **Web:** *www.delta.edu/planet/. Hours: Call or visit website for schedule. Admission: $3.00-$3.50 per person.* A wonderful place to teach children the fun of star-gazing. The planetarium is state-of-the-art and the rooftop observatory seats over 100 people. The audience actually gets to choose what to see in the solar system. Look for programs about sky pirates or cowboys or Garfield.

## WILDERNESS TRAILS ANIMAL PARK
### 11721 Gera Road - M-83 (I-75 to Birch Run Exit)
**Birch Run 48415**

❑   Phone: (989) 624-6177
❑   Hours: Monday-Saturday 10:00am-6:00pm, Sunday 11:00am-5:00pm (summer). Open until 5:00pm (May, September, October).
❑   Admission: $8.00 adult, $5.00 senior (60+), $5.00 child (3-12).
❑   Miscellaneous: Picnic area. Playground.

One of the most popular privately owned animal exhibits in the state, Wilderness Trails offers over 50 acres and 60 different types of animals. See lions, a Siberian tiger and bear, bison, elk, black bears, and deer just to name a few. Two gravel walking trails wind through park or a horse drawn covered wagon is available for a small charge. Kids can have fun touching and feeding the baby animals in the petting area.

## JUNCTION VALLEY RAILROAD

7065 Dixie Highway (I-75, exit 144 south - Just before you turn to head into Frankenmuth), **Bridgeport** 48722

❑ Phone: (989) 777-3480, **Web: www.jvrailroad.com**

❑ Hours: Monday-Saturday 10:00am-6:00pm, Sunday 1:00-6:00pm. (Memorial Day Weekend-Labor Day Weekend). Weekends Only (September & October & Special events).

❑ Admission: $4.50-$5.50 per person (age 2+).

❑ Miscellaneous: Picnic area and playground. You'll pull into a business parking lot, but the ride into the woods is cute, especially over the trestles.

See and ride the world's largest ¼ scale railroad. Voyage on rides through the woods, past miniature buildings, through a 100 foot long tunnel, and over 865 feet of trestles (one has diamonds underneath). Look for the roundhouse with a turntable and the 5-track switch yard.

## SLEEPER STATE PARK

**Caseville** - *6573 State Park Road (5 miles east of town on SR 25), 48725. Web: www.michigandnr.com/parksandtrails/parklist.asp. Phone: (989) 856-4411. Admission: $6.00-$8.00 per vehicle.* Hundreds of acres of woods and beachfront with camping make this a fun park. Also featured are hiking trails, winter sports, mini-cabins, fishing, & boating.

## DURAND UNION STATION (MICHIGAN RAILROAD HISTORY MUSEUM)

**Durand** - *200 Railroad Street, 48429. Phone: (989) 288-3561. Web: http://durandstation.org/. Hours: Tuesday-Sunday 1:00 - 5:00pm.* Visitors stop at the Durand Depot to study area history or maybe catch an Amtrak train roundtrip from Chesaning-to-Owosso. Learn about the Great Wallace Brothers Circus Wreck of 1903 or the Knights Templar Wreck of 1923. Do you know which presidents have made "whistle stops" here?

## *SILVER RIDGE SKI RESORT*

**Farwell** - *1001 Mott Mountain (off Old US 10), 48622. Phone: (989) 588-7220.* 9 runs, ski lessons, rentals, and night skiing. Restaurant overlooks the slopes.

# *FLINT CULTURAL CENTER*

### 1221 East Kearsley Street (I-475, exit 8A)

### Flint 48503

❑ Phone: (810) 237-7330 or (888) 8CENTER, **www.fcccorp.org**

❑ Hours: Tuesday-Friday 10:00am-5:00pm, Saturday & Sunday Noon-5:00pm. Open Mondays in July & August (Closed Holidays).

❑ Admission: $5.00 adult, $4.00 senior, $3.00 child (4-11).

❑ Miscellaneous: Museum Store. Café.

The SLOAN MUSEUM (810-237-3450 or **www.sloanmuseum.org**) highlights include: "FLINT AND THE AMERICAN DREAM" - 20<sup>th</sup> Century Flint beginning with the birth of General Motors, United Auto Workers, and then neon colorful advertising. Also 1950's - 70's typical household furnishings. Check out the 1950's station wagon (a Buick Super) that was available before today's vans and sport utility vehicles. "HOMETOWN GALLERY" - the area's early history with displays on fur trading, pioneer life, lumbering, and carriage making. Look for the 10,000 year old mastodon and Woodland Indian wigwam. Weekend hands-on history activities. "SCIENCE DISCOVERY CENTER" - hands-on science, weekends only.

Also in the same complex (recommended for grade school and up):

❑ FLINT INSTITUTE OF ARTS - 1120 East Kearsley. (810) 234-1695. FREE.

❑ LONGWAY PLANETARIUM - 1310 East Kearsley. (810) 237-3400 or **www.longway.org**. Monday - Friday 9:00 am-4:00pm, Saturday & Sunday 1:00-4:30pm. Free displays. $4.00-5.00 for light & astronomy shows. 3D Digistar II projector in Sky Theater.

❑ SHOWCASE SERIES, (THE) - Whiting Auditorium. Broadway, dance, classic theater & holiday shows. **www.flintyouththeatre.com**

*For updates & travel games, visit:* **www.KidsLoveTravel.com**

## FLINT GENERALS HOCKEY

**Flint** - *3501 Lapeer Road (IMA Sports Arena), 48503. Phone: (810) 742-9422. Web: www.flintgenerals.com. Admission: General $8.00-13.00.* A UHL team plays mid-October thru March. Breakfast and post-game skates with players, occasionally. Seasonal characters and promos.

## FLINT SYMPHONY ORCHESTRA

**Flint** - *1244 East Kearsley Street (Whiting Auditorium), 48503. Phone: (810) 237-7333 or (888) 8CENTER. Web: www.thefim.com.* Professional orchestra performs family concerts and a free summer parks concert series.

## FLINT CHILDREN'S MUSEUM

1602 West 3$^{rd}$ Street, Kettering University Campus (I-75 exit 118 - Corunna Rd. east. Left on Ballenger Hwy., right on Sunset Drive, turns into 3$^{rd}$), **Flint** 48504

- ❑   Phone: (810) 767-5437, **Web: www.flintchildrensmuseum.org**
- ❑   Hours: Tuesday-Friday 10:00am-4:00pm, Saturday 10:00am-5:00pm. Closed major holidays.
- ❑   Admission: $4.00 general (age 1+).
- ❑   Miscellaneous: Recommended for ages 2-10. Gift shop.

Over 100 exhibits focused on science, technology, and the arts. Kids' favorites are the Crazy Mirrors and the Lego table. Be sure to check out the different theme rooms: Grocery Room, Transportation Room, Playhouse, News Room, and Health Room – x-rays, listen to heart, face masks and Stuffee.

## CROSSROADS VILLAGE & HUCKLEBERRY RAILROAD

6140 Bray Road (I-475, exit 13 - follow signs), **Flint** 48505

- ❑   Phone: (810) 736-7100 or (800) 648-PARK
  **Web: www.geneseecountyparks.org/crossroadsvillage.htm**
- ❑   Hours: Wednesday 10:00am-8:00pm. Thursday-Sunday & Holidays 10:00am-5:00pm (late-May to early September). Weekends in October and December for seasonal events.

Crossroads Village & Huckleberry Railroad (*cont.*)

❏    Admission: $10.00 adult, $9.00 senior (60+), $8.00 child (3-12) - Village. Village only tickets discounted $2.00-3.00. (add $1.00-$2.00 weekends)

❏    Miscellaneous: Mill Street Warehouse, Cross Roads Café, Concessions, Carousel, Venetian Swing, Ferris Wheel and Wagon Rides (pulled by ponies) - rides additional charge. Seasonal events keep the village open throughout the year - see Seasonal Chapter.

The 1860's era living village is a collection of 30 authentic buildings that were relocated here to form a village. Friendly, costumed villagers fill you in on the events of the day and answer questions. For example, the barber shop (still operational) staff will share their charges for a cut, shave or bath. We learned that they let a dental patient (yes, they were the town dentist then) take a swig of vanilla extract (full tilt variety!) before they extracted a tooth. The fellas at the cider and sawmill will remind you of characters from "Little House on the Prairie" as they demonstrate their craft. Be sure to buy a cup of cider there - all natural with no added sugar. You'll also meet the town blacksmith, printer (try your hand printing a souvenir off the "kissing" press), doctor, storekeeper at the General Store (with cute, old-fashioned novelties for sale), and toymaker (try your hand walking on stilts - we have a video and George did it!). Before you leave, take a relaxing slow ride on the Huckleberry Railroad. The original line went so slow that passengers claimed they could get off - pick huckleberries along the tracks (still growing plentifully today) and catch the caboose a few minutes later. Watch out for the playful train robber skit - (don't worry…even pre-schoolers won't be scared!).

GENESSEE BELLE: a paddle-wheel riverboat, offers scenic cruises on unspoiled Mott Lake. The Genesee Belle has an open-air upper deck for unobstructed sightseeing and the lower deck is climate-controlled in summer and fall. Although the Genesee Belle is a replica of the steamboats that traveled during the era of Mark Twain, it is very safe and especially designed for sightseeing and relaxation. 45 minute cruises on the lake.

## *GENESEE RECREATION AREA*

**Flint** - *(I-475 exit 13), 48506. Phone: (800) 648-7275. Web: www.geneseecountyparks.org. Admission per activity.* This area includes Stepping Stone Falls on Mott Lake on Branch Road which are lit with color evenings between Memorial Day and Labor Day. You can also find Mott's Children's Farm, camping, hiking, boating, fishing, beach swimming, bicycle trails, and winter sports. Hours vary by activity (mostly dawn to dusk). (Memorial Day-October).

## *FOR-MAR NATURE PRESERVE & ARBORETUM*

**Flint (Burton)** - *2142 North Genesee Road, 48509. Web: www.geneseecountyparks.org/formar.htm. Phone: (810) 789-8567 or (800) 648-7275 Hours: Wednesday-Sunday 8:00am-5:00pm. Trails 8:00am -Sunset. Special programs on Saturdays.* A 380 acre preserve with 7 miles of trails. Visitor Center with Gift Shop. Cross-country skiing in winter.

## *BAVARIAN BELLE RIVERBOAT TOURS*

**Frankenmuth** - *South Main Street (RiverPlace), 48734. Phone: (866) 808-BOAT. Web: www.bavarianbelle.com. Hours: Departures 11:00am until dusk (May - October). Admission: $7.50 adult, $3.00 child (3-12).* One hour sightseeing cruises narrated about the Cass River folklore and history. Open air canopied upper deck and enclosed lower salon (air-conditioned and heated). Snack bar and restrooms on board.

## *BRONNER'S CHRISTMAS WONDERLAND*

25 Christmas Lane (I-75, northbound to exit 136, southbound to exit 144 - follow signs off Main Street M-83), **Frankenmuth** 48734

- ❑ Phone: (989) 652-9931 or (800) ALL-YEAR **Web: www.bronners.com**
- ❑ Hours: Monday-Saturday 9:00am-5:30pm, Sunday Noon-5:30pm, Open Friday until 9:00 pm (January-May). Monday-Saturday 9:00am-9:00pm, Sunday Noon-7:00pm (June-December). Closed Winter holidays including Easter & Good Friday.
- ❑ Admission: FREE

Bronner's Christmas Wonderland *(cont.)*

❑   Miscellaneous: "Season's Eatings" snack area.

A visit to Michigan wouldn't be complete without seeing the "World's Largest Christmas Store" that hosts over 2,000,000 visitors each year! View nativity scenes, 260 decorated trees, and 200 styles of nutcrackers. As dusk approaches drive through "Christmas Lane" that sparkles with over 40,000+ lights. While you're there be sure to check out the "World of Bronners" (an 18 minute multi-image slide show) that highlights the design and production of their selection of trains. Visit "Bronner's Silent Night Memorial Chapel" - named after the famous song (the chapel was originally made in Austria). Kids seem to be most fascinated with the "It Feels Like Christmas" drive around the vast parking lot and the animated displays of seasonal bears, elves, and children playing around the upper perimeter of each theme room. Be sure to get at least one ornament to keep - but "oh" -  how to decide!

## FRANKENMUTH CHEESE HAUS

561 South Main Street

**Frankenmuth 48734**

❑   Phone: (989) 652-6727, **http://frankenmuthcheesehaus.com**
❑   Hours: Daily 9:30am-6:00pm. Open until 9:30pm (summer).
❑   Admission: FREE

Lots of tasting going on here! Ever tried "Chocolate" or "Strawberry" cheese? Not only will you sample some…you can also try cheese spreads (smooth, creamy and fresh tasting) or over 140 different kinds of cheese. Watch a video of the cheesemaking process, or if you time it right, actually see the ladies make it from scratch. They have giant photographs of each step of the process, so if the kids can't see it all they can still understand the process from the pictures. Yummy samples of cheese spreads in varieties from Garden Vegetable to Jalapeno! You will want some to take home (although this souvenir will soon be eaten with a box of crackers!)

# FRANKENMUTH HISTORICAL MUSEUM

613 South Main Street (I-75 to Frankenmuth Exit - Next to the
Visitor's Center, Fischer Hall), **Frankenmuth** 48734

❑   Phone: (989) 652-9701

**Web: http://frankenmuth.michigan.museum/museum.html**

❑   Hours: Monday-Thursday 10:30am-5:00pm, Friday 10:30am-
7:00pm, Saturday 10:00am-8:00pm, Sunday 11:00am-5:00pm.
(April-December). Shorter hours (January-March). Closed winter
holidays.

❑   Admission: $1.00-$1.50 per person.

❑   Miscellaneous: Museum Gift Shop with folk art and toy objects.

Exhibits depict the area's German ancestry and history from Indian
mission days to a town called "Michigan's Little Bavaria". Begin
with a scene from the immigrants' ship travel from Bavaria to the
Saginaw Valley. They designed this museum along the trend of
"hands-on" activities and there are a few interactive stations in
realistic settings.

# FRANKENMUTH WOOLEN MILL

570 South Main Street (I-75 to Frankenmuth Exit - Follow signs to
downtown), **Frankenmuth** 48734

❑   Phone: (989) 652-8121

**Web: www.frankenmuthwoolenmill.com**

❑   Hours: Daily 10:00am-9:00pm (Summer). Daily 10:00am-
6:00pm (Winter).

❑   Admission: FREE.

❑   Miscellaneous: Video of wool processing plays continuously
when workers aren't in, but the store is open.

We've all seen freshly shaven sheep and probably own wool
clothing. But how is it processed? Here's your unique chance to
see how it all happens. They began here in 1894 and the mill has
produced over 250,000 hand-made, wool-filled comforters since
then. See the mill in action where you can begin by looking
through a window of the wash basins (great viewing for smaller
children) where they clean wool brought in from farmers. Washed
fleece is then air dried (it gets really fluffy that way) and then put

through a "carding machine". The wool passes through wire-spiked rollers until it is untangled and meshed together to form a sheet. Comforters are assembled according to Bavarian tradition (hand-tied). Throughout the tour, your guide will let you handle samples of wool at different stages of the process. The kids will find "raw" wool disgusting, but love the way that it turns out. This "hands-on" activity keeps their interest throughout the demonstration.

## GRANDPA TINY'S FARM

7775 Weiss Street (across from Bronners), **Frankenmuth** 48734

- ❑ Phone: (989) 652-KIDS (5437)
  **Web: www.grandpatinysfarm.com**
- ❑ Hours: Monday-Saturday 10:00am-6:00pm, Sunday noon-5:00pm. (April-October)
- ❑ Admission: $5.00 (age 3+). Maximum Family Price $20.00 (Price includes horse drawn wagon ride.)

Step back in time at this working Historical Farm and Petting Farm. Hold cuddly baby bunnies and chicks. Watch playful lambs and goats. Feed and play with the farm animals, gather your own eggs and take a horse-drawn wagon ride! Enjoy seasonal demonstrations of draft horses plowing, planting and harvesting. Special activities are scheduled, weather permitting.

## RIVERPLACE

**Frankenmuth** - *925 South Main Street, 48734. Phone: (800) 600-0105. Web: www.frankenmuth-riverplace.com. Hours: Sunday-Thursday 10:00am-8:00pm, Friday-Saturday 10:00am-9:00pm (September-December, May). Slightly more limited hours (January-April). Daily 10:00am-9:00pm (June-August). Admission: Varies with activity.* Gameroom, toy stores and treats shops, too. A-MAZE-N-MIRRORS - life size maze of mirrors and glass. BAVARIAN BELLE - see separate listing. LIGHTS FANTASTIC - nightly laser-light shows in amphitheater. FREE. COSMIC CARS - Experience this unique combination of music and lights as you challenge your family and friends in one of our state of the art bumper cars. The only 3,000 square foot indoor, year-round bumper car track of its kind.

## APPLE MOUNTAIN SKI AREA

**Freeland** - *4519 North River Road, 48623. Phone: (989) 781-6789 or (888) 781-6789. Web: www.applemountain.com. Hours: Daily 10:00am-10:00pm (mid-December to mid-March). 12 runs.* Night skiing, snow boarding, equipment rental, and instructions are available. Golf and restaurant available.

## LAKEPORT STATE PARK

**Lakeport** - *7605 Lakeshore Road SR 25 north, 48059. Web: www.michigandnr.com/parksandtrails/parklist.asp. Phone: (810) 327-6224. Admission: $6.00-$8.00 per vehicle.* Located along the shore of Lake Huron, the park has two distinct units separated by the village of Lakeport. Camping/cabins, hiking trails, boating, and fishing.

## METAMORA-HADLEY STATE RECREATION AREA

**Metamora** - *3871 Hurd Road (off SR 24 south), 48455. Phone: (810) 797-4439. www.michigandnr.com/parksandtrails/parklist.asp. Admission: $6.00-$8.00 per vehicle.* The park consists of 723 acres with 80-acre Lake Minnewanna in the center. Camping, hiking trails, boating, fishing and swimming.

## CHIPPEWA NATURE CENTER

**Midland** - *400 South Badour Road, 48640. Phone: (989) 631-0830. Web: www.chippewanaturecenter.com. Hours: Monday-Friday 8:00am-5:00pm, Saturday 9:00am-5:00pm. Sunday and most Holidays 1:00-5:00pm. Admission: Donation.* Site includes a modern visitor center with indoor exhibits. Outdoors, there's a wildlife viewing area, wildflower walkway, scenic river overlook, 1870 Homestead Farm (cabin, schoolhouse, heirloom/herb garden, farm animals) and The Arboretum of Michigan Trees and Shrubs. 1000 acres of trails run through the forest, meadows, ponds, and rivers. The Archeological District is the site of a territorial Indian battle.

## DOW GARDENS

1018 West Main Street (corner of Eastman Ave. and West St. Andrews Street, next to the Midland Center for the Arts)

**Midland** 48640

- ❑   Phone: (800) 362-4874, **Web: www.dowgardens.org**
- ❑   Hours: 9:00am - just before sunset, daily except Winter holidays.
- ❑   Admission: $5.00 adult, $1.00 student (6-17).

These gardens were started in 1899 as landscaping around Dow's home. Now there are 100 acres of gardens featuring flowers, trees, rocks and water. Seasonal tulips and wildflowers are pretty to look at. The Barnyard Garden is home to the hog sculpture, ponytail grass, lambs ears and an array of other plants with farm animal names. The Children's Garden has a treehouse and fountains. No food or pets allowed.

## H.H. DOW HISTORICAL MUSEUM

3100 Cook Road (US Business 10 into town. Head NW on Main Street from downtown to Cook Road south),

**Midland** 48640

- ❑   Phone: (989) 832-5319, **www.mcfta.org/historical_society/**
- ❑   Hours: Wednesday-Saturday Noon-4:00pm, Sunday 1:00-4:00pm.
- ❑   Admission: $4.00 adult, $2.00 child.

First of all, please purchase the Children's Guidebook and use it as you go through the museum. It's sure to keep the kids attention because each page has an activity for them to do. You'll want to start at the replica of Evens Flour Mill Complex - the original Midland Chemical Company. This is where young Dow pioneered experiments of separation of bromine from brine using electrolysis. See a prototype of his first lab. Wood scraps were used to build electrolysis boxes that feed onto "spread beds" that feed into a wood tower full of scrap metal. The metal catches the bromine liquid vapor. The museum has many clever interactive (holograms, manual, conversation) displays conveying why Midland, Michigan was an ideal spot to experiment, how Dow's parents felt about his work (proud Dad, worried Mom), and his supportive wife. See a scene where Herbert is running his business yet trying not to be a workaholic. We feel the exhibits will inspire cleverness, tenacity, association with other great wise minds, hard work, and, in some, a zest for making money with science.

## HALL OF IDEAS (MIDLAND CENTER FOR THE ARTS)

1801 West Saint Andrews Road, **Midland** 48640

- ❑ Phone: (989) 631-5930, **Web: www.mcfta.org**
- ❑ Hours: Tuesday-Saturday 10:00am-5:00pm, Sunday 1:00-5:00pm, except Holidays.
- ❑ Admission: $5.00 adult, $3.00 child (ages 4-12).
- ❑ Miscellaneous: Art Gallery, Peanut Gallery (Theatre Guild's family division).

What's 10 feet tall, 10,000 years old, hairy and wears size 80 sneakers? See, touch, hear, explore the world's natural wonders of science, history, and art. "Captain" a Great Lakes fishing boat or set off a mine blast! Ride a John Deere combine (cab of one with panoramic view of field in front of you). Create computer music, visit an old-time theater and say "hi" to an American mastodon skeleton with size 80 feet!

## DEER ACRES

2346 M-13 (I-75 to exit 164, go north on M-13), **Pinconning** 48650

- ❑ Phone: (989) 879-2849, **Web: www.deeracres.com**
- ❑ Hours: Daily 10:00am-6:00pm, Weekends until 7:00pm (early May-Labor Day). Weekends Only 10:00am-7:00pm (after Labor Day to mid-October).
- ❑ Admission: $7.75-$9.75 (age 3+). Additional fee for rides.

Watching your children's eyes light up as they see a deer eating out of their hand is something that you'll never forget. At Deer Acres, the deer are so tame that they even know to come toward you when they hear the food dispensers clicking! Additional fun attractions (small additional fee) include several amusement rides (antique cars, Ferris wheel, carousel, moonwalk) and a narrated safari trip (don't miss the monkeys). Story Book Village brings all of your child's fantasy characters to life like "The Three Little Pigs", "Old Woman In a Shoe", "Old Mother Hubbard" and many others.

## MISS PORT AUSTIN

**Port Austin** - *(at M-53 in downtown), 48467. Phone: (989) 738-5271. Web: www.thumbtravels.com/missptaustin.htm. Admission: $35.00 per person. 20% discount for families and weekday trips. Tours: Leaves dock at 7:30 am and 2:30 pm (starting in July). Call for other times and types of trips. Trips last 4 ½ hours.* A home town fishing expedition is what the summer is all about. Join Captain Fred Davis (and up to 20 guests) on a quest for perch. Once the captain finds you a school of fish, you'll "bait up" using the minnows that he provides and then it's all up to you! A great, casual way to introduce your kids to fishing (and how to tell a fish story...).

## PORT CRESCENT STATE PARK

**Port Austin** - *1775 Port Austin Road (along M-25, 5 miles southwest of town), 48467. Phone: (989) 738-8663. Web: www.michigandnr.com/parksandtrails/parklist.asp. Admission: $4.00 per vehicle.* Port Crescent State Park is located at the tip of Michigan's "thumb" along three miles of sandy shoreline of the Saginaw Bay. Some of the modern campsites offer a waterfront view, either of Lake Huron or the Pinnebog River. A 900-foot boardwalk and five picnic decks offer scenic vistas from the top of sand dunes in the day-use area. A unique feature is their undeveloped beaches and sand dunes contrasted with many forest hiking trails. Camping and mini-cabins plus these activities are available: fishing, swimming, winter sports.

## BLUE WATER TROLLEY

(Off I-94, I-69 to Military to the Black River), **Port Huron** 48060

❑     Phone: (810) 987-8687 or (800) 852-4242 , **www.bluewater.org**

A nostalgic, narrated tour of historic sites including the THOMAS EDISON DEPOT on the St. Clair River (under the Blue Water Bridge). Young Tom moved here at the age of seven and began his road to self-education here. Admission: 10 cents. Season: June-September.

*For updates & travel games, visit:*   **www.KidsLoveTravel.com**

## COAST GUARD CUTTER BRAMBLE

**Port Huron -** *(Port Huron Seaway Terminal on the St. Clair River), 48060. Phone: (810) 982-0891, Web: www.phmuseum.org. Hours: Daily 11:00am-5:00pm (summer). Open Thursday-Monday (spring and fall). Closed January-March. Admission: $5.00 adult, $3.00 senior (55+) and student (7-17). Discount combo pricing with Lightship & Port Huron Museum.* The Coast Guard Cutter Bramble was commissioned in 1944. Following World War II, the Bramble participated in "Operation Crossroads," the first test of an atomic bomb's effect on surface ships. In 1957, along with the cutters Spar and Storis, she headed for the Northwest Passage, traveling through the Bearing Straits and Arctic Ocean. These three surface vessels were the first to circumnavigate the North American Continent, an ambition mariners have had for more than 400 years. In the 1960s, the Bramble was used for search and rescue, icebreaking, and law enforcement throughout the Great Lakes. Decommissioned in the early 2000s, it now serves as an historical museum.

# *EDISON DEPOT MUSEUM*

Thomas Edison Parkway (under the Blue Water Bridge)

**Port Huron** 48060

❑     Phone: (810) 982-0891, **Web: www.phmuseum.org**
❑     Hours: Thursday-Monday 11:00am-5:00pm. Summer hours:
        Daily 11:00am-5:00pm.
❑     Admission: $5.00 adult, $3.00 senior (55+) and student (7-17).
        Discount combo pricing with Lightship & Port Huron Museum.

The Museum is housed inside the historic Fort Gratiot depot. Exhibits portray Edison's boyhood story of creativity, family support, adversity, perseverance, and ultimate triumph as the greatest inventor of our times. While living in his boyhood home along the shores of Lake Huron (age 7-16), Tom Edison conducted some of his first science experiments here (see demos of them) and also sold candy and hand-printed newspapers to train passengers. The story traces young Tom's boyhood and school experiences, his avid curiosity and scientific study fostered by his mother, adolescent entrepreneurial efforts and his work on trains - and in this very depot. Outside the depot, a restored baggage car rests on a spur of railroad track. Inside this baggage car, visitors discover a re-creation of young Edison's mobile chemistry lab and printing shop. See actual artifacts from Tom's lab (glass bottles) and lead type from his printing press. The movie played in the simulated Black Maria (Tom's name for the first movie theatre) is very well done and easy to follow. The museum flows thru his life at a very nice pace. The dioramas and multitude of hands-on opportunities here qualify this Edison Museum as a new favorite.

### FORT GRATIOT LIGHTHOUSE

**Port Huron -** *(Lake Huron near the mouth of the St. Clair River), 48060. Phone: (810) 982-3659. Web: www.phmuseum.org. Tours: FREE tours from May to September with USCG. permission (by reservation). Please note that there are no restroom facilities available at the lighthouse or park and sandals and open-toes shoes are not permitted.* This lighthouse, the oldest in Michigan, was constructed north of the fort in 1829. Originally sixty-five feet high, the white painted brick tower was extended to its present height of eighty-six feet. The green flashing light that was automated in 1933 may be seen for seventeen miles. Today, Coast Guardsmen are stationed at this point and occupy the keeper's house. The lighthouse watches over one of the busiest waterways in the world.

## HURON LADY II SCENIC CRUISES

800 Military Street (On Black River behind Standard Federal Bank - Formerly Michigan National Bank), **Port Huron** 48060

- ❑   Phone: (810) 984-1500 or (888) 873-6726, **www.huronlady.com**
- ❑   Hours: Seasonal (early summer thru early October). See website for schedule.
- ❑   Admission: $14.00 adult, $13.00 senior (Age 60+), $8.00 child (Age 5-12).
- ❑   Tours: Seating up to 100 people. 2 or 3 hour sightseeing tours. Reservations recommended.

Huron Lady II Scenic Cruises (*cont.*)

This well-narrated boat tour passing giant oil refineries, limestone factories and many passing freighters. When passing the freighters (closely), the captain will tell you about their cargo and capacity (did you know it costs less than a Big Mac and Fries to move each item across the Great Lakes by freighter – very efficient). Maybe catch a freighter in the "repair shop" or wave to the Coast Guard by the Fort Gratiot lighthouse (FREE tours May-September 810-982-3659) or a Captain aboard the Lightship or Edison depot...even pass the Canada coastline. Very clean, comfortable all-weather boat with a modest snack bar. Maybe have the kids bring along a sticker book, coloring book or small toys to play with as you sail.

## *HURON LIGHTSHIP MUSEUM*

(End of I-94 east - Moored at Pine Grove Park along the St. Clair River), **Port Huron** 48060

- ❑   Phone: (810) 982-0891, **Web: www.phmuseum.org**
- ❑   Hours: Daily 11:00am -5:00pm (Summer). Thursday-Monday only (fall and spring). Closed January-March.
- ❑   Admission: $5.00 adult, $3.00 senior (55+) & student (7-17). Discount combo pricing with 2 other Port Huron museums.
- ❑   Miscellaneous: Nearby is the PORT HURON MUSEUM - 1115 Sixth Street, that traces 300 years of local history, especially American Indian and marine history (step into a real ship's pilot house). Same hours.

Your entire family will really enjoy the brief tour of this unique lighthouse. It is the last "floating lighthouse" to sail the Great Lakes (decommissioned in 1970) called the "Huron". Used where it wasn't practical to build a lighthouse, it was built in 1920 and was operated by a crew of 11 who took 3 week turns (16 days out, 5 days in). Board the boat that bobbed through thick fog and rode out heavy storms to warn passing freighters of treacherous shoals ahead in the channel. Listen to the fog horn's "heeeee....ooohhhh" deep sound that bellows that sound of the ship's heart. What has replaced the Huron? Find out with self-guided tours of the interior hull, mess hall, captain's quarters, and then experience a panoramic view of the Blue Water Bridge from the pilothouse on top of the boat. It was most interesting to hear stories of freighters like the famous "Edmund Fitzgerald" and to know the dangers of being in a smaller boat that is calling giant ships right to you!

## SANILAC COUNTY HISTORICAL MUSEUM & VILLAGE

228 South Ridge Road - (SR25)

**Port Sanilac** 48469

❑   Phone: (810) 622-9946, **Web: www.sanilacmuseum.com**
❑   Hours: Tuesday-Friday 11:00am-4:30pm, Weekends Noon-4:30pm (mid-June - Early September).
❑   Admission: $2.00-$5.00.

Start at the 1875 Victorian Home with original home furnishings, period medical instruments, original post office cancellation stamps, and an "American" sewing machine (later they changed their name to "Singer"). The Dairy Museum features cheesemaking equipment and you can wander through the Log Cabin where they used some charred logs from the tragic Thumb Area fire of 1881. See an old schoolhouse and stop at the General Store (really cute - try a bottle of old-fashioned "body splash" or some penny candy - lots of licorice!)

### JOHNNY PANTHER QUESTS

**Saginaw** - *(meet near the Shiawassee National Wildlife Refuge), 48601. Phone: (810) 653-3859 (Voice Phone). Admission: $80.00 to $120.00 per couple. $30.00 to $40.00 per additional person depending on trip scheduled. Tours: Boat tours last 3-4 hours.* The Everglades in Michigan? Just a few short moments from downtown Saginaw is one of the greatest examples of wildlife and wetlands that you and your kids will ever see. Take a private boat tour that is personalized for your family. A quiet day with nature…floating along…with a chance to see deer, beaver and maybe even a bald eagle. As owner says, "Eliminate the stress…get out of the mainstream and go on a Quest!"

## *SAGINAW CHILDREN'S ZOO*

1730 South Washington (I-675 to 5$^{th}$/6$^{th}$ Exit to Celebration
Square), **Saginaw** 48601

❑    Phone: (989) 759-4200,  **Web: www.saginawzoo.com**

❑    Hours: Monday-Saturday 10:00am-5:00pm, Sunday & Holidays
11:00am-6:00pm. (Mother's Day weekend - September).
Weekends only in October.

❑    Admission: $4.00 -$5.00 per person (age 3+).

This "kid-sized" zoo features all the fun animals including:
monkeys, bald eagles, alligators, and farm animals. Take a
miniature train or pony ride and then a chance to see and ride a
unique, locally built carousel. After choosing your mount (from
horses, rabbits, ponies or sea horses), enjoy the views of hand-
painted panels depicting scenes of Saginaw's history.

## *SHIAWASSEE NATIONAL WILDLIFE REFUGE*

**Saginaw** - *Green Point Environmental Learning Center is at 3010
Maple Street in town. (Refuge is 6 miles south of town, west of
SR13), 48601. Phone: (989) 777-5930 or (989) 759-1669
(Learning Center)  Web: http://midwest.fws.gov/Shiawassee/
Hours: Dawn to Dusk.* The 9000 acre Refuge provides food and
rest for a variety of birds and other wildlife. This includes 250
species of birds, 10 miles of observation trails to walk, two
observation     decks     with     scopes,     and     The     Green     Point
Environmental Learning Center. The Center offers 2.5 miles of
hiking trails, indoor exhibits and many displays. For Shiawassee
Flats "Michigan Everglades" Boat Trips, call Johnny Panther
Quests (listed on previous page).

## *SAGINAW ART MUSEUM*

**Saginaw** - *1126 North Michigan Avenue, 48602. Phone: (989)
754-2491. Web: www.saginawartmuseum.org. Hours: Tuesday-
Saturday 10:00am-5:00pm, Sunday 1:00-5:00pm. Closed holidays.
Admission: Donations.* Housed in an early 1900's mansion, you'll
mostly find 19$^{th}$ and 20$^{th}$ century American art. The Visionarea
Hands-On Room is the best place to spend time with kids (kids
making easy art jewelry, prints or art science).

### SAGINAW BAY SYMPHONY ORCHESTRA YOUTH THEATRE

**Saginaw** - *Saginaw County Event Center (Heritage Theatre), 48607. Phone: (989) 755-6471. www.saginawbayorchestra.com. Admission: $5.00 per person.* Family-and-kid-friendly productions like Amelia Bedelia and favorite fairy tales.

### SAGINAW SPIRIT HOCKEY

**Saginaw** - *Dow Event Center, 48607. Phone: (989) 497-7747.* **Web: www.saginawspirit.com.** Experience the excitement of OHL hockey and the Saginaw Spirit when they play at home. Meet with the mascot Sammy Spirit and join the Kids Club. Season tickets are available. Individual tickets range from $8.50-15.50. Season: September-March.

### MARSHALL M. FREDERICKS SCULPTURE GALLERY

**Saginaw (University Center) -** *7400 Bay Road (SR84) (Arbury Fine Arts Center on Saginaw Valley State University), 48710. Phone: (989) 790-5667.* **Web: www.svsu.edu/mfsm/.** *Hours: Monday-Saturday Noon-5:00pm. Closed university holidays. Admission: FREE.* Home to more than 200 sculptures by the same artist. He is known nationally and internationally for his impressive monumental figurative sculpture, public memorials and fountains, portraits, medals, and animal sculptures. Free-standing sculptures, drawings and portraits, and photos of bronze pieces are displayed. Plaster models used to cast the sculptor's work in bronze constitute the bulk of the collection indoors. There's a sculpture garden and fountain, too.

## SUGGESTED LODGING AND DINING

**HOLIDAY INN EXPRESS**, **Port Huron.** 1720 Hancock Street (under the bridge to Canada), just off Pine Grove Avenue North. (810) 987-5999. They offer an indoor heated swimming pool, jacuzzi, children's playland, fitness center and a complimentary Breakfast Bar served each morning with a big smile and welcome. There are clean, open eating and playing areas. Ask about their Jungle Room suite complete with frig, micro, 2 TVs (one in the kid's room) w/ VCRs & gobs of videos, and especially the separate bunk bed room for the kids with a jungle animal motif. The staff here are the friendliest you'll ever find!

**BAVARIAN INN**. **Frankenmuth**. 713 South Main Street. (800) BAVARIA or **www.bavarianinn.com**. A famous Frankenmuth restaurant (established in 1888) offering family style dinners. An authentically dressed server (aren't their hats cute?) will help introduce your kids to all the menu offerings they will like such as potato pancakes, veal cutlets, baked chicken, etc. (except maybe the sauerkraut). None of the food is over-seasoned…all kid friendly…but the adults may want to use extra all purpose seasonings available at each table. Also see the Glockenspiel Clock Tower (with performances telling the Pied Piper of Hamelin story in music) and the Doll and Toy Factory (see dolls created before your eyes). The Lodge has five pools and overnight accommodations. Hours: Daily Lunch, Dinner or Overnight.

# Chapter 2
## *Central West Area*

# Our Favorites...

\* Dune Rides & Dune Centers

\* Musical Fountain - Grand Haven

\* Frederik Meijer Gardens - Grand Rapids

\* Windmill Island - Holland

\* Wooden Shoe Factory - Holland

\* S.S. Badger - Ludington

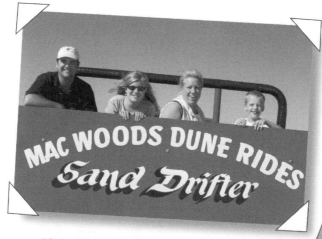

*Miles of Sand...Oh What Fun!*

## *SHRINE OF THE PINES*

M-37 (along the Pere Marquette Riverbanks)

**Baldwin** 49304

❑   Phone: (231) 745-7892, **Web: www.shrineofthepines.com**

❑   Hours: Monday-Saturday 10:00am-6:00pm, Sunday 1:30-6:00pm
    (May 15-October 15).

❑   Admission: $1.00-$3.75 (age 6+).

❑   Miscellaneous: Walk...woodland paths among towering white
    pines and enjoy the abundance of wildlife along the Pere
    Marquette River.

It was Raymond W. Overholzer's (a hunting and fishing guide)
vision to create a shrine to the white pine trees that once covered
Michigan. He began hand-carving and hand-polishing stumps,
roots, and trunks (using the simplest of tools). Over 30 years of
"works of art" are shown here including candlesticks, chairs,
chandeliers, and beds. There is even a 700 lb. table with drawers
carved from a single stump!

### *CANNONSBURG SKI AREA*

**Cannonsburg** - *6800 Cannonsburg Road NE (10 miles east of US-
131 on West River Dr), 49317. Phone: (616) 874-6711.* **Web:**
*www.cannonsburg.com.*   Day and night skiing with 10 runs.
Lessons and equipment rental are available. Cannonsburg offers
the highest vertical in Southwest Michigan.

## *COOPERSVILLE & MARNE RAILWAY*

Train Departs from Downtown (I-96 to Exit 16 or 19)

**Coopersville** 49404

❑   Phone: (616) 997-7000, **Web: www.coopersvilleandmarne.org**

❑   Admission: $10.00 adult, $9.00 senior, $6.00 child (2-12).

❑   Tours: Tuesdays (or Wednesdays) & Saturdays 11:00am &
    1:00pm (May - October).

A great way to introduce your children to rail travel at a relaxed
pace. The summer rides offer a 5 mile tour though rural Michigan
to the town of Marne and then returns on the same line. There are

special theme rides that include The Great Train Robbery with Chuck Wagon Barbecue, The Pumpkin Train (in October), and The Santa Train (in December).

## GRAND HAVEN STATE PARK

**Grand Haven -** *1001 Harbor Avenue (Take US-31 into Grand Haven and follow the "waterfront" signs. Go south at the waterfront to the park entrance), 49417. Phone: (616) 847-1309* **Web:** *www.michigandnr.com/parksandtrails/parklist.asp. Admission: $6.00-$8.00 per vehicle.* 48 acre park with the beautiful sandy shore of Lake Michigan along the west side of the park and the Grand River along the north side of the park. The park consists entirely of beach sand and provides scenic views of Lake Michigan and the Grand Haven pier and lighthouse. There's also boating, fishing and swimming.

## HARBOR STEAMER

**Grand Haven -** *301 North Harbor Drive (off US 31 - head West), 49417. Phone: (616) 842-8950. Web: www.harborsteamer.com. Hours: Daily (except Mondays) cruises afternoons and evenings (Memorial Day-Labor Day). Admission: $7.00-$13.00 (age 5+). Meal or entertainment cruises more.* This cute replica paddlewheel boat offers tours of Spring Lake and the lower Grand River. Choose from a 45 minute waterfront or 90 minute scenic narrated lunchtime (or brown-bag lunch) tour. The lower deck is enclosed, snack items are available, and there are restrooms on board.

## MUSICAL FOUNTAIN

(Downtown Riverfront. Viewing best at Grandstand at Harbor and Washington Streets), **Grand Haven** 49417

❑ Phone: (616) 842-2550
**Web: www.grandhaven.com/fountain.shtml**
❑ Hours: Summers at dusk-approximately 9:30pm. Weekends only in September and May.
❑ Admission: Donations.

❑ Miscellaneous: Tri-Cities Museum is in front of the grandstand and is open most evenings until the concert begins. It contains displays on railroading, shipping, pioneers, the lumber industry, Coast Guard and Maritime vessels in a former railroad depot.

The world's largest synchronized light, water and music show. For 30 years now, jets of water up to 125 feet high go through a series of pipes to create displays that change color to the beat of music. We thought some looked like angel wings and sunrises. The show lasts approximately 20 minutes.

## FISH LADDER SCULPTURE

**Grand Rapids -** *(US131 East to exit 87 - turn right onto Front Street - On Grand River at junction of 4th and Front Streets), 49503. Phone: (800) 678-9859. Hours: Daily, daylight hours. Admission: FREE.* A concrete, 5 step ladder (actually a series of steps) was built by a local artist to assist salmon in jumping up a 6 foot dam to reach their popular spawning grounds further upstream. Leaping fish can be seen anytime, but the best time is late September to late October. If you spend about 20 minutes there you will witness at least one fish make it up all five steps! We sure are glad that Grand Rapids decided to help these pretty "fishies" out!

## GRAND RAPIDS CHILDREN'S MUSEUM

22 Sheldon Avenue NE (Division to Library Street, downtown)

### Grand Rapids 49503

❑ Phone: (616) 235-4726, **Web: www.grcm.org**
❑ Hours: Tuesday-Saturday 9:30am-5:00pm, Sunday Noon-5:00pm. Also Family Night on Thursday from 5:00-8:00pm.
❑ General Admission: $4.00 (ages 2+). Family Night: $1.00

A well supported hands-on museum focuses on learning. Parents and kids truly learn the art of play here. Besides the great "light table" (with clear, colored Legos - you can never play enough with Legos!), they also have giant Tinker Toys and another play table to build a Lincoln Log town! The "dress up" area includes a dressing room and large stage w/ ticket booth to "role-play" perform. Dress up in all kinds of clothes, choose an array of backgrounds and watch as your image is transformed from in front of a green screen to in front of a weather map or city scapes and more. Bubbles, Bees and a Farm Market, too.

## GRAND RAPIDS CIVIC THEATRE

**Grand Rapids** - *30 North Division Street, 49503. Phone: (616) 222-6650. Web: www.grct.org.* Children's Theatre with productions like Frog and Toad or the Wizard of Oz. The second largest community theatre in the U.S. Season runs year round now.

## GRAND RAPIDS GRIFFINS HOCKEY

**Grand Rapids** - *130 West Fulton (Van Andel Arena), 49503. Phone: (616) 774-4585. Web: www.griffinshockey.com. Admission: $5.00-$25.00.* This IHL team plays in March and April. Affiliate of Detroit Red Wings.

## GRAND RAPIDS RAMPAGE FOOTBALL

**Grand Rapids** - *130 West Fulton (Van Andel Arena), 49503. Phone: (616) 222-4000. Web: www.rampagefootball.com.* This Arena Football League plays mid-February through mid-May. Tickets $10.00-$30.00.

## GRAND RAPIDS SYMPHONY/YOUTH SYMPHONY

**Grand Rapids** -*169 Louis Campau Promenade, Suite One (DeVos Hall), 49503. Web: www.grsymphony.org. Phone: (616) 454-9451.* Family and Lollipop Series available September-May. Picnic Pops. Holiday Pops. Youth Symphony concerts feature the 100+ member ensemble (ages 12-21) performing classical favorites. Admission charged.

## BLANDFORD NATURE CENTER

**Grand Rapids** - *1715 Hillburn Avenue NW (US 131 to Leonard Street exit west to Hillburn), 49504. Phone: (616) 453-6192. Web: http://web.grps.k12.mi.us/blandford/home.html. Hours: Monday-Friday 9:00am-5:00pm. Weekends 1:00-5:00pm. Closed major holidays. Trails are open from dawn to dusk. Free admission.* The visitor center is probably where you'll start. Learn about their wildlife care program and then go out on the grounds along self-guided trails to see wildlife. A total of 140 or so acres of fields, forests, ponds and streams can be leisurely explored. Other trails pass the Carriage Barn, Sugar House, Blacksmith, General Store, Barn & Log Cabin (most open summertime). The trails turn into cross-country ski areas in the winter.

## *GERALD FORD MUSEUM*

303 Pearl Street NW (I-196 to US131 to Pearl Street Exit - East - on the West bank of the Grand River), **Grand Rapids** 49504

- ❑  Phone: (616) 451-9263, **Web: www.ford.utexas.edu**
- ❑  Hours: Daily, 9:00am-4:45pm. Closed New Year's Day, Thanksgiving Day, and Christmas Day.
- ❑  Admission: $5.00 adult, $4.00 senior (62+), Children FREE (under 16).

This display of history through artifacts is outstanding to parents, but kids will gravitate to only a handful of displays. As you may have to race through some interesting exhibits, be sure to help your kids look for these (hey…tell them it's a scavenger hunt!): See Elvis' suit, James Dean's motorcycle, Bert and Ernie, A pole sitter, the first video game, Mr. Roger's sweater, and those "groovy" platform tennis shoes (since they are now back in style they may be wearing something similar!). The best areas for kids:

- ❑  OVAL OFFICE REPLICA - See the room that very few people ever see and listen as you eavesdrop on a typical day in the Ford Presidency.
- ❑  HOLOGRAPHIC WHITE HOUSE TOUR - Tour (using photographs taken by the Fords) up to 11 rooms usually off limits to the public. Attend a White House State Dinner or play in the Solarium.
- ❑  CAMPAIGNS - Deliver a speech like the President using a teleprompter or stand on the floor of a political convention. We have a great video of this memory!

## JOHN BALL PARK ZOO

1300 West Fulton Street (Take I-196 to Lake Michigan Drive or Lane Street exit, follow signs), **Grand Rapids** 49504

- ❑ Phone: (616) 336-4300, **Web: www.johnballzoosociety.org**
- ❑ Hours: Daily 10:00am-6:00pm (mid-May to Labor Day). Daily 10:00am-4:00pm (rest of the year). Closed Christmas Day only.
- ❑ Admission: $4.00 adult (14-62), $2.50 (63+), $2.50 child (5-13). No admission is charged in December-February.

See more than 1000 specimens (you know…animals, fish, amphibians, etc.) from around the world at the state's second largest zoo. In addition to the usual lions, tigers, and bears there is a special exhibit on Nocturnal Animals and a petting zoo with farm animals for the young kids. Newer additions include the Spider Monkeys, Bongo, Penguins, and a sassy Hornbill. Look for octopus and moon jellies (w/ their 3 life cycles). The monkeys antics are fun to watch. The camel rides are back, too.

## VAN ANDEL MUSEUM CENTER

272 Pearl Street NW (US131 to Pearl Street, exit 85B)

**Grand Rapids** 49504

- ❑ Phone: (616) 456-3977
  **Web: www.grmuseum.org/vamc/museum.htm**
- ❑ Hours: Monday-Saturday 9:00am-5:00pm, Sunday Noon-5:00pm.
- ❑ Admission: $9.00 adult, $7.00 senior, $3.00 child (3-17).
- ❑ Miscellaneous: Planetarium and laser shows (additional charge). Museum Café. Curiosity Shop. Carousel rides for small fee.

Exhibits that depict heritage and manufacturers of the region. Best picks for children might be:

- ❑ FURNITURE CITY - a partially operational reconstruction of an early 1900's furniture factory and displays of artistic and funky chairs.
- ❑ THE 1890's DOWNTOWN - a recreated street with a theater and shops plus the sights and sounds of transportation and people's conversations as you wait with them at the train station.

❑ AMERICAN INDIANS - Anishinabe people were the first inhabitants of the area. Why do they re-tell the stories of their ancestry so much? Great storytelling theme here.

Be on the lookout for the 76 foot finback whale skeleton which greets you at the entrance in the main hallway. Also, you'll feel like you're in the movie "Back to the Future" when you see the Giant Clock taken from Old City Hall (it's transparent so you can see the mechanisms - and it's still keeping time).

## *FREDERIK MEIJER GARDENS & SCULPTURE PARK*

1000 East Beltline NE (I-96 to East Beltline exit - go north)

**Grand Rapids** 49525

❑ Phone: (616) 957-1580, **Web: www.meijergardens.org**
❑ Hours: Monday-Saturday 9:00am-5:00pm. (until 9:00 on Tuesday). Sunday Noon-5:00pm. Closed only Christmas and New Years.
❑ Admission:$12.00 adult, $9.00 senior (65+) & student, $6.00 child (5-13). Small admission for preschoolers. Outdoor tram rides for about $1.00 each - weekends only.
❑ Tours: Start with a walk or tram tour (sm. Extra fee) around the outdoor themed gardens and lifelike sculpture.
❑ Miscellaneous: Gift shop and café. Current special events are available on their website.

A 125-acre complex featuring indoor (5 stories tall) and outdoor gardens. Inside, children seem to find the most unusual shapes in the Arid Climate Garden w/ cacti that look like spaghetti and skinny fingers. Outside, see tropical and various plants from five continents on nature trails. The sculpture park offers 25 works by renowned artists. The collection is subdivided into two categories: the Sculpture Park and Gallery Collection focuses on work from the era of Auguste Rodin to the present, while the Garden Trails and Conservatory Collection focuses primarily on representational, animal imagery displayed in natural surroundings (change color with the seasons). The Michigan Farm Garden is a replica farm like Mrs. Meijer grew up on. It's fairly "allergy-free" as farms go because all the animals are bronze sculptures. In the big barn they have games for kids like: Tool ID, posing as the famous farmer couple (complete with apron, pitchfork, and farmhouse backdrop), Chore Champions (try gathering eggs, churning butter), Farm Animal drawings, Paper Patchwork quilts and leather Braiding. The Children's Garden is one of the largest in the nation with a: Kid Sense Garden, Water Garden (Great Lakes shape), Wetland Tower (shows natural filtration process of storm water), Quarry (geologists), Log Cabin, Tree House Village (rope bridges and boardwalks), Butterfly Maze and Overlook, Sculpture Walk and a Storytelling Garden.

## WEST MICHIGAN WHITECAPS BASEBALL

**Grand Rapids** - *US 131 & West River Drive (Fifth/Third Ballpark - Old Kent Park), 49544. Phone: (616) 784-4131 or in Michigan (800) CAPS-WIN. Web: www.whitecaps-baseball.com. Admission: $4.00-$8.00.* A baseball stadium with lawn seats? Bleacher and box seats are also available too. The Whitecaps are the Class "A" farm team for the Detroit Tigers and always offer a great family fun value. Meet Crash the River Rascal. Playland. (April - September).

## GRAND LADY RIVERBOAT CRUISES

**Grandville** - *4243 Indian Mounds Drive SW (I96 to exit 70 west/ Wilson Ave to right on Indian Mounds), 49418. Phone: (616) 457-4837. Web: www.river-boat.com. Admission: $10.00 adult (for sightseeing tours). Children ages 3-11 are ½ price except on weekends. Longer tours available.* Their 1½ hour sightseeing cruise tells the story of sites you view and riverboat landings you pass between Grand Rapids & Grand Haven. One of the main features of early riverboats was the giant paddlewheel. The Grand Lady has two identical sternwheels, which may be operated independently. This allows her to be easily maneuvered in the narrow channels and sandbars of the river. The paddle wheels also allow her to operate in very shallow water (as little as 2 ½ feet), where a modern vessel would be grounded. Call or visit website for seasonal schedule of events. Sightseeing tours Daily, subject to prior charters (May-October).

*For updates & travel games, visit:* **www.KidsLoveTravel.com**

## *WILSON STATE PARK*

**Harrison** - *910 North First Street (BR-27 one mile north of Harrison), 48625. www.michigandnr.com/parksandtrails/parklist.asp. Phone: (989) 539-3021. Admission: $6.00-$8.00 per vehicle.* Situated on 36 beautifully wooded acres with a sandy beach, Wilson State Park is located on the north end of Budd Lake in Clare County. Camping/cabins, boating and boat rental, fishing and swimming.

## *HOLLAND MUSEUM*

**Holland** - *31 West 10<sup>th</sup> Street (downtown), 49423. Phone: (888) 200-9123.* **Web: *www.wowcom.net/commerce/museum.*** *Hours: Monday, Wednesday, Friday, Saturday 10:00am-5:00pm, Thursday 10:00am-8:00pm, Sunday 2:00-5:00pm. Admission: $3.00 general, $7.00 family.* As you enter, you'll be mesmerized by the collection of miniature glass churches built by Dutch immigrants for a World's Fair. Most all the displays are "no touch" but kids take an interest in the Dutch Fisherman's Cottage (kids sleep in bunks in the walls) and the carousel made by a Dutch sailor for his kids. They've also developed an interactive experience for children of all ages to learn about Holland and its history through hands-on activities. Watch a video, try on clothing, complete a craft, and have fun. Activities change regularly.

## *WINDMILL ISLAND*

7<sup>th</sup> Street and Lincoln Avenue (US 31 to 8<sup>th</sup> Street)

### Holland 49423

- ❑ Phone: (616) 355-1030, **Web: www.windmillisland.org**
- ❑ Hours: Daily 10:00am-5:00pm (late-April – early October). Extended hours during tulip time.
- ❑ Admission: $7.00 adult, $4.00 child (5-12).
- ❑ Miscellaneous: Candle, sweets, and gift shop. Every windmill product you could imagine is in there. Some activities are for summer only.

*Windmill Island (cont.)*

"DeZwann" (Dutch for the swan) is a 230+ year old, 12 story high, working, authentic Dutch windmill. It's the only one operating in the United States…they produce graham flour almost daily and sell it at the complex. Take a tour of all of the floors, learn how they change the direction of the windmill, see the mechanical wood gears turn (if there's at least a 15 MPH wind) and learn how the miller worked upstairs and sold product on the first floor at the same time. After your tour, Klompen (wooden shoe) dancers perform to organ music as those wooden shoes "klomp" to the beat. The Posthouse museum is an exact architectural replica of a 14<sup>th</sup> century wayside Inn and features a 12 minute slide presentation of Windmills, The Netherlands and our "De Zwaan". See a display of the Netherlands in miniature. The kids won't believe how many water canals are used as streets.

## DEKLOMP WOODEN SHOE AND DELFTWARE FACTORY

12755 Quincy Street - US31

**Holland 49424**

❑   Phone: (616) 399-1900, **Web: www.veldheertulip.com**
❑   Hours: Daily 9:00am-5:00pm.
❑   Admission: FREE
❑   Miscellaneous: Veldheer Tulip Gardens. Colorful tulips, peonies, daylilies, iris, Dutch lilies, daffodils. Admission charged for gardens (when in season).

The Dutch began making wooden shoes as a replacement for leather which was too expensive and deteriorated quickly because of all the exposure to water in the Netherlands. Watch local craftsmen carve "Klompen" (wooden shoes) on machines brought over from the Netherlands. Sizes from Barbie (they really fit!) to Men's size 13. Plain or hand decorated they are great for gardening or decoration. Lots of sawdust!  Delftware began being made by potters in the city of Delft in the 13<sup>th</sup> Century. It is known for its delicately hand-painted blue and white porcelain. This is the only U.S. factory that is producing replica Chinese porcelain and it's just beautiful! While you're having your wooden shoes or small souvenir magnet burned with a special personalization, be sure to take the time to watch the artist use Delft colored paints to decorate plain pieces.

## DUTCH VILLAGE

### 12350 James Street (US 31 and James Street)

### Holland 49424

- ❑ Phone: (616) 396-1475, **Web: www.dutchvillage.com**
- ❑ Hours: Daily 9:00am-5:00pm. (late April - Mid-October)
- ❑ Admission: $10.00 adult, $5.00 child (3-11).
- ❑ Miscellaneous: Café. Ice cream shop. Specialty shops.

You'll feel like you're in Europe (Netherlands) as you see the quaint Dutch Style buildings, canals and flower gardens. Klompen Dancers perform to the music of the Amsterdam Street Organ and wooden shoe crafters are working in their shops with old tools that shape logs into shoes. Demonstration every 15 minutes! In the museum, you can learn how the famous Dutch cheeses of Gouda and Edam are made. There are museums and historical displays (w/ 20 minute movie about the Netherlands) plus the kids favorite spot (and Michele's when she was little)...STREET CARNIVAL - Wooden Shoe Slides, Dutch Chair Swing, and antique Dutch pictured carousel. There's also a farmhouse with "pet and feed" animals.

## HOLLAND STATE PARK

**Holland** - *2215 Ottawa Beach Road (west off US 31 on Lakewood Road), 49424. www.michigandnr.com/parksandtrails/parklist.asp. Phone: (616) 399-9390. Admission: $6.00-$8.00 per vehicle.* Drawn to the beaches and swimming along with the beautifully well-kept, bright red, lighthouse is the reason most come. The park is divided into two separate units; one along Lake Michigan and the other along Lake Macatawa. Almost 150 campsites, boating, fishing, swimming, and bicycle trails are also available.

## SAUGATUCK DUNES STATE PARK

Holland - *2215 Ottawa Beach Road (Off US 31 north), 49424. Web: www.michigandnr.com/parksandtrails/parklist.asp. Phone: (269) 637-2788. Admission: $6.00-$8.00 per vehicle.* Over 2 miles of secluded shoreline along Lake Michigan. In addition, the park has fresh water coastal dunes that are over 200' tall. The park's terrain varies from steep slopes to rolling hills. Hiking trails, swimming, winter sports, and dunes, of course.

## IONIA STATE RECREATION AREA

Ionia - *2880 West David Highway (I-96, Exit 64), 48846. Web: www.michigandnr.com/parksandtrails/parklist.asp. Phone: (616) 527-3750. Admission: $6.00-$8.00 per vehicle.* Rolling hills, babbling brooks, open meadows, forested ridges, a lake nestled in the hills and a river winding its way through woods and fields. Camping/cabins, hiking, boating, fishing, swimming, bicycle trails and winter sports.

## LUDINGTON CITY BEACH

Ludington - *North Lakeshore Drive, 49431. Phone: (231) 845-0324. Hours: Daylight (Memorial Day-Labor Day). Free admission.* A great summer place to cool off featuring swimming and miniature golf.

## LUDINGTON STATE PARK

Ludington - *M-116, 49431. Phone: (231) 843-8671 or (231) 843-2193 (boat rental). www.michigandnr.com/parksandtrails/parklist.asp. Admission: $6.00-$8.00 per vehicle.* Over 300 campsites or cabins, plenty of beaches (one with surfing waves), and extensive hiking trails are big hits here. Lots of dunes here and a great canoe trail, boating, swimming, and fishing. Many love the cross-country skiing and the nature center. Big Sable Point Lighthouse on M116 (2 miles north of the State Park entrance - 231-845-7343 or **www.bigsablelighthouse.org**) is open May thru October for tours of the Tower. Small admission.

# *S.S. BADGER*

701 Maritime Drive (off US 31, Ludington exit into town. Follow
signs for car ferry), **Ludington** 49431

❑   Phone: (800) 841-4243, **Web: www.ssbadger.com**

❑   Hours: Depart times vary (usually morning departure from MI,
    afternoon departure from WI). Call for details (early May - early
    October). Be sure to call or visit their website for information on
    travel packages.

❑   Admission: $47.00-$82.00 adult, $44.00-$76.00 senior (65+),
    $22.00-$38.00 child (5-15), add $53.00 vehicle transport. Ages 4
    and under are FREE. (All rates are per person, round trip and
    subject to change). One way rates available, too.

❑   Tours: The 410-foot "SS Badger" is one of the only Great Lakes
    car ferry boats running today and can carry over 600 passengers
    and 180 vehicles. The current voyage is a 4-hour tour that travels
    from Ludington to Manitowoc, Wisconsin and back, at least once
    per operating day.

Ready for a giant cruise on a giant lake? You have to experience
the S.S. BADGER. With the excitement and romance of a sea
voyage, plus uninterrupted time with family and friends....the
journey is as much fun as the destination. The Badger has
expanded their focus on family amenities designed to appeal to
passengers, children and even pets. Parents have more time to
enjoy the cruise while their children have entertaining things to do.
The expanded children's program (best for school-aged) includes a
KidsPort playroom, face painting, a free activity book (coloring
prizes), and always Badger Bingo and trivia for prizes. The Badger
has also added a few new perks for pets including a special
bandanna, treats and ventilated kennels. Adults head for the
spacious deck areas ("steel beach") for walking or relaxing in the
fresh air (a great place to avoid motion sickness, if you're prone –
they also offer Sea Bands), two food service areas (serving really
good food, beverage and snacks), private staterooms for naps and
private bathroom (extra fee), and satellite television or quiet rooms
(new place for reading or comfortable cat napping). The Main
Lounge and Midship is where kids gravitate to. They watch movies

in the theatre; browse in the nautical ship's store (even have travel games for kids to purchase); but mostly participate in the Activity Director's games – mostly Badger Bingo. Kids can also navigate and track the steamship's progress over open water.

## WHITE PINE VILLAGE

### 1687 South Lakeshore Drive, **Ludington** 49431

❑   Phone: (231) 843-4808 **Web: www.historicwhitepinevillage.org**
❑   Hours: Tuesday-Saturday 10:00am-5:00pm (Early May to mid-October). Mondays in the summer.
❑   Admission: $5.00-$7.00. Slightly higher admissions for special events (i.e. Brunches, pioneer dinners)

A reconstructed 1800's village that features over 20 buildings including a courthouse, hardware store, fire hall, schoolhouse, chapel, and logging and maritime museums. The Exhibit Building has numerous antique transportation vehicles. They have an old-fashioned ice cream parlor, too. Outside are two more wooden boats and railroad carts used for moving heavy rail freight. Along with the automobiles are various tools from the era of the corner garage during the early days of the automobile repair business.

## HART-MONTAGUE TRAIL STATE PARK

**Mears** - *9679 West State Park Road (along US31), 49436. Phone: (231) 873-3083.* A paved, 22-mile trail passing through rural forested lands. It showcases the beauty of Oceana county - from patchwork fields of asparagus, cherries, apples to marshlands…all with no motor vehicles. Picnic areas and scenic overlook areas are available along the trail.

## MAC WOOD'S DUNE RIDES

### West Silver Lake Drive ( US 31 to Shelby Road exit east to B15 north), **Mears** 49436yes

❑   Phone: (231) 873-2817, **Web: www.macwoodsdunerides.com**
❑   Hours: Daily rides 9:30am-Dusk (Memorial Day-Labor Day). Daily rides 10:00am-4:00pm (mid-May - Sunday before Memorial Day & Labor Day - early October).
❑   Admission: $14.50 adult, $9.50 child (3-11).

Got Dunes? Well, ride on or from the Dunes of Lake Michigan as you spend some lazy days along US 31. Maybe start at Mac Woods Dune Rides. Your guide takes you on smooth, perfect sand dunes with easy dips and more than one gorgeous view of Silver Lake and Lake Michigan. Even drive through Lake Michigan! Nearly 70 years ago Malcolm "Mac" Woods created the thrill of dune buggying. Today, your modern vehicle is a multi-passenger, modified, convertible truck "dune scooter". Hang on as you begin a fun and educational 40 minute, 8-mile ride that helps you understand the dunes and why people have come to love this sport.

## SANDY KORNERS JEEP RENTALS

**Mears -** *1762 North 24th Avenue (US 31 Hart/Mears exit, follow signs to Lake), 49436. Web: www.sandykorners.com. Phone: (231) 873-5048. Hours: Daily 10:00am-5:00pm (May-October). Extended sunset tours in the summer. Admission: 4-5 passenger jeeps rent $85.00 per hour on guided tours.* Enjoy the thrill of driving your very own Jeep up and over the sand dune mountains at Silver Lake. It is 60 minutes of fun driving over the great sweeps of sand ridges and valleys near the shores of beautiful Lake Michigan. An experienced guide will make sure you get the most fun and see all of the remarkable sights in this unique area. Make a stop or two to take pictures and if desired, change drivers. They also have Fall Color Tours thru dunes and forest. Car seats are welcome.

## SILVER LAKE STATE PARK

**Mears -** *9679 West State Park Road (US 31 exit Shelby Road west), 49436. www.michigandnr.com/parksandtrails/parklist.asp. Phone: (231) 873-3083. Admission: $6.00-$8.00 per vehicle.* Lots of campsites along the dunes is one draw but dune buggy riding is considered the best here. The dune ridges and valleys are mostly windblown sand and lack trees, scrub brush, and dune grass. The dune area is sometimes compared to a desert. Silver Lake State Park contains more than four miles of Lake Michigan shoreline and boasts a large sandy beach. Look for the Little Sable Point Lighthouse (great for pictures at sunset or dawn) and participate in swimming, boating, fishing, and hiking trails on and off dunes.

## WEST MICHIGAN SAND DRAGWAY

**Mears** - *7186 W. Deer Road (Take Hart Exit West off of US-31, Follow the Signs - 2 Miles down Deer Rd.), 49436. Phone: (231) 873-3345. Web: www.sanddragways.com.* Sand Drag Race programs include top fuel dragsters, funny cars, 4 X 4's ATV's dune buggies, Jr. Dragsters, Jr. ATV's and Mighty Midgets. Tickets: $7.00-$13.00 (age 11+).

## SS MILWAUKEE CLIPPER

**Muskegon** - *2098 Lakeshore Drive, Phone: (231) 755-0990. Web: www.milwaukeeclipper.com. Admission: $6.00 adult, $3.00 student (age 6+). Tours: Friday-Sunday 2:00-7:00pm.* Enjoy a guided tour of this 1904 361-foot vessel (built 7 years before the Titanic), the last American passenger ship left on the Great Lakes.

## MUSKEGON COUNTY MUSEUM

**Muskegon** - *430 West Clay Avenue, 49440. Phone: (231) 728-4119. Web: www.muskegonmuseum.org. Hours: Monday-Friday 9:30am-4:30pm, Saturday-Sunday 12:30-4:30pm.* History of Muskegon County with features of Lumbering, Industry and Wildlife, Native Americans, and a favorite kid spot - Hands on Science Galleries with Body Works. The Coming to the Lakes exhibit examines why various groups of people have migrated to this region for the last 10,000 years. Educational Gift Shop. HACKLEY HOSE COMPANY NO. 2 - (231) 722-7578. Wednesday-Sunday Noon-4:00pm (May-October). Tour a replica Fire Barn, complete with firefighting equipment artifacts, horses stalls, firemen's living room. Youngsters can sit up in an old pumper.

## MUSKEGON FURY HOCKEY

**Muskegon** - *955 Fourth Street (L.C. Walker Arena). 49440. Phone: (231) 726-3879. Web: www.furyhockey.com. Admission: $7.00-$11.00.* United Hockey League professional team plays here October - April. The Muskegon Sports Hall of Fame is located in the Arena. Meet Furious Fred, the team's mascot and join the Hot Shotz Kids Club.

# HOFFMASTER STATE PARK / GILLETTE DUNE CENTER

6585 Lake Harbor Road (I-96, exit 4 west - Pontalune Road)

**Muskegon** 49441

- ❑  Phone: (231) 798-3711 or (231) 799-8900 center
  **Web: www.michigandnr.com/parksandtrails/parklist.asp**
- ❑  Hours: Center: Tuesday-Saturday 10:00am-5:00pm. Open
  Sundays in the summer thru October. Center closed in December
  and January. Park is open 8:00am - Dusk.
- ❑  Admission: $6.00-$8.00 per vehicle.
- ❑  Miscellaneous: Winter hosts cross country skiing, sledding, and
  snowshoeing. Campsites on shaded dunes. Fishing, boating, and
  swimming.

P.J. Hoffmaster State Park features forest covered dunes along nearly 3 miles of Lake Michigan shore. Its sandy beach is one of the finest anywhere. A focal point of the park is the Gillette Visitor Center. The Center has exhibits and hands-on displays. See a multi-media presentation that illustrates and explains both dormant and living dunes. Nature trails to observation decks (one is handicap and stroller accessible). Towering dunes with a dune climbing stairway to the top overlook (it's a workout). The Center has lots of live turtles and frogs, similar to ones that live in dune environments. The favorite for our kids was the giant crystal of sand and the samples of different types and color of sand found around America. Do you know what 3 things are needed to form dunes?

## PORT CITY PRINCESS CRUISES

**Muskegon** - *1133 West Western Ave (off US-31 - Downtown), 49441. Phone: (231) 728-8387 or (800) 853-6311. **Web:** www.portcityprincesscruises.com. Admission: General $15.00. Tours: Daily at 2:00pm. 90 minutes. (Memorial Day - Labor Day)* A sightseeing tour of Muskegon Lake and if the weather is good a brief look at Lake Michigan.

## USS SILVERSIDES

1346 Bluff at Pere Marquette Park (Southside of Channel Way)

**Muskegon 49443**

❑   Phone: (231) 755-1230, **Web: www.silversides.org**
❑   Hours: Daily 10:00am-5:30pm (June-August). Monday-Friday
    1:00-5:30pm, Saturday & Sunday 10:00am-5:30pm (May &
    September). Saturday & Sunday 10:00am-5:30pm (April &
    October).
❑   Admission: $5.00-$7.00 (age 5+). FREE for Active Military.
❑   Miscellaneous: Watch out if you're claustrophobic. Difficult to
    take pre-schoolers around on poor footing, cramped quarters.

A restored, famous WW II submarine that was once used for sinking ships. At Great Lakes Naval Memorial & Museum, you can open up to the thrill of going back to WW II and taking part in an authentic submarine experience. Go through the sub's compartments and see how sailors work and live in such cramped quarters (for up to 2 months). Explore decks, engine rooms, and battle stations. Also, a Camp Aboard program is available for a real fun time!

## MICHIGAN'S ADVENTURE AMUSEMENT PARK & WILDWATER ADVENTURE

4750 Whitehall Road (I-96 to US-31)

**Muskegon 49445**

❑   Phone: (231) 766-3377, **Web: www.miadventure.com**
❑   Hours: Daily 11:00am-9:00pm. (Memorial Day weekend - Labor
    Day weekend). Hours vary slightly throughout the season. Call or
    visit website for complete schedule.
❑   Admission: General $24.00 (under 2 Free). Admission is good
    for both parks. Season passes available. Parking $6.00.

Summer…thrill rides, waterparks and food…right? Michigan's largest amusement park awaits your family for a day (or 2) of summer's best. With over 40 rides with names like Mad Moose, Big Dipper, Wolverine Wildcat, and Shivering Timbers (the 3<sup>rd</sup> largest wooden roller coaster in the country), you can be sure that your day will be fun-filled! Don't worry there are also some "calmer" rides (7 are made just for younger children) including the Zachary Zoomer, a special scaled down coaster just for younger children. A tree house and play areas are also included for younger children. Wildwater Adventure admission is also included (the state's largest waterpark) with the Lazy River water tube ride, a wave pool, the new Grand Rapids family water ride, and Michigan's longest waterslide.

## *COUNTRY DAIRY*

3476 S. 80$^{th}$ Ave. (US 31 to New Era exit. Take MI 20 east)

**New Era** 49446

❑    Phone: (231) 861-4636 or (800) 243-7280
     **Web: www.countrydairy.com**

❑    Tours: $3.00-$6.00 per person (age 3+). During the off-season, <u>call ahead</u> to schedule a tour on Monday, Tuesday, Thursday, Friday, and Saturdays, 9am, 11am, and 1pm.

❑    Miscellaneous: Farm Store and Deli serving Ice Cream (made on premises) for dessert. Their ice cream combinations all sound yummy.

Come visit the ShowBarn, which houses 50 top-producing, prize-winning Holstein cows. Take a guided, tractor-pulled wagon tour of a "working" dairy farm and milk processing facility. On your tour, you will be able to see how cows are milked, how milk is bottled or (on certain days) turned into cheese and ice cream. At the close of your tour, you can sample their famous Premium Chocolate Milk, or try some "Moochies" (cheddar cheese curds). Spiced Monterey Jack cheese (many varieties) is their specialty.

## *NEWAYGO STATE PARK*

**Newaygo** - *2793 Beech Street (US131, exit 125 West), 49337.* *Web: www.michigandnr.com/parksandtrails/parklist.asp. Phone: (231) 856-4452.* Wooded rustic campsites, boating, and swimming access to Hardy Dam Pond.

## DUCK LAKE STATE PARK

**North Muskegon** - *3560 Memorial Drive (US-31, take the Whitelake Drive (Duck Lake State Park) exit, west and go a half-mile to Whitehall Road), 49445. Phone: (231) 744-3480. **Web: www.michigandnr.com/parksandtrails/parklist.asp.** (Day use park only). Admission: $6.00-$8.00 per vehicle.* Duck Lake State Park is a 728 acre day use park, located in Muskegon County. Featuring a towering sand dune, the park stretches from the northern shore of Duck Lake to Lake Michigan. A public beach with swimming and boating; fishing and hiking.

## MUSKEGON STATE PARK

**North Muskegon** - *3560 Memorial Drive (US-31 to M-120 exit), 49445. **Web: www.michigandnr.com/parksandtrails/parklist.asp.** Phone: (231) 744-3480. Admission: $6.00-$8.00 per vehicle.* Features over 2 miles of shoreline on Lake Michigan and over 1 mile on Muskegon Lake. The vast expanse of Great Lakes sand beach ranks among the most beautiful in the world. Forested dunes that join miles of Great Lakes shoreline. Check out their four luge runs. Camping, hiking trails, boating, fishing, swimming, and winter sports.

## MUSKEGON WINTER SPORTS COMPLEX

**North Muskegon** - *(Inside Muskegon State Park), 49445. Phone: (231) 744-9629. **Web: www.msports.org.** Hours: Friday night, Saturday, Sunday. Admission: Park vehicle pass is $6.00-$8.00. All day passes $20.00 - 30.00. Skating/Skiing $3.00-$8.00. Thursdays $10.00 Family Night.* Are Mom and Dad ready to re-live their glory days of winter fun? Of course there is the normal winter fun of ice skating and cross-country skiing trails, but that's only where the fun begins. Two luge tracks (ice covered with banked turns) allow beginners and advanced sledders to go at their own pace (starting at different ascents on the tracks). Speeds range from 25 - 45 MPH! Hang on!

## *MEARS STATE PARK*

**Pentwater** - *West Lowell Street (US-31, take the Pentwater exit and go west on Lowell Street), 49449. Phone: (248) 869-2051. Web: www.michigandnr.com/parksandtrails/parklist.asp. Admission: $6.00-$8.00 per vehicle.* Located on Lake Michigan with a several hundred yards of white sandy beach. Camping, hiking, fishing and swimming.

## *DOUBLE JJ RESORT*

### 5900 South Water Road (US 31 to Exit 136 - East)

### **Rothbury** 49452

❏ Phone: (800) DOUBLEJJ or (231) 894-4444
   **Web: www.doublejj.com**

❏ Admission: Prices are all inclusive for a week stay and are subject to change. $400.00-$600.00 (age 5+), 4 and under Free. Meals are included in rates. Call or visit website for weekend, one-day festival and 3-day rates. Family cabins, tent camping, RVs, covered wagons or teepees, too.

Did you know that Michigan has "Dude Ranches"? Well...Double JJ is actually more than a dude ranch. Daily rides are offered and staffed by experienced "cowpokes" who will teach you all the skills along the way. There is even a rodeo at the end of the week where you can test your newly acquired talent. There is something for all ages. Adults and children (with supervision) can learn separately at there own pace. Some of the attractions and fun include a swimming hole with 145-foot waterslide, a petting farm, riding center, Wild West Shows for the adults in the dance hall (kids have their own shows), fishing, hot tubs, pools, and an award-winning 18-hole golf course. Winter activities include mushing, treking, snowshoeing, snowmobiling and cross-country skiing. Aaahhh...the life of a cowboy!

## *SHELBY MAN-MADE GEMSTONES*

**Shelby** - *1330 Industrial Drive (off US 31), 49455. Phone: (231) 861-2165. Web: www.shelbygemfactory.com. Hours: Showroom: Monday-Friday 9:00am-5:30pm. Saturday Noon-4:00pm. Admission: FREE.* In a 50 seat theatre you can learn the fascinating manufacturing process of how man can actually create gemstones such as diamonds, rubies, and sapphires. They are the largest manufacturer in the world of simulated and synthetic gemstones in the world. See how they can process smaller gems into larger ones at a much lesser cost. If your kids are into rocks (especially pretty colored ones, like our daughter) they'll love this place!

## WHITE RIVER LIGHT STATION MUSEUM

**Whitehall** - *6199 Murray Road (US-31 to White Lake Dr. exit (west) to South Shore Dr., turn left and follow Museum signs), 49461. Web: www.whiteriverlightstation.org. Phone: (231) 894-8265. Hours: Tuesday-Friday 11:00pm-5:00pm. Saturday-Sunday Noon-6:00pm (Summer). Weekends only in September. Small admission fee.* At one time, the Muskegon/White Lake area was known as "The Lumber Queen of the World". Shipping over the Great Lakes was the primary means of transporting this lumber. This historic lighthouse was built in 1875 and your family can still climb the old spiral stairs to the top for a view of White Lake and Lake Michigan. Made of Michigan limestone and brick, it features photographs, paintings, artifacts and maritime stories.

## SUGGESTED LODGING AND DINING

**HAMPTON INN OF MUSKEGON**, **Muskegon**. (US 31 at Sternberg exit, **www.hampton-inn.com/hi/muskegon** or 231-799-8333). Their clean space, complimentary deluxe breakfast bar, warm indoor pool and whirlpool and location right near the mall and major routes is great.

**JOHNNY CARINOS**, **Norton Shores**. Hungry for a nearby Italian feast? We loved Johnny Carinos (just south of the hotel, directly across from the mall at Sternberg exit off US 31, 231-798-6363, 5607 Harvey St. **www. www.carinos.com**). We loved all the kid's choices and highly recommend spicy dishes or Johnny's Combo for adults. Big portions, bold flavors and a focus on giving the guests a taste of what it is like to enjoy the Italian countryside…at a fair price. Kids Menus include games and puzzles ($3.99 junior meals, $5.99-$6.99 offering pasta, pizza and cheese entrees).

**SIERRA SANDS AT THE DUNES**, **Silver Lake**. (7990 W Hazel Road, 231-873-1008 or **www.sierrasands.com**, US 31 to Shelby exit to B15 around the east side of Silver Lake). Want to stay near Silver Lake? With friendly owners and amenities like: a heated outdoor pool and whirlpool, a playground, kiddie and mini-suites available, a Backyard! With tether ball, basketball, horseshoes, a campfire pit and plenty of lawn – this is an oasis from concrete, boring hotels. Just a short walk to town shops and restaurants and game centers. Plus, they offer discounted admission to amusements, bike rentals, water sport rentals, dune riding and horseback riding – order them right from the front office.

**RADISSON NORTH**, **Grand Rapids**. When touring Grand Rapids w/kids, maybe stay close to most everything at the Radisson North off US 131 & 270 Ann Street. They have a large, recently remodeled indoor pool, whirlpool and game room and pizza delivery room service.

**ONE TRICK PONY RESTAURANT** - **Grand Rapids**. 136 East Fulton Street. **www.onetrick.biz/**. Just a block away from the Children's Museum is One Trick Pony Restaurant with a children's menu. This place is the oldest building in Grand Rapids used for businesses from dress makers to meat markets...every business has done one thing well...including the current specialty pizzas made here now.

**ROBINETTES APPLE HAUS**, **Grand Rapids**. After visiting Meijer Gardens, head up the East Beltline (3142 Four Mile Road, (616) 361-5567) for a light meal and see this historic restaurant/cider mill and gobs of apple & cherry trees. Try a homemade sandwich or soup topped off with real apple cider or cherry juice and a fresh apple dessert with ice cream! Nicest folks and they give group tours of the orchards in large wagons (by appointment).

# Chapter 3
## *North East Area*

# Our Favorites...

\* Hartwick Pines State Park - Grayling

\* Mackinac Island Carriage & Bike Tours

\* Mackinac Bridge & Museum - Mackinaw City

\* Mackinac State & Historic Parks

\* Mackinaw Trolley Tours

\* Presque Isle Lighthouses - Presque Isle

*Biking fun on Mackinac Island*

# *JESSE BESSER MUSEUM*

491 Johnson Street (Off US 23 near Alpena General Hospital)

**Alpena** 49707

❑     Phone: (989) 356-2202

      **Web: www.oweb.com/upnorth/museum**

❑     Hours: Tuesday-Saturday 10:00am-5:00pm, Sunday Noon-
      5:00pm.

❑     Admission: $5.00 adult, $3.00 senior and child (5-17).

❑     Miscellaneous: Planetarium $1.00 extra. Planetarium programs
      are Sunday at 2:00pm (Under age 5 not admitted to Planetarium).

Mostly local history with a re-created 1800's street of shops and
cabins. If you come during a festival or special event weekend,
make sure you see the display on the role of concrete in the area.
The concrete block-making machine was perfected here in a land
rich with limestone. Other permanent exhibits include: Gallery of
Man, Lumbering and Farming, a Focult Pendulum, Area Fossils
and Restored Historic Buildings.

## *CLEAR LAKE STATE PARK*

**Atlanta** - *20500 M-33 (M-33 nine miles north of Atlanta), 49709.*
***Web: www.michigandnr.com/parksandtrails/parklist.asp.** Phone:*
*(989) 785-4388. Admission: $6.00-$8.00 per vehicle.* Located in
elk country, Clear Lake State Park is a quiet, secluded retreat
offering a sandy beach and a shallow swimming area that is ideal
for children. Camping, hiking, boating, fishing, and winter sports.

## *WILDERNESS STATE PARK*

**Carp Lake** - *898 Wilderness Park Drive (west of Mackinaw
City by CR 81), 49718. Phone: (231) 436-5381. **Web:**
www.michigandnr.com/parksandtrails/parklist.asp. Admission:
$6.00-$8.00 per vehicle.* Rough campsites and cabins. Hiking,
boating, fishing, swimming, and bicycle trails.

## ALOHA STATE PARK

Cheboygan - *4347 Third Street (M-33 South), 49721. Web: www.michigandnr.com/parksandtrails/parklist.asp. Phone: (231) 625-2522 Admission: $6.00-$8.00 per vehicle.* The largest freshwater lake in Michigan (Mullett Lake) is here along with activities such as camping/cabins, boating, fishing, and swimming.

## CHEBOYGAN COUNTY HISTORICAL MUSEUM

Cheboygan - *404 South Huron Street, 49721. Phone: (231) 627-9597. Web: www.cheboyganmuseum.com. Hours: Monday-Friday 1:00-4:00pm. Admission: $2.00 adult (18+).* The county sheriff used to call this place home from 1882 - 1969 - it even was the area jail complete with 8 cells. Today, these cells have become exhibit areas featuring local history including: lumbering, farming, and lifestyle. See a recreated late 1800's "parlor room", bedrooms, and even a schoolroom.

## CHEBOYGAN STATE PARK

Cheboygan - *4490 Beach Road, 49721. Phone: (231) 627-2811. Web: www.michigandnr.com/parksandtrails/parklist.asp. Admission: $6.00-$8.00 per vehicle.* One of the main highlights of the park is the Cheboygan Point Light or the Duncan Bay Beach. Camping/cabins, fishing, hiking, swimming and winter sports.

## COAST GUARD "MACKINAW" TOURS

Cheboygan - *Coast Guard Drive (SR 27 to US 23 South, across bridge), 49721. Phone: (231) 627-7183.* Home port of Mackinaw along the Cheboygan River. The boat is not always in port (it visits around the Great Lakes). When commissioned, Mackinaw was the most powerful and capable icebreaker in the world. She is still the standard by which other icebreakers are measured. If in port, hop aboard and take a look around. Note the narrow spacing in the ship's steel ribs that distinguish her as an icebreaker.

## *CORSAIR SKI AREA*

**East Tawas** - *218 West Bay Street, 48730. Phone: (989) 362-2001 or (800) 55-TAWAS.* **Web:** *www.skinordic.org/corsairski.* Admission: Donation to pay for trail grooming. A cross country ski area with over 35 miles of groomed trails. Visit their warming cabin for a well deserved and welcome respite after an invigorating day of skiing. All skill levels. Rentals are available in town. Great picnic area and hiking in summer and fall. Help your kids try their luck at trout fishing in the Silver Creek.

## *TAWAS POINT STATE PARK*

**East Tawas** - *686 Tawas Beach Road (3 miles east of town off US 23), 48730. www.michigandnr.com/parksandtrails/parklist.asp. Phone: (989) 362-5041. Admission: $6.00-$8.00 per vehicle. Additional $2.00 per person for lighthouse tour.* Check out the 1876, 70 foot lighthouse, Tawas Point Lighthouse. The lighthouse is open to the public for viewing by appointment or on special occasions. The lighthouse stands 70 feet above Lake Huron and the walls at the base are 6 feet thick. The Coast Guard station adjacent to the park on Lakeview Drive was also built in 1876 and is the only surviving example of the First Series Life Saving Stations built on the Great Lakes. The park overall has been referred to as the "Cape Cod of the Midwest". Mini-Cabins and campsites, beach, birding (best in May), nature trails, boating and fishing are there, too.

## MICHIGAN AUSABLE VALLEY RAILROAD

230 South Abbe Road (I-75 exit 202 north. Off SR33, 3.5 miles south of the blinker light in town), **Fairview** 48621

❑    Phone: (989) 848-2229
     **Web: www.michiganausablevalleyrailroad.com**
❑    Hours: Weekends and Holidays 10:00am-5:00pm. (Memorial Day-Labor Day)
❑    Admission: $4.00 (ages over 2).
❑    Tour: 1 and ½ mile trip is approximately 18 minutes long. Perfect for smaller kids.

Michigan Ausable Valley Railroad (*cont.*)

❑     Miscellaneous: Quaint depot and gift shop where you can
      purchase tickets and fresh, hot popcorn.

This ¼ scale train offers visitors a calm, scenic tour which travels
through a jackpine forest (Huron National Forest) and overlooks
the Comins Creek Valley. You'll get to pass through a 115 foot
wooden tunnel and over two wooden trestles (one of them is 220
feet long). Some passengers get a glimpse of wildlife such as deer,
hawks, heron, beaver and maybe even elk or bear!

## CALL OF THE WILD MUSEUM

**Gaylord** - *850 South Wisconsin Avenue (I-75 exit 282, then east on
Main Street, then south on Wisconsin), 49735. Phone: (989) 732-
4336 or (800) 835-4347. Web: www.gocallofthewild.com. Hours:
Daily 8:30am-9:00pm. (mid-June-Labor Day), Daily 9:30am-
6:00pm. (Rest of year). Admission: $4.00-$6.00. Miscellaneous:
Also at location are Bavarian Falls Adventure Golf, Go Carts,
Krazy Kars Tot Ride (additional fee). Gift shop.* The museum is
full of dioramas of over 60 North American Animals in natural
settings. As you look over displays of elk, moose, black bear,
timber wolves, etc., you'll learn about their behavior and habitat
and sounds. The Michigan History area has stories recounted by an
early fur trapper named Joseph. The Four Seasons Display of
Michigan changes as you watch. They have an observation beehive
there, too. Before you begin your adventure into the museum,
make sure you pick up an activity sheet to help you discover a little
more as you go through. Once you are finished going through the
museum, you can turn in each activity sheet for a prize.

## OSTEGO LAKE STATE PARK

**Gaylord** - *7136 Old 27 South (off I-75 south, Take I-75 to the
village of Waters, Exit 270, and go west to Old 27. Go north on
Old 27 five miles to park), 49735. Phone: (989) 732-5485. Web:
www.michigandnr.com/parksandtrails/parklist.asp.     Admission:
$6.00-$8.00 per vehicle.* "The Alpine Village." The park is shaded
with large oak, maple and pine. The park encompasses 62 acres
and provides more than a half mile of sandy beach and large sites

near or within sight of the lake. Camping/mini cabin, boating, fishing, swimming (mid-April to early November).

## GRAYLING FISH HATCHERY

### North Down River Road (I-75 to exit 254)

### Grayling 49738

❑     Phone: (989) 348-9266, **Web: www.graylingfishhatchery.com**

❑     Hours: Daily Noon-6:00pm (Memorial Day-Labor Day).

❑     Admission: $1.50 adult, $1.00 child (6-17), $6.00 family.

It's always fun to watch kid's eyes light up at a "fish farm". See 11 ponds that contain more than 40,000 trout. See fish ranging from tiny aquarium size (2 inches long) to several pounds (28 inches long), and yes, you can even buy some to take home (priced by the inch). Fish food is available from dispensers for a nominal fee and is a great way to really bring the fish to life. Entertainment and demos every Sunday at 2:00pm.

## HARTWICK PINES STATE PARK

### 4216 Ranger Road (I-75 exit 259 - on M-93), **Grayling** 49738

❑     Phone: (989) 348-2537 center or (989) 348-7068 park

**Web: www.michigandnr.com/parksandtrails/parklist.asp**

❑     Hours: Park open 8:00am-10:00pm. Museum buildings 9:00am-
4:00pm (May-October) (until 7:00pm in summer). Also open
select weekends for special events. Logging Museum is closed
November - April.

❑     Admission: $6.00-$8.00 per vehicle.

❑     Miscellaneous: Bike trails, Braille trails, hiking, camping,
fishing, picnic areas, winter sports, small gift shop. Summers-
living history programs along the Forest Trail.

Some call it an "outdoor cathedral of nature", walking along the Old Growth Forest Foot Trail as it winds through the forest behind the Visitor Center. Along the 1¼ mile long trail, you can stop (¼ mile from Visitor Center) at the Logging Museum (open May-October only). Depending on the event, you'll see logging wheels and other logging equipment, a steam sawmill, plus logger's quarters in use. Be sure to stop in the Michigan Forest Visitor

Center before your walk out into the pines. See the history of logging - both past cut and run phases - and modern conservation forestry. The audiovisual show gives you a great overview. Did you know, today, there is more paper recycled than made from trees cut down? Find hands-on exhibits on computer (Forest Management Simulation), dioramas (Reading the Rings, Sounds of Birds), and the talking "Living Tree"... or talking Loggers and Rivermen displays. Their guides and programs have a great reputation.

### SKYLINE SKI AREA

**Grayling** - *4020 Skyline Road (I-75 to exit 251), 49738. Phone: (989) 275-5445. Hours: Thursday evenings, Friday-Sunday & Holidays 10:00am-9:00pm.* 14 runs. Rentals, lessons and ski shop.

### WELLINGTON FARM PARK

**Grayling** - *97 Michigan Avenue (west end), 49738. Phone: (989) 348-4461. **Web: www.wellingtonfarmpark.org**. Hours: Monday-Saturday 10:00am-4:00pm (Summer). Admission: $1.50 per person.* Located in the former Michigan Central Depot, the museum details local history from Camp Grayling military history to lumbering and fire fighting. The museum also has a railroad caboose, a farm shed, a trapper's cabin and a display dedicated to the greatest archer of all time - Fred Bear. Audio visual tapes of some of the area's old-timers telling family histories and stories of the early days.

### HARRISVILLE STATE PARK

**Harrisville** - *248 State Park Road (US-23 South of M-72), 48740. **Web: www.michigandnr.com/parksandtrails/Parklist.asp**. Phone: (989) 724-5126. Admission: $6.00-$8.00 per vehicle.* Harrisville State Park features a campground/mini-cabins and day-use area nestled in a stand of pine and cedar trees along the sandy shores of Lake Huron. The park is within walking distance of the resort town of Harrisville. Over ½ mile of Lake Huron frontage with Cedar Run Nature Trail, boating, fishing, swimming, bicycle trails, and winter sports.

## NEGWEGON STATE PARK

**Harrisville** - *248 State Park Road, 48740. Phone: (989) 724-5126  Web: www.michigandnr.com/parksandtrails/parklist.asp.* *Miscellaneous: Small gift shop.* A rustic, undeveloped area for hiking. No camping, no services.

## STURGEON POINT LIGHTHOUSE

Sturgeon Point Road (5 miles north of Harrisville State Park entrance, off US 23, Lakeshore Drive, follow signs)

**Harrisville** 48740

❑    Phone: (989) 724-5056
❑    Hours: Daily 10:00am-4:00pm (Memorial Day-September).

An 1869 lighthouse. Tour the restored lighthouse keeper's house, but not the tower (it's still in use). The stark contrast of the white painted bricks against the bright red trim makes the building very photogenic. Sitting on the shore end of a long and rocky submerged finger of land that juts into Lake Huron, it is plain to see why a lighthouse was needed here.

## BURT LAKE STATE PARK

**Indian River** - *6635 State Park Drive (I-75 exit 310 west to SR 68 to Old US 27), 49749. Phone: (231) 238-9392. Web: www.michigandnr.com/parksandtrails/parklist.asp.    Admission: $6.00-$8.00 per vehicle.* Burt Lake State Park is open from April to November (depending on the snowfall). It is located on the southeast corner of Burt Lake with 2,000 feet of sandy shoreline. Great beaches on the state's third largest lake, the park has numerous campsites and cabins, boating and rentals, fishing, swimming, and winter sports.

## ROMANIK'S RANCH

**Levering** - *10941 Weadock Road (I-75 exit 326, 13 miles south of Mackinaw), 49755. Web: www.romaniksranch.com. Phone: (231) 627-6106. Hours: Daily 10:00am-4:30pm (mid-May to Labor Day). Thursday-Sunday 10:00am-4:30pm (September-October). Admission: $9.00 adult, $8.00 senior, $6.00 child (5-12).* See donkeys, cows, goats, peacocks, ponies, sheep, pigs, horses, Koi fish ponds, chickens, prairie dogs and rabbits. Now touch and feed farm animals or take a hayride on the mile-long trail to see buffalo and elk herds in Michigan woodlands. There's also a playground, rustic barn, chuckwagon, and gift shop. Maybe try a buffalo burger or buffalo chip cookies?

## BUTTERFLY HOUSE

**Mackinac Island** - *1308  McGulpin Street (Huron Street north to Church Street west to McGulpin), 49757. Phone: (906) 847-3972.* **Web:** *www.mackinac.com/butterflyhouse. Hours: 10:00am-7:00pm (Summer), 10:00am-6:00pm (Labor Day- late October). Admission: $5.00 adult, $2.00 child (6-12).* See several hundred live butterflies from Asia, Central and South America and the United States in free flight. A great setting of tropical gardens. One of America's first butterfly houses featured in popular magazines.

# FORT MACKINAC STATE HISTORIC PARK
(on the bluff above downtown Mackinac Island)

### Mackinac Island 49757

❑    Phone: (906) 847-3328

     **Web: www.mackinacparks.com**

❑    Hours: Daily 9:30am-8:00pm (mid-June to mid August). Daily until 4:30pm (early May to mid-June and mid-August to mid-October).

❑    Admission: $9.50 adult, $6.00 student (6-17). Combo admission with Colonial Mackinac, Old Lighthouse and Mill Creek sites available for discount.

❑    Miscellaneous: Food available at Tea Room (lunch).

Your carriage is greeted by a period dressed soldier inviting strangers to visit. Children and families will want to see the short audio visual presentation in the Post Commissary Theater. It's quick and simple but enough to "pull you in". Next, if it's close to the top of the hour, be sure to check out the kid-friendly, wonderfully amusing, cannon firing and rifle firing demonstrations. Maybe volunteer to help the soldiers (check out the funny, pointed hats). The Post Hospital and Officer's Quarters (costumes/hands-on or "Hanging with Harold") and Blockhouses (short narrative by an animatronic figure) will intrigue the kids. In the new exhibit space, Military Medicine, you can hear through a giant stethoscope, visit with a virtual Post Surgeon on rounds, and take a look at a frostbitten foot! On your way in or out of the complex, be sure to visit the Soldier's Barracks exhibits featuring "Mackinac: An Island Famous in These Regions". Mackinac Island history from Furs (touch some) to Fish (step on a dock and listen to the fishermen come into port) to No Cars (1898 law) to Fudge! Oh, by the way, be sure to check and see if your ancestor was a Victorian soldier at Fort Mackinac.

## *MACKINAC ISLAND CARRIAGE TOURS*

### (Across from Arnold Ferry Dock - Main Street, Downtown)

### Mackinac Island 49757

- ❏   Phone: (906) 847-3307, **Web: www.mict.com**
- ❏   Hours: Daily 9:00am-5:00pm (mid - June - Labor Day). Daily 9:00am-4:00pm (mid-May to mid-June and Labor Day to October).
- ❏   Admission: $19.00 adult, $8.00 child (5-12).
- ❏   Tours: 1 hour & 45 minutes. You also have on/off privileges at several "hot spots".
- ❏   Miscellaneous: Since motor vehicles aren't permitted on the Island, this is one fun way to leisurely see the sites. It keeps the island quaint to have the clip-clop sound of carriages - we think you'll agree!

It's guaranteed you'll hear amusing stories of the history (past & present) of the island. The multi-seated carriages stop at all of these highlights: Arch Rock (which story of formation do you believe?), Skull Cave, the Governor's Mansion, Grand Hotel, Fort Mackinac, Surrey Hill shops and snacks (including Wings of Mackinac Butterfly House), and the horse's stable area. Look for several "parking lots" full of bikes and carriages! We recommend this tour on your first trip to the island.

## MACKINAC ISLAND STATE PARK

**Mackinac Island** 49757

❑   Phone: (906) 847-3328

    **Web: www.mackinacparks.com**

❑   Admission: FREE for center. Tours require fee.

❑   Tours: Summers- guided tours w/ costumed interpreters. Beaumont Memorial (dedicated to the studies of human digestion), Blacksmith, Biddle House (crafts), McGulpin House, Indian Dorm are off premises but part of package fee in the summer ($5.00-$6.00)

❑   Miscellaneous: Visitors Center located downtown on waterfront. Maps of numerous different trails to bike and/or walk (and easy-reading history of places you'll see) is available on many ferries or at the Visitors Center.

Most of Mackinac Island is preserved as a state park. Stretching eight miles around the island's perimeter, M-185 is a scenic shoreline road and the nation's only state highway without motor vehicle traffic. There are 70 miles of roads and trails within Mackinac Island State Park, most of which are wooded inland trails for hikers, bikers and horseback riders in spring, summer and fall. There are 1,800 acres under canopies of cedars, birches and crossings of creatures like butterflies. The prehistoric geological formations, Arch Rock and Sugar Loaf, are natural limestone wonders that tower over the Straits. These can be viewed from below on biking trails or from a walking overview. Fort Holmes features a panoramic view of the Fort Mackinac and the Straits of Mackinac at the island's highest point - 320 feet above Lake Level. Look for historic caves and nature trails around most every turn.

### WINGS OF MACKINAC

**Mackinac Island** - *(Surrey Hill Shops, just past Grand Hotel), 49757. Web: www.wingsofmackinac.com. Phone: (906) 847-WING.* Free-flying butterflies in a lush garden paradise setting. See exotic butterflies from around the world including: White Peacocks, Long-Tailed Skippers, Painted Ladies, Spice Bush Swallowtails, Graphium Decolors, Ruddy Daggerwings, Blue Morphos, Tiger Swallowtails and Monarchs. Curators available to answer questions. Admission: $2.50-$5.00 (age 5+).

## *COLONIAL MICHILIMACKINAC STATE HISTORIC PARK*

102 Straits Ave (Downtown under the south side of Mackinac Bridge - Exit 339 off I-75), **Mackinaw City** 49701

- ❑    Phone: (231) 436-5563, **Web: www.mackinacparks.com**
- ❑    Hours: Daily 9:00am-4:00pm (May to early October). Extended hours until 6:00pm (mid-June to mid-August).
- ❑    Admission: $9.50 adult, $6.00 youth (6-17). Combo tickets for Fort Mac, Colonial Michi and Mill Creek are available at great discounts.
- ❑    Miscellaneous: Many festivals are held here including encampments and Colonial weddings.

"Join the Redcoats (if you promise to grow). Watch a Dig. Dance a Jig". In the Summer, costumed docents (in character) demonstrate musket /cannon firing, cooking, blacksmithing, barracks living, church life, and trading. Pies cook near fireplaces, chickens roam free, and an amusing soldier leads you on a tour of the village. Originally occupied by the French, then the British, even the Indians - an audiovisual program will explain the details. Archeological digs are held in the summer to look for ongoing significant finds. Be sure to check out the updated "Treasure From the Sand" exhibit as it takes you to a unique underground tunnel display of subterranean artifacts recovered. In the Soldiers Barracks hands-on building: Dress up, stir the pot, lie in a bunk, try on coats, play a game or go into the "Black Hole" - a dark "time-out". Many areas of this park engage the kids interest - how cool to play (and learn) in a real fort!

## *HISTORIC MILL CREEK*

South US 23 (5 minutes southeast of town)

**Mackinaw City** 49701

- ❑    Phone: (231) 436-7301, **Web: www.mackinacparks.com**
- ❑    Hours: Daily 9:00am-5:00pm (mid-June to mid-August). Daily 9:00am-4:00pm (May to mid-June) & (Labor Day to late September).

Historic Mill Creek (*cont.*)

❑    Admission: $7.50 adult, $4.50 youth (6-17). Good combo rates
     when add Fort Michilimackinac, Old Lighthouse or Fort
     Mackinac.

❑    Miscellaneous: Cook house Snack Pavilion. Museum Store.
     Forest trails with working beaver dam.

As you walk along wooden planked paths, notice the different tree
names - Thistleberry, Ironwood, etc. You'll have an opportunity to
see a replica 18th century industrial complex - the oldest sawmill
yard to provide finished lumber - in the Great Lakes Region.
Water-powered sawmill and sawpit demos are given daily
(Summers -lumberjack demos). Participants can help demo old &
"newer", easier techniques to saw wood (which would you rather
do?). There's also a reconstructed millwrights' house on site along
with a museum. The audiovisual orientation is only 12 minutes
long and is a great way to understand Michigan lumber history.
Did you know a local amateur historian discovered this site,
accidentally, in 1972? Creatures of the Forest is a naturalist
outdoor "forest" talk - dress up as a beaver (why the raincoat?) and
learn how creatures and trees co-exist.

## *MACKINAC BRIDGE MUSEUM AND "MIGHTY MAC" BRIDGE*

231 East Central Avenue (Downtown within view of bridge)

**Mackinaw City** 49701

❑    Phone: (231) 436-5534, **Web: www.mackinacbridge.org**

❑    Hours: Daily 10:00am-9:00pm (May-October). Bridge open 24
     hours.

Go to the upstairs museum at Mama Mia's Pizza (donations only).
Watch the all new digitally re-mastered movie covering the history
and construction of the Mackinac Bridge back in the mid-1950's.
Why build the longest bridge ever - the "bridge that couldn't be
built"? When you see the black & white photos of the long lines,
staging cars to get on ferry boats to cross over the lake to the
Upper Peninsula, you'll see the reason. On display, are the original
spinning wheels that spun and ran cable (41,000 miles of it!) across

the bridge; the original wrench (9-10 feet long) used to tighten anchor bolts on the towers; and most interesting, the hard hats of the numerous iron workers. Now, pay the $2.50 toll and cross the 5 mile long steel super-structure! P.S. On a windy day the bridge bows or swings out to the east or west as much as 20 feet!

## *MACKINAC ISLAND FERRY SERVICES*

(Stops/Dock Pickups are clearly marked)

**Mackinaw City** 49701

Call for season schedules. Rain or shine. (early May - mid to late October). Note: Budget $9.00 for kids (age 5-12). $19.00 for adults. (Round Trip)

**ARNOLD LINE FERRY**. (800) 542-8528 or **www.arnoldline.com**. Smooth trips, large ships, comfortable seats and cabins. Restrooms.

**SHEPLER'S FERRY**. (800) 828-6157 or **www.sheplersferry.com**. Fast trips with very courteous and efficient staff. Restrooms. Narrative on the way over.

**STAR LINE FERRY**. (800) 638-9892 or **www.macinacferry.com**. Newest fleet. Most scheduled daily departures. Restrooms.

## *MACKINAW THEATER*

**Mackinaw City** - *248 South Huron Avenue (Mackinaw Crossings entertainment/shop complex), 49701. Phone: (231) 436-2200 or (877) 43-STAGE. Web: www.mackinawtheater.com. Showtimes: Tuesday-Sunday Mid-afternoon and early evening shows (May - mid-October). Admission: Average $23.00-$28.00 adult. Children half price.* Their signature "Reflections" show allows each guest to travel back to the "I remember when" places of your heart through two hours of tempos and tunes celebrating the impact of all forms of music on the memorable moments of our lives. It is the kind of show that makes you feel better about life and love. Kids like the silly sounds of songs and cool dance moves. Other artists are brought in several times per summer. Many are "reflection" era performers or impersonators.

## *MACKINAW TROLLEY TOURS*

(pickup at hotels), **Mackinaw City** 49701

❑   Phone: (231) 436-7812, **Web: www.mackinawtrolley.com**

❑   Miscellaneous: Kids of all ages get to ring the trolley bell (and get a sticker, too). If you climb Castle Rock, you get a sticker for that, too! This is a wonderfully organized tour with amusing stories and enough stops along the way to keep the kids attention from wandering. Try a different trip each visit!

HISTORICAL TOUR OVER THE BRIDGE: Ride through history on the Mackinaw Trolley as they narrate happenings and events along the way. Fort Michilimackinac area, Old Mackinac Point Lighthouse, Train and Car Ferry Docks, The Mackinac Bridge, Father Marquette's Mission and Grave Site at St. Ignace, Indian lore at Ojibwa Museum and the magnificent view from Castle Rock. 2½ hours. Departs 10:00am daily (mid-May to mid-October). Additional departure at 1:00pm during summer. Rates $7.00-$20.00 (age 3+).

LIGHTHOUSES OF NORTHERN LAKE HURON: Visit the Great Lakes Shipwreck Museum at Whitefish Point on Lake Superior to see artifacts and exhibits of shipwrecks, including the famous Edmund Fitzgerald, and many other ships that went down in the cold waters of Lake Superior. Tour the original Whitefish Point Lighthouse, and then venture along the Lake Superior shore line and through the Hiawatha Forest to climb and explore the famous Point Iroquois Lighthouse and tower. Enjoy the freighter watching from both lighthouses as the shipping lanes are just off shore.   Lunch included. 5 ½ hours (late June-late September). Rates $35.00 (part of group of 15+)

MACKINAW TROLLEY TRAIL: Ride along the desolate shores of sparkling Lake Michigan, walk the Wild Sand Dunes and through Forests in the faded footsteps of moccasins. View fields of rare wildflowers. Visit the McCormick Mansion overlooking historic Cecil Bay on Mackinac Headlands. Enjoy a delightful Polish-American lunch at the unique Legs Inn overlooking Lake Michigan. 3 hours. Departs Wednesday & Saturday 9:30am (mid-May-mid-June). Rates $7.00-$14.00 (part of group of 15+)

FALL COLOR TOUR: See Northern Michigan's brilliant fall colors and visit a scenic working farm producing 100 acres of pumpkins, gourds, Indian corn, and vegetables. Pick a pumpkin or a bucket of gourds right out of the field. Ride down back roads to Lakeshore Drive's famous tunnel of trees and view Michigan in all of her glory. Stop at a very special farm and store with garden fresh herbs, spices, vegetables, homemade preserves and canned goods, cut and dried flowers and other fall specialties (mid-September to mid-October). Rates $7.00-$20.00.

## *OLD MACKINAC POINT LIGHTHOUSE*

(just east of the Colonial Michilimackinac Visitor's Center in Mackinaw City near the south end of the Mackinac Bridge)

### **Mackinaw City** 49701

❑ Phone: (231) 436-4100 **Web: www.MackinacParks.com**

❑ Hours: Daily 9:00am-4:00pm (mid-May to early October). Extended until 5:00pm in summer.

❑ Admission: $6.00 adult, $3.50 student (6-17). We encourage checking out the discount combo deals with other Mackinac Historic Parks.

❑ Tours: Tours to the top of the lighthouse tower are available. The climb is about 4 stories via 51 steps and an 11-rung, vertical ladder through a narrow access opening. You should be over 4 feet tall and wear shoes that have no chance of falling off your feet while climbing the stairs and ladder (no bare feet or flip-flops).

Recently re-opened for the first time in over 50 years, the entire first floor of the structure and the tower is open for touring. Visitors will see original artifacts from the station, including the brass and glass Fresnel lens that lit the Straits of Mackinac for more than 60 years. Built in 1892, the light guided ships through the dangerous straits until the navigation lights from the Mackinac Bridge rendered it obsolete. Take a peek at the restored, fully furnished kitchen of the keeper's dwelling in its 1910 appearance. Guides in historic costumes are stationed within the lighthouse to provide historical information, conduct tours of the grounds and lead small groups up the tower. Enjoy a panoramic view of the Mackinac Straits with unique photographic perspectives of the Mackinac Bridge and Mackinac Island.

## THUNDER FALLS FAMILY WATERPARK

(off I-75 exit 337 or 338 and turn right), **Mackinaw City** 49701

❑    Phone: (231) 436-6000

     **Web: www.thunderfallswaterpark.com**

❑    Hours: Open daily 11:00am-8:00pm (summer).

❑    Admission: General Admission Rates: $16.00-$22.00. Twilight Special (Starts at 4pm) $13.95.

Visit one of Michigan's largest and newest Waterpark attractions, Thunder Falls Family Waterpark. Discover your favorite among 12 slides or enjoy the leisurely pace of our Lazy River. Cool off and relax in Michigan's best wave pool by riding the 4 foot waves, or enjoy the arcade, lounge areas, food court and interactive children's play areas. Water temperatures are comfortably heated.

### ONAWAY STATE PARK

**Onaway** - *3622 North M-211 (M-211 six miles north from the City of Onaway), 49765. Phone: (989) 733-8279.* **Web:** *www.michigandnr.com/parksandtrails/parklist.asp. Admission: $6.00-$8.00 per vehicle.* One of the oldest State Parks in Michigan is located on the southeast shore of Black Lake. The park covers 158 acres of rugged land, including sand cobblestone beaches, large unique rock outcroppings and a diversity of trees including a stand of virgin white pines. Known for game fishing, they also have camping, hiking trails, boating, and swimming. Just 10 miles east of the park is the picturesque Ocqueoc Falls, the largest waterfall in Michigan's Lower Peninsula.

### AU SABLE RIVER QUEEN

**Oscoda** - *West River Road (6 Miles West Of Oscoda), 48750. Web: www.riverqueencruises.com. Phone: (989) 739-7351 or (989) 728-3775. Admission: $6.00-$12.00 (age 5+). Prices can be slightly higher for fall color tours. Tours: 2 hour tours depart once or twice daily. Call ahead for times. (Memorial Day weekend - 3<sup>rd</sup>*

*weekend in October).* An authentic paddle wheel boat that has been touring this section of the river for over 40 years hosts you for a relaxing and narrated 19 mile trip. "Captain Bill" teaches about the area's history and wildlife along the journey. Glass enclosed decks and a snack bar are also available.

### *IARGO SPRINGS*

**Oscoda** - *(Au Sable River Road Scenic Byway), 48750. Phone: (800) 235-4625. Hours: Daily, year-round. FREE admission.* What once was a spot for tribal ceremonies (the Chippewas believed that the spring had medicinal qualities), today is a great place to take the family into nature. Be sure to tell your kids not use up too much energy as you descend the 294 steps down the banks to the spring (don't worry, there are benches to rest on the way back up!). A new nature boardwalk (with a 30' tall observation deck) and interpretive center are worth a look, too.

## *DINOSAUR GARDENS PREHISTORIC ZOO*
### 11160 US 23 South, **Ossineke** 49766

- ❑    Phone: (989) 471-5477 or (877) 823-2408
- ❑    Hours: Daily 10:00am-6:00pm (mid-May to mid-October).
- ❑    Admission: $3.00-$5.00 per person.
- ❑    Miscellaneous: Miniature golf. Snack bar.

An 80 foot long, 60,000 pound Brontosaurus is one of the many thrills that awaits your kids at this unique family tradition. A mixture of dinosaurs and cavemen with Christianity, as you're greeted by a Christ statue holding the world in his hand. Original owner Paul Domke spent some 38 years creating and sculpting 26 full scale dinosaurs that are "exploring" the forest of trees inside this attraction. A monstrous T-Rex in one exhibit is battling a Triceratops. Several scenes show cavepeople locked in mortal combat with giant snakes and Mastodons. A big-headed Aptosaurus is entered via a staircase. Inside the belly you'll find a heart-shaped Jesus — "The Greatest Heart." Storyboards and sound effects accompany each exhibit to help bring them to life. This is a great way to see the size and scale of the creatures that once walked the earth.

## PRESQUE ISLE LIGHTHOUSE MUSEUMS

East Grand Lake Road (US 23 to CR638)

**Presque Isle** 49777

❑   Phone: (989) 595-9917

❑   Hours: Daily 9:00am-5:00pm. (Mid-May to Mid-October).

❑   Admission: $1.50-$2.50 (age 6+).

❑   Gifts shops at both locations.

OLD LIGHTHOUSE: Supposedly haunted old lighthouse and keepers' house full of artifacts. Built in 1840, you can visit with the "lightkeeper lady" inside the keeper's cottage (so-o cute!). Kids can make noise blowing a foghorn or ringing a giant bell (or as George called it when he visited with his family when he was 2 years old...the Bongy Bell!). Any age can climb the minimal 33 stairs to the top of the lighthouse for a great view.

NEW LIGHTHOUSE: An 1871 lightkeepers' quarters and a larger, more classical lighthouse. At 113' high, New Presque Isle is one of the tallest lighthouses that shines on the Great Lakes. It has a Third Order Fresnel lens and a focal plane of light that is 123 feet above lake Huron. It's a challenge to climb the some odd 133 steps - but what a rush!

### HOEFT STATE PARK

**Rogers City** - *US-23 North, 49779. Phone: (989) 734-2543.* **Web:** *www.michigandnr.com/parksandtrails/parklist.asp. Admission: $6.00-$8.00 per vehicle.* Contains 300 heavily wooded acres with a mile of sandy Lake Huron shoreline in the 654 total acres of park. The park features 4 ½ miles of trails that run through the forest and along the shoreline that is perfect for hiking or cross-country skiing. The park also has mini-cabins available that sleep four people. Visitors can also enjoy swimming in Lake Huron, a picnic area and shelter, a playground, and boating and fishing.

### PRESQUE ISLE COUNTY HISTORICAL MUSEUM

**Rogers City** - *176 Michigan Street, 49779. Phone: (989) 734-4121. Hours:   Weekdays Noon-4:00pm. (June-October). Also Saturdays (July-August). Admission: Donations.* The restored

Bradley House contains exhibits based on local history. In various theme rooms on three floors, see a re-created general store or Victorian parlor. Displays include marine, lumbering and American Indian artifacts.

## THOMPSON'S HARBOR STATE PARK

**Rogers City** - *US23 North, 49779. Phone: (989) 734-2543. Web: www.michigandnr.com/parksandtrails/parklist.asp*. For the rugged outdoorsman in the family, explore over 6 miles of trails in an area that is located on the Lake Huron shoreline. Adjacent to the Presque Isle harbor. Park roads are undeveloped. Call ahead for driving conditions. No camping. No services.

## NORTH HIGGINS LAKE STATE PARK

11252 North Higgins Lake Drive (I-75 or US 27 exits - 7 miles west of town via US 27 and Military Road), **Roscommon** 48653

❑   Phone: (989) 821-6125 or (989) 373-3559 (CCC Museum)
    Web: www.michigandnr.com/parksandtrails/parklist.asp
❑   Hours: Park open dawn to dusk. Museum open summers
    11:00am-4:00pm.
❑   Admission: $6.00-$8.00 per vehicle.

Over 400 acres available for camping/cabins, picnicking, hiking, boating, fishing, swimming, and winter sports. Most people find the Civilian Conservation Corps Museum is the reason for their trip here. During the Great Depression, many men without work were enrolled to perform conservation and reforestation projects throughout Michigan. CCC planted trees, taught and practiced fire fighting, constructed trails, built bridges and even built buildings (some are still standing). Housed in replica barracks, the museum has displays of highlights and techniques of their work. Interpretive, outside walks are available too.

## SOUTH HIGGINS LAKE STATE PARK

**Roscommon** - *106 State Park Drive (I-75 at Roscommon Road south), 48653. Phone: (989) 821-6374. Web: www.michigandnr.com/parksandtrails/parklist.asp. Admission: $6.00-$8.00 per vehicle.* Voted some of the most beautiful lakes in the world, this park caters to families. The beaches are family-friendly and there's plenty of camping sites. Hiking trails, fishing, and winter sports are there too. For information on canoe and boat rentals call (989) 821-5930.

## RIFLE RIVER RECREATION AREA

**Rose City** - *(off M-33 southeast), 48654. Phone: (989) 473-2258. Web: www.michigandnr.com/parksandtrails/parklist.asp. Admission: $6.00-$8.00 per vehicle.* Rifle River Recreation Area is a wilderness located within the AuSable State Forest. Includes Devoe Lake and Grousehaven Lake, Lupton. Camping/cabins, hiking trails, boating, fishing, swimming and winter sports.

## SUGGESTED LODGING AND DINING

**MISSION POINT RESORT**: **Mackinac Island** (from the ferry docks, head east one-half mile). **www.missionpoint.com** or Phone: (906) 847-3312 or (800) 833-7711. This is truly a "family-friendly" resort and with the features they keep adding…it's a destination to stay at for a few days. You can just hang out around the grounds with amenities like: outdoor heated pool, tennis, croquet, horseshoes, video arcade/game room and lawn bowling. Or, sign up for a one hour Island sail or Ferry tour. Now, rent bikes or in-line skates and explore the 8 mile Island trail. They have four eateries and kids 12 & under eat FREE (most restaurants). They have hayrides, picnic games, poolside bingo and Sundae parties, too. Probably the best feature is their children's program: Mac The Moose Kid's Club, open to all youngsters ages 12 and under. Character meets, parties and tuck-in services are available for a fee. The Discovery Club Center has themes like "Space Day", "Nature Day", "Under the Sea", or "Wild West Day". They have a Tweeners club, too (ages 11-14). Rates: Start at $149.00 per night. Open May - October.

**GRAND HOTEL:**   **Mackinac Island** (from the ferry docks, head west one-half mile). (906) 847-3331 or (800) 33-GRAND or **www.grandhotel.com**. At 660 feet, Grand Hotel's Front Porch (full of white rockers) is the world's largest. Self-guided grounds tours are $10.00 per person if not a hotel guest. The kitchen staff of 100 serves as many as 4,000 meals per day. Their gourmet food is unforgettable! Ask to take a Kitchen Tour to see how they do it. Kids won't believe the large number of plates, pies and potatoes they use.  (Kitchen tours by pre-arrangement only or at special events). Recreational activities include: golf, tennis, croquet, bocci ball, swimming (outdoor pool), bicycling, saddle horses, carriage tours, duck pin bowling and a game room. Children's Programs (day or evening-3 hours) include "kids-style" lunches or dinners and fun group games, arts and crafts or a hike or tour. Rebecca's Playroom is open daily for families to enjoy games, crafts, videos and play when they are not conducting a paid program. Off-peak or special family rates begin at around $400.00 per night (includes full breakfast and five-course dinner and gratuities).  Watch the movies "Somewhere in Time" (Christopher Reeve/Jane Seymour) or "This Time for Keeps" (Esther Williams) before your visit to get the feel for the place. If you forget, they have a TV/VCR in every room and a copy of "Somewhere in Time" ready to watch. Remnants of these movies are found throughout the grounds (i.e.. Esther Williams pool or "Is it you?" twin trees). Believe it or not, this place is not stuffy...just casually elegant...best for a special treat or occasion.

# Chapter 4
## *North West Area*

# Our Favorites...

* Huron-Manistee National Forest - Cadillac

* Beaver Island - Charlevoix

* Sleeping Bear Dunes - Empire

* Kilwin's Candy Kitchens - Petoskey

* Petoskey State Park - Petoskey

*Climbing Sleeping Bear Dunes*

## MUSIC HOUSE MUSEUM

**Acme** - *7377 US 31 North (8 miles north of Traverse City), 49610. Phone: (231) 938-9300.* ***Web: www.musichouse.org.*** *Hours: Monday-Saturday 10:00am-4:00pm, Sunday Noon-4:00pm (May-October). Plus Holiday hours Friday-Sunday (mid-November thru December).* Guided tours feature major instruments being played and explained. Rare antique musical phonographs and music boxes.

## SHANTY CREEK RESORT SKI AREA

**Bellaire** - *One Shanty Creek Road (off M-88), 49615. Phone: (231) 533-8621 or (800) 678-4111* ***Web: www.shantycreek.com.*** A resort that features 41 runs, ski lessons, and equipment rentals. Accommodations include a new slopeside hotel. An Arnold Palmer designed golf course awaits your golfing skills in the summer. Great children's ski school. Babysitting is available.

## PLATTE RIVER STATE FISH HATCHERY

**Beulah** - *15120 US-31, 49617. Phone: (231) 325-4611.* ***Web: www.michigan.gov/dnr (click on Fishing).*** *Hours: Monday-Friday 8:00am-4:00pm (year-round).* Fish hatcheries are always a family favorite. The new information center, hatchery building, lower weir harvest facility and the upper weir egg-take station are the best places to learn. Best time to visit is in the fall when thousands of salmon can be seen.

## BOYNE MOUNTAIN & AVALANCHE BAY INDOOR WATERPARK

**Boyne Falls** - *(off US 131), 49713. Phone: (231) 549-6001 or (800) GO-BOYNE.* ***Web: www.boynemountain.com/bm_fr_ss.htm.*** *Hours: Resort is open year-round. Summer is golf, Winter is skiing. Indoor waterpark open all year. Admission: Lodge packages vary. Admission to waterpark begins at $25.00 per person (age 3+).*

MOUNTAIN RESORT: One of the Lower Peninsula's finest resorts, Boyne Mountain 40+ runs, many new trails, rentals, ski lessons, outdoor pool and slopeside lodging/cabins. A children's ski program and baby sitting are also available.

AVALANCHE BAY WATERPARK: Attached to the NEW Mountain Grand Lodge and Spa luxury hotel, Avalanche Bay Indoor Waterpark is BIG, WET, and fully enclosed providing a great year-round family aquatic adventure. Themed as a Swiss-Austrian village, Avalanche Bay Indoor Waterpark will transport guests to a winter wonderland enjoyed at a comfortable 84 degrees! Slides, rides, kid's pools, climbing wall, lazy river, even a surf simulator – there is something for everyone at Avalanche Bay. And for the little ones, Fritz the mascot and his furry friends will be at Avalanche Bay.

## *HURON-MANISTEE NATIONAL FORESTS*

1755 South Mitchell Street (over 960,000 acres in the northern part of the Lower Peninsula), **Cadillac** 49601

- ❑     Phone: (800) 821-6263
      **Web: www.fs.fed.us/r9/hmnf/index.shtml**
- ❑     Hours: Open 24 hours daily.
- ❑     Admission: $3.00 per carload per day.

Popular activities here are swimming in Lakes Huron and Michigan, cross-country skiing, snowmobiling, trout fishing, modern and rough camping, boating and bicycle trails. Popular spots within the forests are:

THE NORDHOUSE DUNES - one mile of undeveloped shoreline along Lake Michigan.

THE LODA LAKE WILDFLOWER SANCTUARY - one mile trail through marsh, forest and orchards. Over 40 miles of trails for hiking along the Manistee River.

THE RIVER ROAD SCENIC BYWAY - runs 22 miles along the south bank of the Au Sable River. View reservoirs, bald eagles, salmon, the Canoeists Memorial and the Lumberman's Memorial and Visitors Center of logging.

TUTTLE MARSH WILDLIFE AREA - Managed 5000 acres of fox, deer, coyote, muskrat, beaver, otter and weasel.

# MITCHELL STATE PARK

6093 East M-115 (3 miles north of US 131)

**Cadillac** 49601

☐   Phone: (231) 775-7911

   **Web: www.michigandnr.com/parksandtrails/parklist.asp**

☐   Admission: $6.00-$8.00 per vehicle.

☐   Miscellaneous: Camping and cabins, boating and rentals, fishing, swimming, and winter sports.

The park is 245 acres and is situated between Lake Mitchell and Lake Cadillac and provides an excellent opportunity to view a variety of wildlife on the outskirts of Cadillac. A historic canal connects the two lakes and runs directly through the park. The Visitor's Center is also called the Carl T. Johnson Hunting & Fishing Center. A full size Michigan elk mount is on display in the exhibit hall, as well as other wildlife species which have been "brought back" by the efforts of sportsperson's organizations. With the push of a button, visitors can hear the call of the elk or other species featured in the wildlife exhibit. Exhibits include a wall-length aquarium and trapping and conservation efforts. Many come here for the birding too. You may see great blue heron, yellow finches and mallards. Center open Tuesday - Sunday 10:00am-6:00pm (May-November). Weekends only the rest of the year.

## SUGAR LOAF RESORT

**Cedar** - *4500 Sugar Loaf Mountain Road (off M-72), 49621. Phone: (231) 228-1553 or (800) 952-6390. Hours: Resort is open year-round, but skiing is usually from December-March. Golf in summer.* 20 runs, an excellent kids' ski schools (toddlers and up), rentals, lessons, and a restaurant. Indoor pool and spa with attached fitness center, and a heated outdoor pool.

## BEAVER ISLAND BOAT COMPANY

**Charlevoix** - *103 Bridge Park Drive, 49720. Phone: (231) 547-2311 or (888) 446-4095.* **Web: www.bibco.com.** *Admission: $33.00 adult, Basically Half Price-child (5-12). Rates are roundtrip. Vehicle transport also available.* Passenger and Car Ferry service from Charlevoix to Beaver Island, the Great Lakes' most remote inhabited island. Tour drivers will guide you through Beaver Island's beautiful scenery & intriguing history, while giving you an idea of why island life is so unique. Beaver Island is home to two lighthouses. Packages include round trip cruises and possible escorted island tours of museums and island lunches. Call for schedule and information (April-December).

### FISHERMAN'S ISLAND STATE PARK

**Charlevoix** - *Bells Bay Road (off US-31 southwest), 49720. Web: www.michigandnr.com/parksandtrails/parklist.asp. Phone: (231) 547-6641. Admission: $6.00-$8.00 per vehicle.* A 2,678-acre park in Charlevoix County that features a park road that travels for two and one-half miles along the Lake Michigan shoreline. Away from the shoreline, the park's terrain consists of rolling dunes, covered with maple, birch, and aspen, broken up by bogs of cedar and black spruce. Camping, hiking, fishing, swimming and bicycle trails.

### YOUNG STATE PARK

**Charlevoix** - *2280 Boyne City Road (US-131, west on M-75), 49720. Web: www.michigandnr.com/parksandtrails/parklist.asp. Phone: (231) 582-7523. Admission: $6.00-$8.00 per vehicle.* Young State Park is located at the east end of beautiful Lake Charlevoix. The park spans over 560 acres in Charlevoix County and is a mix of gently rolling terrain, lowlands, and cedar swamp. Camping, hiking, boating and rentals, fishing, swimming and winter sports.

### LEGS INN

**Cross Village** - *M-119 (US 31 to Carp Lake Village to Gill Road west through Bliss Township to Cross Village), 49723. Phone: (231) 526-2281. Web: www.legsinn.com. Hours: Daily, Lunch and Dinner. (mid-May to mid-October).* Included on the State Historic Register, this restaurant's roof line is ornamented with inverted cast-iron stove legs. The fantasy-like atmosphere of this medieval looking stone, timber and driftwood landmark was created by one man, Polish immigrant, Stanley Smolak. The original Polish owner was also inducted into the Ottawa Indians tribe locally. His

sculptures and whimsy decorating using tree trunks will intrigue
you. The authentic Polish cuisine is the specialty, but delicious
American dishes are also served. Indoor/Outdoor dining but no
A/C. Casual dress. Moderate prices. Children's Menu.

## *SLEEPING BEAR DUNES NATIONAL LAKESHORE*

9922 Front Street (SR 72) (I-75 to M-72 exit, head west. 35 miles
along northwest Lower Peninsula shores), **Empire** 49630

- ❑   Phone: (231) 326-5134,  **Web: www.nps.gov/slbe**
- ❑   Hours: (Visitor's Center) Daily 8:00am-6:00pm (Summer). Daily
      9:00am-4:00pm (rest of year).
- ❑   Admission: $10.00 per week/ per vehicle or $5.00 per person per
      week.
- ❑   Miscellaneous: Visitor's Center in Empire has nice slide show to
      understand area better.

The name of the shore comes from Chippewa Indian stories of a
mom and her two bear cubs separated by a forest fire. The cubs
now stand for the North and South Manitou Islands - still stranded.
Among the dunes are rugged bluffs, ghost forests, and exposed
bleached trees. From late April through early November, take the
Pierce Stocking Scenic Drive route to view the dunes. On South
Manitou Island, climb the 100 foot lighthouse or view the wreck of
a freighter or the Valley of Giants (white cedar trees). The islands
are accessible by ferry from Leland. The Maritime Museum at the
Coast Guard Station in Glen Haven displays maritime area history
and is open summers only. A daily re-enactment of a Life-Saving
Service rescue is the highlight of every afternoon (specifically
directed toward kids!). The ever-popular Dune Climb is a
challenge, but so worth it! (Remember, climbing down is much
easier than climbing up!). Be sure to take pictures once you arrive
on a high summit. Ranger-led walks, campfire programs and other
activities are available in July and August. Fishing, canoeing,
hiking and cross-country skiing are favorite activities here.

## BOYNE HIGHLANDS

**Harbor Springs** - *600 Highlands Drive (I-75 exit 282, west on M-32), 49740. Phone: (800) GO-BOYNE or (231) 526-3000. Web: www.boynehighlands.com.* Besides great family skiing (on your choice of 44 slopes), this resort offers a large heated outdoor pool that is warm even when the outside temperature is below zero. Babysitting, rentals, slopeside lodging (inn and cottages), children's activities and lessons are also available.

YOUNG AMERICANS DINNER THEATRE: talented young performers, ages 15-21, come together from across the nation and make Boyne Highlands their summer home. The show features all styles of music from the past 100 years along with various numbers from the Broadway hits of yesterday and today. They present this unique music and dance experience while serving as your waiters and waitresses. Dinner shows $23.00-$40.00.

## NUB'S NOB

**Harbor Springs** - *500 Nub's Nob Road, 49740. Phone: (800) SKI-NUBS or (231) 526-2131. Web: www.nubsnob.com.* Across the street from Boyne Highlands (see listing), Nub's Nob offers 41 runs, rentals, instructions, and children's activities. Also, for the beginners, be sure to check out the Midwest's only Free LEARN-TO-SKI & SNOWBOARD AREA (all ages) complete with its own chairlift.

## FUN COUNTRY WATER PARK

**Interlochen** - *9320 US-31 South (US 31 & M-137), 49643. Phone: (231) 276-6360. Web: www.funcountrytc.com. Hours: Daily 11:00am-9:00pm. Water slide closes at 6:30pm (Memorial Day - Labor Day). Admission: Day Pass ~$14.00 (age 4+). Toddlers are half price.* Beat the heat by cooling off in one of their three water areas offering a large twisting, turning waterslide that sends you down 300 feet of thrilling fun and a smaller slide for the little ones ending in a wading pool with squirt guns that battle each other. Step into the Splash Zone, an aquatic playground offering dumping buckets, water guns, and many other water features sure to get you soaked. After you get dried off, test your skill on the go kart track. Next, test your skill on our 18 hole adventure golf featuring waterfalls, rivers and bridges. The little ones will love trying out the Power Paddler boats. They also offer an arcade and a full service snack bar serving everything from burgers to ice cream.

## INTERLOCHEN STATE PARK

**Interlochen** - *M-137 (South of US 31), 49643. Phone: (231) 276-9511   Web: www.michigandnr.com/parksandtrails/parklist.asp. Admission: $6.00-$8.00 per vehicle.* Camping on the beach of the lake with bathhouses and boat rentals is popular especially in the summer. Summer Music Camp Shows. Hiking trails, fishing, boating, bicycle trails, and winter sports are available.

## BOTTLE HOUSE MUSEUM

**Kaleva** - *14451 Wuoksi (next to Bethany Lutheran Church), 49645. Phone: (231) 362-3793. Hours: Saturday Noon-4:00pm (Memorial Day weekend-Labor Day weekend). Other times by appointment.* Over 1500 articles of historical interest housed in the beautiful and unique building well known as the "Bottle House." The home was built with over 60,000 soft drink bottles in 1941. It is listed on the Michigan Register of Historical Sites, Ripley's Believe it or Not and the National Register of Historic Sites.

## ORCHARD BEACH STATE PARK

**Manistee** - *2064 Lakeshore Road, 49660. Phone: (231) 723-7422. Web: www.michigandnr.com/parksandtrails/parklist.asp. Admission: $6.00-$8.00 per vehicle.* Lots of reasonable camp site rentals on the dunes, great beaches with swimming, hiking trails.

## WATER BUG, THE

**Manistee** - *Manistee River Walk, South River Bank (west of Maple/Washington St. off River St, behind Department Store), 49660. Web: www.manistee.com/~waterbug/ Phone: (231) 398-0919. Tours: Historical (1:00 & 3:00pm) or Lighthouse (sunset). Closed Mondays and Tuesdays except holidays. Memorial Day weekend-Labor Day. $10.00 adult, $5.00 child.* View the Historical Victorian Port City of Manistee from the water. Trip includes view of Historic Downtown, Wetlands and the beautiful Lighthouse from a 22 passenger riverboat.

## LEELANAU STATE PARK / GRAND TRAVERSE LIGHTHOUSE

15310 North Lighthouse Point Road (north of Traverse City on M-22 through Northport and take M-201 eight miles north),

**Northport** 49670

❑    Phone: (231) 386-5422

   **Web: www.michigandnr.com/parksandtrails/parklist.asp**

❑    Admission: $6.00-$8.00 per vehicle.

The word Leelanau is the Indian word for "A Land of Delight" and could not better describe the area. Along the shorelines, Petoskey stones can be found. Camping/cabins, hiking trails, fishing, swimming and winter sports.

GRAND TRAVERSE LIGHTHOUSE tours along coastal dunes are a big draw (**www.grandtraverselighthouse.com**, daily afternoons May thru October, and November weekends). Today, one can tour the restored lighthouse resembling a keeper's home of the 1920's and 30's. Exhibits on area lighthouses, foghorns, shipwrecks and local history are located in the Lighthouse and Fog Signal Building. The restored air diaphone foghorn is demonstrated throughout the year, and visitors can climb the tower for a spectacular view of Lake Michigan.

## KILWIN'S CANDY KITCHENS

355 North Division Street, **Petoskey** 49770

❑    Phone: (231) 347-3800  **Web: www.kilwins.com**

❑    Admission: FREE

❑    Tours: Monday - Thursday 10:30am, 11:00am, 2:00pm, 2:30 pm. 20 minutes (June - August). Group tours (10+) by reservation during non-peak candy-making (after holidays).

❑    Miscellaneous: Retail store sells over 300 types of mouth-watering candy.

When first arriving, you'll probably park your car where the sign reads, "Chocolate Lovers Parking - All Others Will Be Towed". This is just the right kind of invitation to let you (and the kids) know that you are in for a real treat. Northern Michigan seems to have a real taste for fudge and candy and Kilwan's is one of the area's most respected candy-makers. Get "close to the action" on this tour and see all of the various production processes. The kids will love watching 2 workers stretching 3 foot slabs of peanut brittle!

## *LITTLE TRAVERSE HISTORICAL MUSEUM*

**Petoskey** - *100 Depot Court (Waterfront at Bayfront Park), 49770. Phone: (616) 347-2620. Web: www.petoskeymuseum.org. Hours: Thursday-Saturday 1:00-4:00pm (May-October). Admission: $1.00 adult (over 18). FREE for children.* Housed in an old railroad depot, you'll find information about the area's Okawa Indians and pioneer times. Exhibits about Ernest Hemingway (Much of the exhibit revolves around the time when Hemingway lived in the Petoskey area as a young man) and Civil War author Bruce Catton. Display of Petoskey stones, too.

## *PETOSKEY STATE PARK*

### 2475 M-119 (north of US 31)

#### **Petoskey** 49770

❑    Phone: (231) 347-2311
        Web: www.michigandnr.com/parksandtrails/parklist.asp
❑    Admission: $6.00-$8.00 per vehicle.

Old Baldy Trail includes a stairway that leads up Old Baldy, a stable dune that is one of the attractions in the park. After climbing the dune, the view that is available of the bay is breathtaking. The Portage Trail winds through very diverse terrain where a nature lover may find different species of plants and wildlife. Campsites along Little Traverse Bay with a great beach and trails in and out of wooded dunes. There's well developed nature trails and in Spring, sort through Winter's debris for Petoskey stones (designated Michigan state stone). Look for the coral fossils in the stones and you've probably found one. Boating and winter sports are also available.

## *CRYSTAL MOUNTAIN RESORT*

12500 Crystal Mountain Drive (off M-115), **Thompsonville** 49683

❑ Phone: (231) 378-2000 or (800) 968-7686 Adventure Center
   **Web: www.crystalmtn.com**
❑ Hours: Resort is open year-round. Skiing usually December-
   March. Golf and waterpark in summer.

WINTER: Crystal Mountain is a "family-friendly" resort that offers 34 runs with a children's "learn to ski" program, indoor and outdoor pools, restaurant, and slopeside rooms.

SUMMER: THE PARK AT WATER'S EDGE. One-acre outdoor waterpark complex with large pool with zero-depth entry. Lap lanes, water playground (water cannon, lily pad walk, water basketball and volleyball court, a tumble pail, crawl tube), hot tub and a sand play area. Around $10.00 per person admission. Cottages feature 22 two-and three-bedrooms. Also, Saturday chairlift rides for a great view and supervised tube or canoe trips on the Platte River. Bike rentals and planned family games and recreation available as packages.

### *TALL SHIPS "WESTWIND" & "MANITOU"*

**Traverse City** - *13390 SW Bay Shore Drive (Grand Traverse Bay - West arm), 46984. Phone: (231) 941-2000 or (800) 678-0383. **Web:** www.tallshipsailing.com. Admission: Varies by length of "get-away". 2 hour sails range from $32.00-40.00 adult/ Half price child. Call or visit website for sailing schedules and rates. (Summer)* The Westwind (66') and Manitou (114') ships offer tours and accommodations during the summer months. The Westwind calls Traverse City her home port. From there, she offers fun-filled 2-hour outings, three to four times a day throughout the sailing season. Her bright white sails and hull are a most popular sight on the sparkling waters of West Grand Traverse Bay. The sunset cruises can be breath-taking. "Manitou" is one of the largest sailing ships on the Great Lakes, similar in design to vessels that sailed one hundred years ago. She was built specifically for passenger service, making her one of the most comfortable windjammers afloat. Up to twenty-four passengers can enjoy the pleasure and thrill of sailing aboard "Manitou."

## *CLINCH PARK ZOO*

**Traverse City** - *Union & Grandview Parkway (Next to the beach), 49684. Web: www.ci.traverse-city.mi.us/services/zoo.htm. Phone: (231) 922-4904. Hours: Daily 9:30am-5:30pm (Memorial Day-Labor Day). Daily 10:00am-4:00pm (mid-April - Memorial Day & day after Labor Day - October). Admission: $2.00-$4.00 (age 5+). Train rides additional.* A smaller zoo in the heart of the downtown resort/shopping area that features wildlife that is native to Michigan. Picnic area, concession stands and small train rides (Memorial Day - Labor Day).

## *GREAT WOLF LODGE*

**Traverse City** - *3575 North US 31 South, 49684. Phone: (231) 941-3600. Web: www.greatwolflodge.com.* A Northwoods themed year-round resort with family-sized suite lodging; a huge indoor waterpark (waterslides, a family boat ride, indoor/outdoor pool, children's pool, lazy river, whirlpools and interactive water fort); an arcade and restaurant. This all-in-one resort draws you in to stay in the backwoods, modernly rustic setting. Your stay includes passes to the indoor waterpark, evening storytimes and Cub club activity room. The décor in the lobby and suites are so comfortable.

## *PIRATE'S COVE ADVENTURE PARK*

**Traverse City** - *1710 US-31 North, 49684. Phone: (231) 938-9599. Web: www.piratescove.net. Hours: Daily 10:00am-11:00pm (late April-late October). Admission: $6.00-$9.50 per activity (age 4+). Rides use tokens that can be purchased.* Adventure Miniature golf in a fun-filled setting of lavish landscaping and delightful pirate themes. Putt your way over footbridges, under waterfalls, and through mountain caves. Sharpen your putting skills on Blackbeard's Challenge Course, Captain Kidd's Adventure or The Original Course. A fun park for kids of all ages. Electric cars entertain the youngest kids while go-carts and waterslide (must be 42" tall to use) help keep the older kids entertained. Specially designed to be ridden in your street clothes—if you dare! Maybe try a bumper boat pond with squirt gun-equipped boats.

## *DENNOS MUSEUM CENTER*

**Traverse City** - *1701 East Front Street (On campus of Northwestern Michigan College), 49686. Phone: (231) 995-1055.* **Web: www.dennosmuseum.org.** *Hours: Monday-Saturday 10:00am-5:00pm, Sunday 1:00-5:00pm. Closed on major holidays. Admission: $4.00 adult, $2.00 child (under 18).* A regional hub for arts and culture, this dramatic building features three rotating exhibition galleries, a sculpture court, a gallery of Inuit Eskimo art from the museum's permanent collection as well as the 367-seat Milliken Auditorium, a 32-seat video theater, and a museum store. Highlights of the Discovery gallery include several unique interactive exhibitions including Recollections and Elastic Surgery, The Sound Wall, A Laser Harp and Anti-Gravity mirror plus numerous exhibitions related to light and color. The gallery also features a Hubble Space Telescope theater with ongoing transmission of programming from NASA and the Space Telescope Institute.

## *OLD MISSION PENINSULA LIGHTHOUSE*

**Traverse City** - *(along M-37), 49686.* View this 19$^{th}$ Century lighthouse and step back in time as your kids stand at the geographical point that is exactly halfway between the Equator and the North Pole.

## *SAND LAKES QUIET AREA*

**Traverse City** - *(M-72 to Broomhead Road - South), 49686. Phone: (231) 922-5280. Hours: Always open (year-round). Free admission.* This adventurous place is so "quiet" (as the name implies) because all motor vehicles are banned from the 10 miles of trails that feature fishing and camping. Make your plans to hike in and camp and see how Michigan must have looked to the early pioneers and Native Americans. (Note: Trails are not stroller accessible).

### *TRAVERSE CITY STATE PARK*

**Traverse City** - *1132 US-31 east, 49686. Phone: (231) 922-5270. Web: www.michigandnr.com/parksandtrails/parklist.asp. Admission: $6.00-$8.00 per vehicle.* Almost 350 campsites opposite Grand Traverse Bay with bridge to beach and close to attractions. Hiking trails, boating, fishing, swimming, and winter sports, too.

## *GREAT LAKES CHILDREN'S MUSEUM*

13240 S. West Bayshore Drive (across from Heritage Harbor, on M-22), **Traverse City (Greilickville)** 49684

- ❑   Phone: (231) 932-GLCM  **Web: www.greatlakeskids.org**
- ❑   Hours: Tuesday-Saturday 10:00am-5:00pm, Sunday 1:00-5:00pm. Thursday until 6:00pm.
- ❑   Admission: $4.00 per person (age 2+).

A hands-on interactive children's museum focused on the Great Lakes and water. Exhibits include kid-sized lighthouse, a sailboat, and a periscope. A child can pilot a Great Lakes freighter or navigate the Lakes on the navigation wall. Thoughts Flow area, visitors can interact directly with moving water, channeling and redirecting it in hundreds of different ways. In the Water Cycle children can go up the sunshine climb as they evaporate, condense in the cloud chamber, slide down as precipitation, and then go into the groundwater tunnel. There are over 30 exhibits & activities awaiting.

# Chapter 5
## *South East Area*

# Our Favorites...

* Jiffy Mix Tour - Chelsea
* The Henry Ford Museum - Dearborn
* Greenfield Village - Dearborn
* Ford Rouge Factory Tours - Dearborn
* Lionel Trains Visitor Center - Chesterfield (Detroit)
* Diamond Jack's River Tours - Gross Ile (Detroit)
* Detroit Zoo - Artic Ring of Life - Royal Oak (Detroit)
* Stagecoach Stop USA - Irish Hills
* MSU's Children's Garden & Dairy Plant - E. Lansing
* Michigan Historical Center - Lansing

*A Giant Industrial Lab - Ford Rouge Tour*

## WILD SWAN THEATER

**Ann Arbor** - *416 West Huron Street (performances at Towsley Auditorium), 48103. Web: www.wildswantheater.org. Phone: (734) 995-0530. Admission: $8.00-$10.00 for single tickets.* A professional theater company that performs for family audiences using dance, masks, puppets and music. Productions like "Winnie the Pooh" or "Peter Rabbit" and other famous storybook tales come to life for the kids. Mostly matinees.

## ANN ARBOR HANDS-ON MUSEUM

### 220 East Ann Street (between 4th & 5th Avenue - Downtown)

### Ann Arbor 48104

- ❏ Phone: (734) 995-5439, **Web: www.aahom.org**
- ❏ Hours: Monday-Saturday 10:00am-5:00pm, Sunday Noon-5:00pm.
- ❏ Admission: $7.00 adult (age 2+).
- ❏ Miscellaneous: Explore Store.

Your kid's eyes will light up with amazement as you explore over 250 exhibits on 4 floors in this old firehouse. Watch your skeleton ride a bicycle as you explore human movement, play a song on a walk-on piano, "be one" with a green screen, touch fossils, have bubble fun, climb walls, and whisper across the room to a friend (and they can hear you) are just a few of offerings. Learn "How Things Work" with gears, pulleys and air movement or play a laser harp in "Light & Optics". "Waste to Watts" shows how new environmentally friendly technology can turn our trash into electricity. Let the little ones find their own space in the "Preschool Gallery". (Remember Mom & Dad...you came for the children...but learning sure is fun!).

## DOMINO'S FARMS

### 24 Frank Lloyd Wright / Earhart Road (I-94 to US-23 North. Take US-23 North to Plymouth Road exit (exit 41), Ann Arbor 48106

- ❏ Phone: (734) 998-0182, **Web: www.pettingfarm.com**
- ❏ Hours: Monday-Friday 9:30am-4:00pm, Saturday & Sunday 10:30am-5:00pm.
- ❏ Admission: $4.50-$5.00 per person (age 2+).

Domino's Farms (*cont.*)

❑   Miscellaneous: Picnic area. Domino's Pizza available.

First pass a herd of buffalo or cows grazing on the grounds of the Domino's Pizza World Headquarters. Across the street is Domino Farms, an early 1900's depiction of Michigan farm life. The Petting Farm has 100+ chickens, goats, sheep, peacocks, pot-bellied pigs, and miniature horses. Take a hayride to buffalo fields and stop and get a close look at their shy, huge faces! Many animal demonstrations throughout the day. One of the cleanest farms you'll ever see. Nice outdoor activity to enjoy with a picnic.

## *UNIVERSITY OF MICHIGAN MUSEUMS*

(I-94 to State Street Exit), **Ann Arbor** 48109

❑   **Web: www.umich.edu**
❑   Tours: Many of these facilities are included in a group tour- by appointment.

SPORTS MUSEUM - 1000 South State Street - (734) 647-2583. Captures the spirit of 100+ years of athletic competition with emphasis on the Rose Bowl, Big Ten and U.S. Olympics. Located in the nation's largest college stadium. Weekdays until 4:00pm.

MUSEUM OF NATURAL HISTORY - 1109 Geddes Avenue - (734) 764-0478. Michigan birds and animals. Face to face with prehistoric allosaurus conquering a stegosaurus or a mastodon from Michigan. Evolution of whale's skeletons. Daily until 5:00 pm. Suggested donation $3.00-$5.00. Planetarium.

MUSEUM OF ARCHEOLOGY - 434 South State Street - (734) 764-9304. 100,000+ artifacts from ancient Egypt, Greece and Rome. See a mummy child! Open Daily until 4:00pm, except Mondays.

STEARNS MUSICAL COLLECTION - 1100 Baits Drive - North Campus - (734) 763-4389. 2000+ musical instruments on display from around the world. Open until 4:00pm weekdays.

BOTANICAL GARDENS - 1800 North Dixboro Road - (734) 998-7061. Tropical, warm-tempered or desert plants. Nature trail. Prairie. Daily 10:00am - 4:30pm. Admission $1.00-$3.00.

## ISLAND LAKE RECREATION AREA

**Brighton** - *12950 East Grand River (I-96, exit 151), 48116. Web: www.michigandnr.com/parksandtrails/parklist.asp. Phone: (810) 229-7067. Admission: $6.00-$8.00 per vehicle.* A canoe livery offers relaxing trips down the scenic Huron River. Hiking trails, beaches, boating, fishing, swimming, bicycle trails, winter sports and cabins available.

## MOUNT BRIGHTON SKI AREA

**Brighton** - *4141 Bauer Road (I-96 - Exit 145), 48116. Phone: (810) 229-9581. Web: http://users.iglide.net/mtbrighton/.* A "family friendly" attraction that offer 26 runs of various skill levels. Snowboarding, lessons and rentals are available.

## BRIGHTON RECREATION AREA

**Brighton** - *6360 Chilson Road (I-96 exit 145 south), 48843. Web: www.michigandnr.com/parksandtrails/parklist.asp. Phone: (810) 229-6566. Admission: $6.00-$8.00 per vehicle.* The area has a combination of high, irregular ranges of hills, interspersed with a number of attractive lakes. Oak forest, thick hedgerows and open spaces blend on the uplands while grassy marshes, shrub masses and dense swamp timber mark the lowlands. Beaches, swimming, and trout fishing are most popular here. Other features include hiking, winter sports, modern and rough camping, boating and bicycle trails.

## MICHIGAN INTERNATIONAL SPEEDWAY

**Brooklyn** - *12626 US 12 (1 mile west of M-50), 49230. Web: www.mispeedway.com. Phone: (517) 592-6666 or (800) 354-1010 tickets. Hours: Call or visit website for current schedule. (Summer). Admission: $15.00-$100.00 per person.* Gentlemen (and ladies) start your engines! The thrill of world class professional motorsports is alive and well in Michigan. This speedway is a D-shaped, 2-mile oval that offers high-banked (18 degree) turns to a variety of racing vehicles including NASCAR, CART, and the NASCAR Craftsman Truck Series. Also see the fastest 400 mile race, the annual Michigan 400 or Winston Cup series.

## CALDER DAIRY FARM

9334 Finzel Road (I-275 - Telegraph Road Exit (south), to Stoney Creek Rd - West to Finzel Rd South - follow signs), **Carleton** 48117

❑   Phone: (734) 654-2622 **Web: www.calderdairy.com**
❑   Hours: Daily 10:00am-8:00pm. Winter hours vary.
❑   Admission: FREE
❑   Tours: Pre-arranged @ $6.00 per person (includes hayride and ice cream cone). Minimum group is 15.
❑   Miscellaneous: Farm Store and Ice Cream Shop. Main Store - watch milk arriving and fed through series of pipes for processing.

See how luscious ice cream is made - right from the Brown Swiss Cow's milk! Pet the Holstein and Swiss Cows plus numerous other animals that you're likely to see on a farm (pigs, ducks, sheep). They make creamy ice cream, chocolate milk, eggnog, plus milk right from the cows - fresh in glass bottles. Check out the milking machines behind the store to see cows milked by the dozen. Take a tour in a hay wagon (horse driven) and you'll see fields of llamas, deer and bright peacocks. At the end of your visit to the land of "Babe", be sure to get a generous souvenir cup of fresh ice cream!

## CHELSEA MILLING - "JIFFY MIX"

201 West North Street (I-94 west to Chelsea exit - north - follow signs), **Chelsea** 48118

❑   Phone: (734) 475-1361, **Web: www.jiffymix.com**
❑   Hours: Monday-Friday 9:00am-1:30pm. Closed Holidays.
❑   Admission: FREE
❑   Tour: By appointment only. Age 6 and up (for safety reasons in the plant). 45 person max. Entire tour takes about 1 ½ hours.
❑   Miscellaneous: Souvenir box of Jiffy Mix given with recipe booklet. Chelsea Milling calls itself a complete manufacturer: storing wheat, milling wheat into flour, producing mixes from the flour and even making the little blue boxes.

In a time when manufacturing tours are minimal or eliminated, this is a good, old-fashioned tour! Inside the world headquarters of the internationally known Jiffy Mix Baking Products, you'll begin in the auditorium with a slide show narrated by your tour guide.

Because they're veteran associates, they talk about each operator by name. Learn some history about the company including how they got the name "Jiffy". In 1930, Grandma Mabel Holmes named the famous, low-priced, blue and white baking mix boxes "Jiffy" after hearing cooks exclaim, "The muffins will be ready in a jiffy!". Their flour is from Michigan and is milled using silk material similar to your kid's blanket edging. You'll see the packaging process, first in the slide show, then actually out in the factory. After you have a snack of Jiffy Mix cookies and juice, everyone adorns a hair net and takes a 20 minute walking tour of the packaging process. It's neat to see waxed paper formed in a block, filled, boxed and then sealed. The sealing machine is a cute 8 legged machine. Did you know their #1 selling product is "Corn Muffin" mix? At the end of the tour you can choose from muffin or another mix box to take home…yummies there…yummies at home!

## WATERLOO RECREATION AREA

16345 McClure Road (take I-94 to exit 157 (Pierce Road) and go north to Bush Road), **Chelsea** 48118

❑ Phone: (734) 475-8307

**Web: www.michigandnr.com/parksandtrails/parklist.asp**

❑ Admission: $6.00-$8.00 per vehicle.

The lower peninsula's largest state park, it features cross-country skiing, horse rental and trails, modern and rough camping and cabins, beaches and boating, fishing, bicycle trails, and winter sports. For an additional small charge, you can tour the Farm Museum buildings. There's also long hiking trails and an Audubon Society preserve adjacent. Many visit often to the Eddy Geology center (open Tuesday-Sunday 9:00am-5:00pm, 734-475-3170), where you can view changing samples of geos from the Great Lakes, Michigan and the Midwest. The exhibits include: a "mad scientist lab" with interactive tests of mineral radioactivity, luminescence and computer microscopes; an interactive map of Michigan's bedrock with lift-door samples from prominent sites; and a "fossil graveyard" featuring lift-a-rock models of famous fossilized bones and teeth. Touch-screen computer mineral games challenge users to "where does it come from," and a model ice cave takes the visitor back to the Ice Age through blue-screen technology. There's also a collection station that has rotating rock and mineral collections. Outside, a quarter-mile paved rock walkway features large, outstanding samples of Michigan bedrock. There's also a slide show, hands-on activities and professional demonstrations.

### AUTOMOBILE HALL OF FAME

**Dearborn** - *21400 Oakwood Blvd. (Next to Greenfield Village), 48121. Web: www.automotivehalloffame.org/about/purpose.html. Phone: (313) 240-4000. Hours: Daily 9:00am-5:00pm. (Memorial Day-October). Closed Mondays the rest of the year. Closed major winter holidays. Admission: $3.00-$6.00 (age 5+).* A 60-seat theatre giant-screen theatre features a short film, "The Driving Spirit", that takes an amusing look at the individuals responsible for the creation of the automotive industry (follow the "Spirit-ed" boy on this video journey and through the rest of the museum). Before you leave, be sure to start up a replica of the first gasoline-powered car, listen in on a meeting that led to forming the world's largest corporation, look into the Ransom Olds workshop, and visit a classic 1930's showroom.

### FORD ROUGE FACTORY TOUR

(The Henry Ford Museum departures out front), **Dearborn** 48124

❑   Phone: (313) 982-6001 **Web: www.thehenryford.org**

❑   Hours: Monday-Saturday 9:30am-5:00pm. Open some holiday weekend Sundays and all summer Sundays (mid-April thru Labor Day), too. Closed Thanksgiving and Christmas Days.

❑   Admission: Timed tickets: $14.00 adult, $10.00 child (3-12)

You've already prepurchased your timed ticket for the factory tour, now head over to the bus depot to depart at your assigned time. Motor coach rides over include audio and video presentations featuring key historic sites along the route. Tell the kids to look and listen. Your tour bus actually drives through the Steel Stamping Plant. Next, visitors are led to the Legacy Theater where you view a 12-minute film made from historic photos and films, which tells the story of both Henry Ford and the Ford Rouge complex (great Industrial Revolution learning here, parents). A short walk away, visitors enter the next theater, the Art of Manufacturing. This 360-degree, multi-screen theatre-in-the-round gives viewers the sensation of actually being a part of the manufacturing process through the film which incorporates the traditional visual experience with sound, touch and scent (new car smell)! Visitors feel the heat of the blast furnace and the gentle mist of the paint shop. Get stamped and welded, too! Station Three, the eighty-foot high Observation Deck, offers an impressive view of the entire Rouge Center, including the world's largest living roof covering much of the Dearborn Truck Plant. Finally, visitors take a walkway to the Ford F-150 truck assembly plant for a panoramic, self-guided view of the modern industrial factory (stroller accessible). Along the one-third of a mile walk (with rest stops and potty breaks, if needed) through the plant, you'll see key points in the final assembly process. Meet actual team leaders (by video) and hopefully Bumper and Blinker are working hard installing windshields. Because it's both entertaining and industrial (not super technical), both parents (esp. Moms) and kids will enjoy this tour.

## *GREENFIELD VILLAGE*

20900 Oakwood Blvd. (I-94 to SR 39 north to Oakwood Blvd.)

### Dearborn 48124

❏ Phone: (313) 982-6100 or (313) 982-6150 info
   **Web: www.hfmgv.org**

❏ Hours: Daily 9:30am-5:00pm (April 15 - October 31). Saturdays until 9:00pm (early July until late August). Friday-Sunday 9:30am- 5:00pm (November-December).

❏ Open New Year's Day. Closed Thanksgiving and Christmas Days.

❏ Admission: $20.00 adult, $19.00 senior (62+), $14.00 child (5-12) for each museum. (Combo prices and additional attractions are available). Horse-drawn carriage rides, sleigh rides, steam train or steamboat rides available for additional fee.

❏ Miscellaneous: IMAX Theatre (800-747-IMAX) where you'll learn of fascinating innovations and interesting modern science (avg. $10.00-$12.00 per ticket).

Greenfield Village (*cont.*)

The American Experience examines so much of American history it's hard to believe it's all in one village. Henry Ford's genius in choosing the best authentic and reproduced historic buildings.

Greenfield Village Highlights:

<u>HENRY FORD BIRTHPLACE</u> - he certainly loved and cherished his mother. See what he played with as a boy.

<u>FORD COMPANY</u> - the hostess recommends you don't buy the model A, but wait for the Model C (better radiator).

<u>COHEN MILLINERY</u> - try on hats of olden days.

<u>GEORGE WASHINGTON CARVER - PEANUTS!</u> A great look at the possibilities of products made with peanuts. Carver helped find industrial uses for peanuts to help poor Southerners find new crops to grow and new uses for the crops they had.

<u>WRIGHT BROTHERS CYCLE SHOP & HOME</u> - just think of the boys "tinkering" around the shop.

<u>MATTOX HOUSE</u> - Recycling before the work existed! Newspaper wallpaper, license plate shingles, and layered cardboard ceilings.

<u>EDISON'S MENLO PARK LAB</u> - Learn about Edison's brilliant and showy sides. Using a loud child as a volunteer, they demonstrate a real Edison phonograph (it really worked) and souvenir piece of tin foil used as the secret to the phonograph's success.

<u>TASTE OF HISTORY RESTAURANT</u> -Choose from favorites such as Abraham Lincoln's Chicken Fricassee or George Washington Carver's dish-of-choice. Or, try a Railroaders Lunch made with hobo bread just like 19th century railroad workers ate - round raisin nut bread filled with turkey and cheese. Sounds funny but it's really good!

Compared to our visits as children years ago, we noticed a much more interactive, kid-friendly environment. The guides and actors really are skilled at engaging the kid's curiosity and use kids, not adults, as part of their demos.

# *HENRY FORD (THE)*

20900 Oakwood Blvd. (I-94 to SR 39 north to Oakwood)

**Dearborn** 48124

❑    Phone: (313) 982-6001 or (800) 835-5237

**Web: www.thehenryford.org**

❑    Hours: Daily 9:30am-5:00pm.

❑    Admission: $14.00 adult, $13.00 senior (62+), $10.00 child (5-12). Combo discounts available for Rouge Factory tour or Greenfield Village.

America's largest indoor-outdoor museum examines our country from rural to industrial societies. A special focus is placed on accomplishments and inventions of famous Americans.

The Henry Ford Museum highlights:

HOME ARTS - evolution of home appliances.

MADE IN AMERICA - production of goods in the USA.

INNOVATION STATION - interactively be an innovator or team project player. Really hands-on! Furniture Fun Packs.

YOUR PLACE IN TIME - explore the 1900's from your own life history experiences. Kids find it silly to see what was considered "technology" years ago. For example, The Dymaxion House was built and sold in the mid-1900's as a solution to the need for a mass-produced, affordable, easily transportable and environmentally efficient house. The house was shipped in it's own metal tube and used tension suspension from a central point. From the outside, it looks like a mutated Airstream or flying saucer! A Sales Rep greets you at the entrance and shares the features of the efficient home with your family – want to buy one?

HEROES OF THE SKY -  With a blend of education and entertainment, it literally allows visitors to become a wingwalker at the county fair, see just how far the Wright Brothers flew on their first flight, or test the principles of aviation as you prepare and test flight your special paper plane. Fifteen historic airplanes interpret storylines that bring to life the lofty accomplishments of America's pioneering aviators.

The Henry Ford (*cont.*)

<u>HENRY'S TREASURES</u> - Lincoln's Chair (the rocking chair he was assassinated in) and Rosa Park's Bus (the one that started the Civil Rights movement). They will stop you in your tracks!

<u>CAFÉ</u> - Check out the Weiner Mobile (even make a Mold-A-Rama w/ the kids or grab a snack at the Weiner Mobile Café).

Compared to our visits as children years ago, we noticed a much more interactive, kid-friendly environment. The guides and actors really are skilled at engaging the kid's curiosity and use kids, not adults, as part of their demos.

## *FAIR LANE*

4901 Evergreen Road (Hwy 39, exit 7. On the campus of University of Michigan, Dearborn), **Dearborn** 48128

❑ Phone: (313) 593-5590. "The Pool" - (313) 436-9196
   **Web: www.henryfordestate.org**

❑ Hours: Tuesday-Saturday 10:00am-3:00pm, Sunday 1:00-4:30pm. (April-December). Monday-Friday tour available only at 1:30pm (January-March). Closed winter holidays plus Easter.

❑ Admission: (Guided Tours- 90 minutes) $10.00 adult, $9.00 senior, $6.00 child (5-12).

❑ Miscellaneous: Self-guided outdoor tour: Ford Discovery Trail, an Estate walking loop to discover the "Wizards of Fair Lane," includes treehouse, bathhouse, boathouse, and scenic vistas. Open daily, mid-June through Labor Day. $2.00 per person.

Much more than just another mansion tour…this was the home of visionary, Henry Ford. In many ways, our lives have been shaped and changed by decisions and visions that Henry Ford saw and created. A 90 minute  tour takes you into the fascinating 6-level mansion which had many innovations. The on-site electric generating power plant (the Rouge River was the energy source) produced enough electricity to power the mansion and part of the university campus! See many of Ford's personal vehicles in the garage that include the famous Model A and Model T, an early 1900's innovative "camper" (some people say that he started the RV industry), a "Fordson" tractor, and even an electric car that he was going to partner into production with Thomas Edison. Kids, look for the mini- electric cars used by the grandkids to drive around the property and the one lane bowling alley. Check out the giant wrench in the generator room. What was Mr. Ford's favorite plant? (soybeans). Complete your tour with lunch at "The Pool" restaurant (since it was built over the estate's swimming pool - open weekdays, lunchtime only).

## *DETROIT SPORTS*

### Detroit

**DETROIT TIGERS BASEBALL**: Comerica Park. (313) 471-BALL or **www.detroittigers.com**. Major league baseball played April-September. Game's biggest scoreboard. Home runs - two huge tigers with glowing eyes growl and aquatic fireworks fountain performs. Outside - 30 hand-painted tigers on carousel and Italian Ferris wheel. Inside - main concourse has a visual tour of baseball and lifestyle history.

**DETROIT LIONS FOOTBALL**: Ford Field. (248) 325-4131 or **www.detroitlions.com**. NFL football (over 70 seasons) season runs September-December. Giant glass wall in new dome stadium.

**DETROIT RED WINGS HOCKEY**: Joe Lewis Arena. (313) 396-7575 or **www.detroitredwings.com**. NHL top five team in the League play September-early April. Call or visit website for ticket availability.

**DETROIT PISTONS BASKETBALL**: The Palace of Auburn Hills. (248) 377-0100 or **www.nba.com/pistons**. NBA team with all star players.

**DETROIT SHOCK WOMEN'S BASKETBALL**: The Palace of Auburn Hills. (248) 377-0100 or **www.wnba.com/shock/**. WNBA play in the spring.

## DETROIT SYMPHONY ORCHESTRA

**Detroit** - *3663 Woodward Avenue #100, 48201. Tickets: (313) 576-5111 or Office: (313) 576-5100. www.detroitsymphony.com.* Be sure to ask about "Young People Series".

## WRIGHT MUSEUM OF AFRICAN-AMERICAN HISTORY

**Detroit** - *315 East Warren Avenue (off I-94 or I-75), 48201. Phone: (313) 494-5800. Web: www.maah-detroit.org. Hours: Wednesday-Saturday 9:30am-3:00pm. Friday and Saturday until 5:00pm. Admission: Adults $5.00 (18+), $3.00 (17 and under).* A tribute to the history and culture of Detroit's African-American community. The exhibit, "Of the People: The African-American Experience" traces the history and operations of the slave trade. Learn also that Detroit was one of the most active stops in the "Underground Railroad" (a network of safe stops that helped slaves escape from the south before the Civil War). Once reaching Detroit, they could cross the Detroit River into Canada. See the space suit worn by Mae Jemison, the first African-American woman to travel in space in 1992. Other fun and educational exhibits trace the history of African music and how it transformed present American music including the famous Detroit's "Motown Sound".

## DETROIT CHILDREN'S MUSEUM

**Detroit** - *6134 Second Avenue (between Burroughs and Amsterdam), 48202. Web: www.detroitchildrensmuseum.org. Phone: (313) 873-8100. Hours: Monday-Friday 9:00am-4:00pm, plus second Saturdays.* Your kids (target age 4-9) will be encouraged at this museum to test their imagination and creativity at its various interactive attractions. Be sure to ask for the "Treasure Hunt Game" that gets kids involved in a discovery adventure throughout the building. Younger children will find lots to do in the Discovery Room where they can test their skills with many interactive teaching toys. Parents hang on tight to those little ones!

# DETROIT HISTORICAL MUSEUM

5401 Woodward Avenue (Woodward and Kirby. SR 1)

**Detroit** 48202

❏   Phone: (313) 833-1805, **Web: www.detroithistorical.org**
❏   Hours: Wednesday-Friday 9:30am-3:00pm, Saturday 10:00am-
     5:00pm, Sunday Noon-5:00pm.
❏   Admission: $5.00 adult, $3.00 senior (62+) or child (4-18).
     Children under 4 FREE.
❏   Miscellaneous: Free admission on Wednesdays. Train-cam mini-
     train setup is new feature where camera displays the view from
     the little train going around the town.

After you've wondered through Frontiers to Factories: Detroiters at
Work before the Motor City; and the Streets of Old Detroit, be sure
to plan most of your time in the Motor City exhibits. See the first
car in Detroit - a horseless carriage that was driven down
Woodward Avenue. Then, around the corner, you can crank up a
Model T and then sit in it (great photo op!). The best part of this
exhibit has to be the Body Drop! First, watch it happen on video
(actual footage from a Ford Assembly plant). Then see the 70 foot
section of actual assembly plant and the performance of the final
steps of production. Some mannequins are in the pits below, some
workers are above one floor as they "drop" the car body onto the
chassis below. Did you know that Mr. Cadillac's full name is
Antoine de la Mothe Cadillac? - No wonder they're so fancy!

# DETROIT INSTITUTE OF ARTS (DIA)

5200 Woodward Avenue (off I-94 or I-75, Cultural Center)

**Detroit** 48202

❏   Phone: (313) 833-7900, **Web: www.dia.org**
❏   Hours: Wednesday-Friday 11:00am-4:00pm, Saturday and
     Sunday 11:00am-5:00pm. Friday nights until 9:00pm.
❏   Admission: Donations. Suggested - $6.00 adult, $3.00 child (14
     and under).
❏   Tours: 1:00pm Wednesday - Saturday. 1:00 & 2:30 pm, Sunday.
❏   Miscellaneous: Restaurant and café.

Detroit Institute Of Arts (DIA) (*cont.*)

A great place for kids of all ages to interact and explore. Most exhibits are "kid-friendly" and interactive and there is even a booklet: Animal & Creatures Abound, that encourages kids to "want to discover" the museum and its treasures. See exhibits such as "The American House", "The Spiral Staircase" and even "The Donkey" (which invites kids to hang, climb, and burn up excess energy) while at the museum. Fun, interactive computer programs also entertain and teach. The Great Hall features many suits of armor from the $13^{th}$ to $18^{th}$ century. But, above all, the masked mummy (kept safely in a display case) in the Egyptian art and artifacts exhibit is always a way to get the kids to say "wow" or "wooooo".

## *DETROIT SCIENCE CENTER*

5020 John R Street (I-75 - Warren Exit), **Detroit** 48202

- ❑     Phone: (313) 577-8400, **Web: www.sciencedetroit.org**
- ❑     Hours: Monday-Friday 9:00am-3:00pm, Saturday 10:30am-6:00pm, Sunday Noon-6:00pm. Closed Mondays in the fall.
- ❑     Admission: $7.00 adult, $6.00 senior (60+), $6.00 child (2-12). IMAX is additional $4.00.
- ❑     Miscellaneous: Café.

Just a block away from the Detroit Institute of Arts is another wonderful example of what learning "outside of the books" is all about. Located in the heart of Detroit's Cultural Complex (park once and visit maybe 4-5 museums), the museum still has the IMAX Dome Theatre and Digital Dome Planetarium plus new, dynamic exhibits. Space Laboratory takes you into the sky via space shuttle or telescope. Motion Lab has a "stadium" Science Stage and lots of pulling, pushing physics comparing motion, speed and direction (little engineers thrive here). The Life Science Lab focuses on similarities between the rainforest and city ecosystems. The Matter and Energy Lab has a "caged" Sparks Theatre and exhibits exploring electricity, magnetism, energy conversion, etc. Waves & Vibrations has all the funky lights and sounds. There's even an area for the younger set to explore all the things their older siblings are playing with on a larger scale.

## *BELLE ISLE*

(I-75 to East Grand Blvd. Take MacArthur Bridge over to the Isle
on the Detroit River), **Detroit** 48207

❑ Phone: (313) 852-4075

**www.ci.detroit.mi.us/recreation/centers/M/belle_isle/belleM.htm**

❑ Hours: Dawn to Dusk. See specific hours for special parks
within the Isle.

❑ Miscellaneous: FREE admission to Trails, Picnic areas, beach,
Nature Center. Common to see many deer. There's also a wild
animal hospital and playgrounds.

The well-used 1000 acre park and playground, still in site of the
skyscrapers of Detroit offers:

**AQUARIUM AND CONSERVATORY** - (313) 852-4141. Hours:
Wednesday-Sunday 10:00am-5:00pm. Admission: $2.00-$4.00.
Old aquarium focuses on freshwater species found in Michigan
and the tropics (ex. Electric eel and a stingray). The adjacent
conservatory explores plants and flowers mostly in desert and
tropical settings (ex. Cacti, ferns, palm trees, banana trees and
orchids).

**DOSSIN GREAT LAKES MUSEUM** - 100 Strand Drive (South
Shore of Belle Isle). (313) 833-1805. **www.detroithistorical.org**.
Hours: Saturday - Sunday, 11:00am-5:00pm. Admission: $2.50-
$3.50. You're greeted by two Battle of Lake Erie cannons and the
actual anchor recovered from the Edmund Fitzgerald shipwreck.
Stand in the pilot house of an ore carrier. As the marine radio sends
out requests, turn the ship wheel to steer it on course or use the
periscope. The 1912 Great Lakes Luxury Steamer Lounge Room is
handsome (all oak carvings) - reminiscent of scenes in the movie
"Titanic".

### *HISTORIC FORT WAYNE*

**Detroit** - (downtown, riverfront), 48207. Phone: (313) 833-1805
**Web: www.detroithistorical.org**. Hours: Saturday and Sunday
11:00am-4:00pm (Memorial Day-Labor Day weekends). Enjoy
special guided tours of the Historic Fort Wayne grounds at a price
of $2.00 per person. Leaving regularly from the Fort's Visitors

Center, the tours will include the Star Fort built in the 1840s, the Commanding Officer's House, and the Spanish-American War Guardhouse. Secured parking is $5 per vehicle. Picnic lunches and coolers are permitted on the Fort grounds, which offer a nice view of the Detroit River, the Ambassador Bridge and Canada. However, alcohol, grills, pets and fishing are not permitted.

### MOTOWN HISTORICAL MUSEUM

**Detroit** - *2648 West Grand Blvd. (M-10 to West Grand Blvd. Exit), 48208. Web: www.recordingeq.com/motown/motown.htm. Phone: (313) 875-2264. Hours: Sunday & Monday, Noon-5:00 pm, Tuesday-Saturday, 10:00am-5:00pm. (Closed holidays). Admission: $7.00 adult, $4.00 child (12 and under).* In two homes that are next to each other, the music world was changed forever by Berry Gordy, composer and producer. The original recording studio "A" not only helped to build the "Motown" sound, but discovered and built the careers of the Stevie Wonder, the Temptations, the Four Tops, Diana Ross, and Marvin Gaye, just to name a few. A great stop in musical history.

### PEWABIC POTTERY

**Detroit** - *10125 E. Jefferson Avenue (across from Waterworks Park and exactly 1.5 miles east of the Belle Isle Bridge), 48214. Phone: (313) 822-0954. Web: www.pewabic.com. Gallery Hours: Monday-Saturday 10:00am-6:00pm. Admission: FREE. Tours: Self-guided tours of the pottery's kiln room and other production areas are during regular business hours. Groups must call ahead to make reservation (sm. Fee).* Nationally renowned for its handcrafted ceramic vessels and architectural tiles and its unique glazes, Pewabic Pottery is located in the Detroit area. They make a wide range of vases, candlesticks and unique embossed tiles. Four of the 13 People Mover stations are adorned with ceramic murals created at Pewabic.

# *RAINFOREST CAFÉ EDUCATIONAL TOURS*

4310 Baldwin Road (I-75, exit 84 - Great Lakes Crossing)

**Detroit (Auburn Hills)** 48326

❑    Phone: (248) 333-0280, **Web: www.rainforestcafe.com**

❑    Hours: Daily, Lunch and Dinner.

❑    Tours: Usually begin at 10:00am and include lunch. Must be scheduled in advance.

A theme restaurant and wildlife preserve filled with live and mechanical animals; ongoing rainstorms (even thunder and lightning); a talking rainforest tree; giant "walk-through" aquarium (really cool!); hand-sculpted "cave like" rock everywhere. Preschoolers and younger love the fish tank but are a little uneasy with the motorized large gorillas and elephants (request seating on the other side of the dining room). Did you know they give Educational Group Tours? What a "light-hearted" way to introduce your kids to the animals, plants and environs of the rainforest! The Fun Field Trip Adventure uncovers why elephants have big ears & why the Café's resident crocodile collects pennies for charity. What is your favorite fish in the coral reef? You can also include a group lunch afterwards in your plans (for an ~$8.00 per person fee). Nibble on Jurassic Tidbits and Paradise Pizza plus other kid-friendly food, drink and dessert. Although your food bill will be above moderate - it's the epitome of a theme restaurant.

## *WALTER P. CHRYSLER MUSEUM*

**Detroit (Auburn Hills) -** *1 Chrysler Drive (northwest corner of Featherstone & Squirrel Roads on Daimler-Chrysler campus), 48326. Phone: (888) 456-1924 or (248) 944-0001.* **Web:** *www.chryslerheritage.com. Hours: Tuesday-Saturday 10:00am-6:00pm, Sunday Noon-6:00pm. Admission: $6.00 adult, $3.00 senior, $3.00 child (6-12).* The Museum contains 55,000 square feet and displays 75 vehicles. It tells the stories of Walter P. Chrysler and his love of trains, brothers John and Horace Dodge and their mechanical genius, and such industry notables as Carl Breer, Virgil Exner and Lee Iacocca. It covers everything from the Detroit Tank Arsenal to Roadrunners, Vipers and Prowlers.

Several interactive displays explain brake systems, aerodynamics, power steering, platform team design and more. Interactive computer kiosks timeline the decades from 1920-1980 using vintage news footage, classic commercials and audio clips.

## CRANBROOK ART & SCIENCE MUSEUMS

1221 North Woodward Avenue (I-75 exit to Square Lake Road (West) to Woodward, I-696 exit - Woodward),

### Detroit (Bloomfield Hills) 48303

❑ Phone: (877) GO-CRANB, **Web: www.cranbrook.edu**

❑ Hours: Art: Wednesday-Sunday 11:00am-5:00pm. Science: Daily 10:00am-5:00pm. Friday until 10:00pm.

❑ Admission: $6.00-$7.00 adult, $4.00-$5.00 senior(65+) and child (3-17).

❑ Miscellaneous: Picnic areas. Planetarium and Laser Shows. $3.00 extra. Café. Gift shop. Seasonal gardens with fountains, ponds and sculpture.

Different areas to check out are: Our Dynamic Earth (15 foot T-Rex, wooly mastodon), Gem & Mineral Hall, Nature Place (live reptiles, turtles, and bugs - native to Michigan), Art (metalwork, realism sculpture "Body Builder", outdoor sculpture), Physics Hall (hands-on experiments about lasers and light, movement, and air).

## LIONEL TRAINS VISITOR'S CENTER

26750 Russell Smith Drive (23 Mile Road) (I-94 to Exit 243)

### Detroit (Chesterfield) 48051

❑ Phone: (586) 949-4100, **Web: www.lionel.com**

❑ Admission: FREE

❑ Tours: (For reservation call: (586) 949-4100 ext. 1211) Wednesday & Thursday 10:00am, 3:00 and 4:00pm. Friday 10:00am, 1:30, 2:30pm. Saturday 10:00, 11:00am & Noon. Gift Shop is open during all tours.

Since 1900, Lionel has been delighting hearts (both young and old) with the illusionary world of model train villages. Not only will you have fun watching and learning each step of the manufacturing process (by video), but this tour allows plenty of time to "play" with the creations that make Lionel so special. See 10 trains running (on a 14 X 40 layout) simultaneously from village to village, over bridges and through tunnels just like a miniature movie set. Kids can interact with the display by pushing several buttons that create a movement or reaction in the display. There is also a smaller children's layout where kids get to operate the trains. If you're a collector (or about to become one), be sure to buy one of the Visitor's Center boxcars that are available only in the gift shop.

## *MORLEY CANDY MAKERS*

23770 Hall Road (I-94 to Hall Road M-59 Exit)

### Detroit (Clinton Township) 48036

❑    Phone: (586) 468-4300 or (800) 682-2760
     **Web: www.morleycandy.com**
❑    Admission: FREE
❑    Tours: Self-guided Monday - Friday 9:00am - 3:00pm
     (observation hallway only). Guided group tours with video are
     available Monday - Friday between 10:00am - 1:00pm. Call to
     schedule appointment.

One of Michigan's largest candy makers, this tour is sure to delight chocolate lovers of all ages. Both educational and fun, see Morley's cooking chocolate in huge copper kettles (gallons at a time). Much of that chocolate gets poured over the famous caramel used to make both vanilla caramels and, when mixed with fresh southern pecans, their spectacular Pecan Torties® ! Did you know chocolate doesn't like sudden temperature changes? How do they keep it from "turning"? The 70 foot long observation hallway is a great way to see all the candy making in action. Don't leave without your edible souvenirs!

## MARVIN'S MARVELOUS MECHANICAL MUSEUM

31005 Orchard Lake Road (I-696 exit Orchard Lake Road North)

### Detroit (Farmington Hills) 48334

- ❑ Phone: (248) 626-5020, **Web: www.marvin3m.com**
- ❑ Hours: Monday-Thursday 10:00am-9:00pm, Friday-Saturday 10:00am-11:00pm, Sunday Noon-9:00pm.
- ❑ Admission: FREE. Each device takes a quarter to operate.
- ❑ Miscellaneous: Concessions. Modern pinball and interactive games are there too.

Pass back in time to an old-fashioned carnival full of antique slot and pinball machines, mechanical memorabilia and games. It's a very busy place with lights flashing and marionette music playing all around you. Here are some games that were really unique: a bulldozer mechanical game, Old Time Photos, Marionette and Clown Dancing Shows, and miniature carrousel and Ferris wheel. Marvin's is listed in the World Almanac's 100 most unusual museums in the U.S. Once you're inside, it's hard to know what game to play first! P.S. - Grandparents can get real sentimental here.

## DIAMOND JACK'S RIVER TOURS

25088 Old Depot Court (Hart Plaza, foot of Woodward, downtown)

### Detroit (Grosse Ile) 48138

- ❑ Phone: (313) 843-9376, **Web: www.diamondjack.com**
- ❑ Hours: Thursday-Sunday (early June-Labor Day).
- ❑ Admission: $14.00 adult, $12.00 senior, $10.00 child (6-16).
- ❑ Tours: 2-hour leisurely narrated cruise departs at 1:00pm and 3:30pm.
- ❑ Miscellaneous: Snacks and beverages available on board. Safest parking available at the Renaissance Center.

The 65-foot "mini-ship" cruises down the Detroit River around Belle Isle and back to Ambassador Bridge. This is the world's busiest international waterway along the U.S. and Canadian shorelines. There's a good chance that large freighters and ocean ships will pass by. You'll see a great view of both the Detroit and downtown Windsor, Canada skylines and pass by (with stories told by captain) the historic Warehouse District, Mayor's Residence (if he's out back, he'll wave), Yacht Clubs, Islands, Bridges and a Fireboat. See the world's only marble Art Deco lighthouse or one of only two International Marine Mailboats in the world. They told us the mailboat has it's own zip code and delivers mail to the freighters by a pail on a pulley.

### GREENMEAD HISTORICAL PARK

**Detroit (Livonia)** - *20501 Newburgh Road (jct. 8 Mile and Newburgh Roads), 48150. Phone: (248) 477-7375.* **Web:** *www.ci.livonia.mi.us. Hours: Grounds open Daily 8:30am-4:00pm (May-October, and in December). Closed holidays. Admission: $1.00-$2.00 per person. Tours: Guided tours are offered only on Sundays between 1:00 - 4:00pm and during special events.* The 95 acre park site was the 1820's homestead of Michigan pioneer, Joshua Simmons. The Simmon's family lived in a modest frame house, while the barn, a building of primary importance was the first major structure completed. Together, the buildings tell the story of farm life in rural Michigan. Eight historical buildings (some plain, some fancy) outline regional history, especially during scheduled events or Sundays. There is a wide variety of items exhibited in the general store. They have stocked the store with goods from the 1913 ledger. This building is a favorite of children of all ages, who enjoy shopping at its candy and trinket counters.

## MOTORSPORTS MUSEUM & HALL OF FAME OF AMERICA

43700 Expo Center Drive (I-96 - exit 162)

**Detroit (Novi)** 48375

❑   Phone: (248) 349-7223, **Web: www.mshf.com**

❑   Hours: Daily 10:00am-5:00pm (Memorial Day-Labor Day). Thursday-Friday only (rest of year).

❑   Admission:$4.00 adult, $2.00 senior and child (under 12).

If there is a racing fan in your family this is a "must stop". See over 100 vehicles including powerboats, motorcycles, "Indy style" racecars, NASCAR style racecars, dragsters, and even snowmobiles. Get their photo taken in the driver's seat of an actual Winston Cup racecar and then take the challenge of racing on the 4-lane scale slot car track or video simulation race car.

## DETROIT ZOO

8450 West Ten Mile Road (I-75 to I-696 West - Woodward Avenue Exit), **Detroit (Royal Oak)** 48068

❑    Phone: (248) 398-0900 info, **Web: http://detroitzoo.org**

❑    Hours: Daily 10:00am-5:00pm (April & September/October). Daily 9:00am-5:00pm (May-Labor Day). Wednesday-Sunday 10:00am-4:00pm. (November-March).

❑    Admission: $11.00 adult, $9.00 senior (62+), $7.00 child (2-12). $5.00 Parking fee.

❑    Miscellaneous: Picnic areas and playground. Strollers and Adult roller chairs available for rent.

Simply put…your family is in for a real day of adventure and fun when visiting the Detroit Zoo. The world's largest polar bear exhibit, the Artic Ring of Life, is a lifelike trek to the North Pole's tundra, open sea and ice mountains. Start outside and curve around the exhibit to the spectacular 70 foot long clear tunnel (Polar Passage) which takes visitors underneath diving and swimming polar bears and seals. Their antics and casual behavior will entertain you for most of the visit (plan 45 minutes to one hour just at this exhibit)! What a fun learning experience for the kids to see the Inuit peoples and their interaction w/ Artic animals. Here's a few of the other, constantly changing exhibits that you'll see: The Mandrill Exhibit (a very colorful baboon), The Wilson Aviary Wing (30 species of birds in a large free-flying building - much like an indoor jungle - there is even a waterfall), The Penguinarium (love that name! - see underwater views of these birds that cannot fly), and The Chimps of Harambee (a forest setting with rock habitats…what a show!), and The Wildlife Interpretive Gallery (huge aquarium, theater, hummingbird and butterfly garden). And if all this wasn't enough…take an excursion on the famous Detroit Zoo Miniature Railroad (it transports over 500,000 passengers a year).

## *SPRING VALLEY TROUT FARM*

**Dexter** - *12190 Island Lake Road (off I-94), 48130. Phone: (734) 426-4772.  **Web: www.springvalleytroutfarm.com**. Because of Michigan weather, the farm is open Spring and Fall on Saturdays and Sundays from 9:00am to 5:00pm. Memorial Day to Labor Day open Wednesday through Sunday from 9:00am-6:00pm. The farm closes end of September each year.* Natural, organic (non-polluted water) fed trout in spring-fed ponds are waiting to be caught. There is even a Children's Trout pond reserved for little anglers under 10 years old. The environment is so perfect in these ponds, they can even guarantee a catch on every outing! They'll clean the fish and pack them in ice to take home. Fees charged ($3.00 per person to fish - age 5+ and a fee per pound of fish caught). Picnic/grilling areas. No license or equipment needed.

## *GREATER LANSING SYMPHONY ORCHESTRA*

**East Lansing** - *Bogue Street & Wilson (MSU Campus - Wharton Center for Performing Arts), 48824. Phone: (517) 487-5001 or (800) WHARTON.  **Web: www.lansingsymphony.org**.* Free Young People's Concerts and music for Broadway shows like "Beauty & the Beast".  Hot Buttered Pops, Jingle Bell Pops, or Play Me A Story.

## *MICHIGAN STATE UNIVERSITY*

West Circle Drive (Off SR 43), **East Lansing** 48825

❏     Phone: (517) 355-7474

   **Web:http://msutoday.msu.edu/directory**

MUSEUM: West Circle Drive. (517) 355-2370. Natural wonders of the Great Lakes, world cultures, animal diversity. 3 stories of special exhibits. Museum store. They offer numerous family programs focused on the history of inhabitants of Michigan.

KRESGE ART MUSEUM: Culturally diverse art. FREE. (517) 355-7631.

BEAUMONT TOWER: Site of Old College Hall - the first building erected for instruction in scientific agriculture. Recently renovated. Weekly carillon concerts.

Michigan State University (*cont.*)

FARMS: Observe milking cows mid-afternoon. Also sheep, horse and swine areas. Weekdays only. (517) 355-8383. South Campus.

HORTICULTURE GARDENS AND GREEN HOUSE: Bogue & Wilson Road (south end of campus). (517) 355-0348. American Trial Garden test site. Children's Garden - 63 theme gardens - garden emphasizes the important part plants play in children's daily lives, from the first cereal bowl in the morning to the last popcorn snack at night. Secret Garden (just like movie), Pizza Garden (wheat for dough, toppings and spices, tomatoes), Peter Rabbit Garden (bunny food favorites), Sensation Garden (guess which plant it is by smell), 2 Treehouses, and a Butterfly Garden. (517) 353-4800. Small Admission donation. Spring/Summer. Parking fee on weekdays. Our favorite garden for kids (in the state and midwest) is so colorful and artistically done (on a kid's level).

DAIRY STORE AND PLANT. South Anthony Hall (Farm Lane & Wilson Road). (517) 432-2479 or http://dairystore.msu.edu/. Hours: Monday-Friday 9:00am-5:00pm, Saturday-Sunday Noon-5:00pm. Closed University holidays. Admission: FREE. Everything you ever wanted to know about "Cheddaring"! This is a great guided (in groups, pre-arranged) or self-guided (with simple explanations) observation deck tour of the pilot plant where students process milk making the famous Spartan cheese and ice cream. After you see the production facility, walk downstairs to the Dairy Store and buy a cone (their Junior cones are still 2 dips) or a light lunch.

BUG HOUSE: Natural Science Building. Farm Lane & East Circle Drive. (517) 355-4662. Noisy cockroaches, millipedes and giant grasshoppers.

ABRAMS PLANETARIUM: Shaw Lane & Science Road. (517) 355-STAR. Small Admission. Weekend matinees are suggested for younger ones.

# MERIDIAN TOWNSHIP'S CENTRAL PARK

5150 Marsh Road

**East Lansing (Okemos) 48864**

❑     Phone: (517) 347-7300 or (517) 349-5777 Nokomis
       **www.nokomis.org or www.meridianhistoricalvillage.com**
❑     Hours: Nokomis Learning Center: Tuesday-Friday 10:00am-
       4:00pm, Saturday Noon-5:00pm. Meridian Historical Village:
       Saturday 10:00am-2:00pm (May-October).

NOKOMIS LEARNING CENTER - center for focus of woodland
Indians of the Great Lakes; specifically the Ojibwa, Ottawa, and
Potawatomi tribes known as the People of the Three Fires. Group
tours & programs recommended. Gift shop.

MERIDIAN HISTORICAL VILLAGE - the only known Plank
Road Tollhouse still around in the state is part of this small village.
It includes a furnished farmhouse and one-room schoolhouse with
a school bell ringing the beginning of class.

## SEVEN LAKES STATE PARK

**Fenton** - *2220 Tinsman Road (I-75, exit 101), 48430. Phone: (248)
634-7271. Web: www.michigandnr.com/parksandtrails/parklist.asp.
Admission: $6.00-$8.00 per vehicle.* The dam, constructed by the
developers, formed one large lake from seven small lakes
(historically known as the DeCoup Lake) hence the name Seven
Lakes State Park. Camping, hiking trails, boating and rentals,
fishing, swimming, bicycle trails, and winter sports.

# CHILDS' PLACE BUFFALO RANCH

12770 Roundtree Road (US-12 : Take Moscow Road North, Left
(West) on Mosherville Road, Right (North) on Rountree Road)

**Hanover 49241**

❑     Phone: (517) 563-8249 **Web: www.horsesandbuffalo.com**
❑     Hours: Tuesday-Sunday 9:00am-4:00pm.
❑     Admission: Buffalo herd visit $5.00 per person. Horseback riding
       $20.00 per hour. Zipline ride $5.00. Mechanical Bull ride $5.00.
       Free Bucking Barrel.

Childs' Place Buffalo Ranch (*cont.*)

❑ Miscellaneous: Be a cowgirl/cowboy for the day (age 10+) or Live on the Ranch overnight. Dress casually.

Here's a visit that your kids are sure to tell their friends about! Take a hay wagon ride out into Gary Childs' pastures to see some of his more than 100 buffalo. The brave kids will usually get the opportunity to reach out and actually touch a live buffalo and feed corn cobs onto their huge tongues! (if the herd is cooperating that day). This ranch was also fortunate enough (1/40 million chance) to have given birth to a white buffalo…(which is a powerful Native American spiritual symbol). The calf died, but they have lots of pictures to show.

## WETZEL STATE PARK

**Harrison Township** - *28681 Old North River (3 miles NW from New Haven), 48045. www.michigandnr.com/parksandtrails/parklist.asp. Phone: (810) 765-5605.* Undeveloped park providing areas for cross -country skiing, snowmobiling & hiking. No camping. No services.

## HOLLY RECREATION AREA

**Holly** - *8100 Grange Hall Road (off I-75 exit 101), 48442. Phone: (248) 634-8811. www.michigandnr.com/parksandtrails/parklist.asp. Admission: $6.00-$8.00 per vehicle.* Approximately 10 miles of hiking and cross country ski trails are in the central portion of the recreation area. Although mountain bikes are prohibited on these trails, there is an extensive mountain bike trail system located in the Holdridge Lakes area of the park, ranging in terrain from easy to advanced. Camping, hiking, boating, fishing, swimming, bicycle trails and winter sports.

## MYSTERY HILL

7611 US Highway 12 (opposite Hayes State Park), **Irish Hills** 49265

❑ Phone: (517) 467-2517, **Web: www.mystery-hill.com**
❑ Hours: Daily 11:00am-6:00pm (Summer). Weekends only (May, September, October).
❑ Admission: Average $5.00 (ages 4+).
❑ Tours: 30 minute guided.

❑      Miscellaneous: Gift shop. Miniature Golf Course, RC Race Cars.

Exhibits seem to defy gravity and your sense of balance goes. Water runs uphill and people stand sideways without falling over. The principles demonstrated are studied and applied by psychology departments of universities everywhere. It's an illusion experiment (or is it real?…) and you're the assistant!

## STAGECOACH STOP WESTERN RESORT & FAMILY FUN PARK

7203 US 12 (head about 20 miles west on US 12 from Ypsilanti)

**Irish Hills** 49265

❑      Phone: (517) 467-2300, **Web: www.stagecoachstop.com**
❑      Hours: Tuesday-Friday 11:00am-5:30pm, Weekends 10:30am-6:00pm (Summer Break). Weekends only (April/May and September/October).
❑      Admission: $12.00 adult, $8.00 child (4-11).
❑      Miscellaneous: Petting zoo, Fort Wilderness playground, picnic area, and kiddie rides. Food. Jamboree Theatre with country music entertainment. Motel/Cabins on premises (includes park admission, evening hayride, and continental breakfast) have lofts for the kids and kitchenettes.

Travel back to the Old West - made to look like an authentic 19th century western village with wooden plank sidewalks and dirt streets. Listen closely to the Marshall when he makes announcements every few minutes about the activity to begin. Maybe start out slow by watching a craftsman blacksmith, glass-blower, or worker in the sawmill. Stop by the petting zoo and then pan for gold with an old prospector (watch out, they're greedy!). Parents can sip on a Sarsaparilla (old-fashioned non-alcohol beverage) as kids play on rides like Runaway Mine Cars or the Incredible Flying Machine. Silly, staged gunfights challenge the Marshall against thieves. Remember, the bad guy always gets it in the end! Wander through the shops of a barber, bank, see magic shows, etc. and stop in a saloon (café) for a chuckwagon meal or treat. Be sure to take a Wild Country Train ride before leaving.

## *WALKER TAVERN STATE HISTORIC COMPLEX*

13220 M-50 (US 12 & M-50), **Irish Hills (Brooklyn)** 48230

- ❑    Phone: (517) 467-4401, **Web: www.michigan.gov/hal**
- ❑    Hours: Wednesday-Sunday 10:00am-5:00pm (Memorial Day - Labor Day). Closed MIS race weekends.
- ❑    Admission: FREE
- ❑    Tours: Approximately 1 hour

In the mid-1800's, the journey between Detroit and Chicago (by stagecoach) was a 5-8 day event (one-way, can you imagine?). This farmhouse tavern was the original stopping point (along what is now known as US 12) where travelers could have a meal, relax, or spend the night. Discover how life was in the 1840's with realistic exhibits that show a barroom, dining room, parlor and kitchen. The Visitor's Center also features a movie about a young boy's travels from New York  to Chicago in the 1840's. Located in the Cambridge Junction Historic State Park. No camping.

### *DAHLEM ENVIRONMENTAL EDUCATION CENTER*

**Jackson** - *7117 South Jackson Road (I-94 to exit 138 - south), 49201. Web: www.jackson.cc.mi.us/DahlemCenter. Phone: (517) 782-3453. Hours: Tuesday-Friday 9:00am - 4:30pm, Saturday & Sunday Noon-5:00pm. Trails open Daily 8:00am - sunset. Miscellaneous: Gift shop. Cross-country skiing in winter.* Over 5 miles of hiking trails allow you to explore the fields, marshes, ponds, and forest of this "piece of nature" just a short drive from the city. All, regardless of age and physical abilities, can explore on the special needs (1/2 mile) trail. (All-terrain wheelchairs are available on request). Call or visit website for details on upcoming nature programs.

## *CASCADES*

1992 Warren Avenue (I-94 exit 138, south on West Avenue),

**Jackson** 49203

- ❑    Phone: (517) 788-4320
    **Web: www.jacksonmich.com/cascades2.html**

❑   Hours: Park open 11:00am-11:00pm. Cascades illuminated dusk -
    11:00pm in the Summer.
❑   Admission: General $3.00-$4.00 (ages 6+).
❑   Miscellaneous: Snack Bar. Gift store and restrooms. Paddleboats,
    mini-golf.

It began in 1932 and you can still view the colorful and musical
waterfalls and fountains. Sound response programs were developed
so that the Cascades lights and fountains change patterns in direct
response to pre-recorded or live music. Use seating provided or
climb to the top and be refreshed by spraying water. Continuously
changing patterns keep it lively. The Cascades Falls history
museum is within the park.

## SLEEPY HOLLOW STATE PARK

**Laingsburg** - *7835 Price Road (off US 27 east on Price Road),
48848. Web: www.michigandnr.com/parksandtrails/parklist.asp.
Phone: (517) 651-6217. Admission: $6.00-$8.00 per vehicle.* A
river winds its way through the woods and fields of the park and
Lake Ovid is nestled in the middle of it all. Lake Ovid is a 410 acre
man-made lake which was developed by making a dam on the
Little Maple River. A "no wake" lake environment is great for
fishing and rough camping. Other features include a beach with
snack bar, boating, hiking and bike trails, and winter sports.

## BALD MOUNTAIN RECREATION AREA

**Lake Orion** - *1330 Greenshield (I-75 exit SR 24 north
approximately 7 miles), 48360. Phone: (248) 693-6767. Web:
www.michigandnr.com/parksandtrails/parklist.asp. Admission:
$6.00-$8.00 per vehicle.* Bald Mountain Recreation Area consists
of 4,637 rolling acres. The picturesque park area has some of the
steepest hills and most rugged terrain in southeastern Michigan.
Beginning with a great kiddie beach at Lower Trout Lake, the park
also features hiking trails, fishing, boating, horseback riding,
winter sports, and cabins for camping.

## MINIBEAST ZOOSEUM

6907 West Grand River Avenue (1/2 mile east of I-96 exit 90 & I-69 exit 8), **Lansing** 48906

- ☐ Phone: (517) 886-0630
  **Web: http://members.aol.com/YESbugs/zooseum.html**
- ☐ Hours: Tuesday-Friday 1:00-5:00pm, Saturday 10:00am-5:00pm (late March to mid-October). Closed holidays.
- ☐ Admission: $2.50-$3.50 (ages 3+).

Michigan's largest insect and spider museum and outdoor classroom. They have computers and cockroaches, tarantulas and trails, even snails. 1000's of specimens...even some hands-on "bugging", too! Try their many educational (like roller ball bug-can you keep him alive?) games.

## MICHIGAN HISTORICAL CENTER

702 West Kalamazoo Street (I-496 exit ML King, exit north follow signs to Capital Loop), **Lansing** 48909.

- ☐ Phone: (517) 373-3559. **Web: www.michiganhistory.org**
- ☐ Hours: Monday-Friday 9:00am-4:30pm, Saturday 10:00am-4:00pm, Sunday 1:00-5:00pm. Closed state holidays.
- ☐ Admission: FREE.
- ☐ Miscellaneous: Museum store. Snack Shop open weekdays.

A great way to understand Michigan society, land, and industry - and all in one building. If your travel plans around Michigan are limited, this would be a history time-saver. We really enjoy museum layouts with untraditional "real life" settings and odd turns and corners. We've found this keeps children's curiosity peaked! Follow the Paleo Indians of the past to industry of the present (Detroit Cars). Play teacher in a one-room schoolhouse. "Don't Misses" include: the look and touch 3840 pound Float Copper that spans 4 feet by 8 feet and is hollow-sounding; entering rooms like the Mine Shaft or Lumber Barons parlor or old-time theater; learning words you may not know like Riverhog; and the Create-A-Car Touch Screen Computer. As you enter the center, you'll find the three-story relief map of Michigan - it's wonderful to gaze at from many angles.

## FENNER NATURE CENTER

**Lansing** - *2020 East Mount Hope Avenue, 48910. Phone: (517) 483-4224. Hours: Tuesday-Friday 9:00am-4:00pm. Weekends 11:00am-4:00pm (year-round).* A visitor's center and gift shop plus self-guided trails. Call or visit website for special seasonal children's programs. Free admission.

## LANSING LUGNUTS

**Lansing** - *505 East Michigan Avenue (Oldsmobile Park, downtown), 48912. Web: www.lansinglugnuts.com. Phone: (517) 485-4500.* Class "A" Midwest League - Toronto Blue Jays Affiliate (Early April - Early September). Admission: $6.50-$8.00. Fireworks/Kids Days. Play area for kids.

# POTTER PARK ZOO

1301 South Pennsylvania Avenue (entrance is just south of the I-496 Freeway, along Red Cedar River), **Lansing** 48912

❑   Phone: (517) 483-4222, **Web: www.potterparkzoo.org**
❑   Hours: Daily 9:00am-6:00 or 7:00pm (Memorial Day-Labor Day). Daily 9:00am (10:00am Winter) - 5:00pm (rest of the year).
❑   Admission: $6.00 adult, $3.00 senior (60+), $2.00 child (3-15). Parking fee. Lansing residents receive discount.
❑   Miscellaneous: Pony or camel rides and petting zoo, too.

More than 400 animals (get a virtual visit on the website) await your family at this great educational and family friendly zoo. Snow Leopards, Black Rhinos, Siberian Tigers, Reindeer, Lemurs, Penguins, and Red Pandas are just a few of the exhibits featured. Welcome the River Otters and Arctic Fox exhibits and new babies here and there. Don't you love the antics of the Primates. Cotton-Tops are the little monkeys that are black and white and look like they have snazzy mohawk hairdos. You can spot the babies clinging to their parents' backs.

### *WOLDUMAR NATURE CENTER*

**Lansing** - *5739 Old Lansing Road (2 miles west of Waverly Rd.), 48917. Phone: (517) 322-0030.* **Web: www.woldumar.org**. *Hours: Center open Monday-Saturday 10:00am-5:00pm. Park open dawn to dusk.* Nature Center facilities and grounds provide programs year round. Tours of Moon Log Cabin also.

## *IMPRESSION 5 SCIENCE CENTER*

200 Museum Drive (Banks of Grand River, off Michigan Avenue, downtown), **Lansing** 48933

- ❑ Phone: (517) 485-8116, **Web: www.impression5.org**
- ❑ Hours: Monday-Saturday 10:00am-5:00pm. Closed major holidays and September.
- ❑ Admission: $5.00 adult, $3.50 senior (62+) and child (3-17).
- ❑ Miscellaneous: Impressions to Go Café. Great Science gift shop, too.

150 displays challenge all five senses (i.e. the reason for Impression 5 name). Although it's smaller than many science centers, it's well worth the lower admission cost. Highlights include: THROWING THINGS - using different principles of physics, kids play with different forms of projectiles and balls...even giant slingshots. We've never seen this before - so many different ways to throw things! HEART WORKS - a walk through Heart Maze with sound effects, push button arteries (clear and clogged), try on a "fat vest" and find out what it feels like to carry an extra 20 pounds around, display of actual horse, cat, and mouse hearts. WATER - Build a water tower, navigate a ship thru locks, assemble a plumbing system and splash. BUBBLES - create bubble walls, circles. LIGHT AND SOUND experiments and COMPUTER LAB AND REAL CHEMISTRY LAB - where techs help you make your own experiment -slime! $1.00 extra and you get to take home your experiment! Outside the lab are "Roundtables" - simple experiments you do as a family.

## *MICHIGAN STATE CAPITAL*

Capital & Michigan Avenues (I-496 exit M.L. King Street. Follow Capital Loop), **Lansing** 48933

- ❑ Phone: (517) 373-2353
  **Web: http://council.legislature.mi.gov/lcfa/x1.htm**
- ❑ Tours: Monday-Friday 9:00am-4:00pm. Tours leave every half hour.
- ❑ Admission: FREE.

The House and Senate Galleries are situated inside a building that looks like the US Capital. Recently restored, the building was originally designed by foremost architect, Elijah E. Myers during the Gilded Age. You'll start out under the dome which is a view upward over 160 feet. This gets the kids' attention. Next, you take a peek in the Governor's Office. It's a very stately, very large office that was cleaned during the restoration with cotton swabs (at least, the ceiling was). The kids try to imagine doing their cleaning chores with only cleaning solution and cotton swabs - sounds impossible! Another highlight of this tour is the Senate Room. Magnificent to view (from the public access balcony), it has so much detail, the kids are mesmerized. They'll also learn about contemporary legislative processes and how citizens get involved.

## *PLANET WALK*

**Lansing** - *River Trail along Grand & Red Cedar River (Outside Science Center - 200 Museum Drive), 48933. Phone: (517) 371-6730.* Travel 93 million miles from the Earth to the Sun, almost another 4 billion miles to the farthest planet, Pluto. Want to walk it? Begin at the scaled down version of the sun (it's about the size of a giant play ball). Each step further out covers 1 million scale miles. Pass earth, the size of a pea, and Jupiter, the size of an orange. The total walking distance from the Sun to Pluto is 2 miles.

## R.E. OLDS TRANSPORTATION MUSEUM

**Lansing** - *240 Museum Drive (Downtown off Michigan Avenue, next to Impression 5), Phone: (517) 372-0529 or (888) ASK-OLDS.* **Web: www.reoldsmuseum.org**. *Hours: Tuesday-Saturday 10:00am-5:00pm, Sunday Noon-5:00pm. Closed major holidays. Admission: $3.00-$5.00 (over age 5).* See the first Oldsmobile (1897), Toronado (first 1966), Stars, Durants and Olds car advertising. See autographed and experimental motors plus an REO Speedwagon or Cloud. So many "old" cars to look at up close…look for the Spartan car. The museum is a reflection of R.E. Olds life and contribution to the transport industry from 1883 to the present are featured, too.

## J & K STEAMBOAT LINE

**Lansing (Grand Ledge)** - *(various departure spots on the Grand River), 48837. Phone: (517) 627-2154. Admission: $8.00-$49.00 depending on the type of cruise. Children (3-12) are at 50% of adult rate.* This cruise line features 3 riverboats and a variety of cruising options. "Spirit of Lansing", "Princess Laura" and the largest, the "Michigan Princess" (which has three levels and luxurious woodwork and crystal). The boat features fully air-conditioned and heated cabins that allow for year-round cruising. Be sure to ask about the "Celebration", luncheon or music cruise.

## ALGONAC STATE PARK

**Marine City** - *8732 River Road (2 miles north of the city on SR 29), 48039. www.michigandnr.com/parksandtrails/parklist.asp. Phone: (810) 765-5605. Admission: $6.00-$8.00 per vehicle.* On the St. Clair River you can watch the large freighters pass by from this park. Algonac's lakeplain prairies and lakeplain oak savannas are considered globally significant. These special habitats include nineteen species that are on the state list of endangered, threatened, and special concern species. Other features include winter sports, hiking trails along a prairie area, fishing (walleye), rough camping, and boating.

### *CLEAN WATER BEACH*

**Milan** - *16339 Cone Road (US 23 to exit 22 - follow signs), 48160. Phone: (734) 439-1818* **Web: *www.heathbeach.com****. Hours: Daily 10:30am-7:30pm (Memorial Day Weekend-Labor Day Weekend). Admission: $6.00 (weekends), $5.00 (weekdays), $3.00 child (9-12), Under 8 FREE (all the time).* Some people see a hole in the ground (in this case caused by the construction of US-23)...others see opportunity. In 1962, area resident Charles Heath gained a 6-acre lake (in his former cow pasture) along the new construction. For years they used this recreation area as a family swimming hole. With the persuading of friends, Charles decided to make some improvements and open it to the public.

## *MILAN DRAGWAY*

10860 Plank Road (US 23 to exit 25)

**Milan** 48160

❑ Phone: (734) 439-7368 **Web: www.milandragway.com**
❑ Hours: Season is April-October. Auto races held in the day, Saturday & Sunday. Motorcycle races held Friday nights.
❑ Admission: Adults $10.00, Children $4.00 (7-12), FREE (ages 6 and under). During special events - rates can be higher. Call or visit website for details.
❑ Miscellaneous: Drag and bracket racing. Events include junior racing, nostalgia days, RAM chargers, Harlet drags and invitationals. There's even a new track for off-road truck races.

A race that lasts 6 seconds or less? Don't blink or you might just miss it! See Michigan (and nationally known) racers compete to see who can travel the fastest on the ¼ mile drag "strip". Special events feature "dragsters" that can reach speeds of over 300 MPH (in a little over 4 seconds!) Be sure to bring earplugs for the kids (& parents) since these "open header" vehicles can be extremely loud! Hey Moms and Dads... Wednesday and Friday allow you (for an entry fee) to see just how fast the family "dragster" can go! Kids can also compete in special miniature drag cars...wow!

# KENSINGTON METROPARK
2240 West Buno Road (I-96 - Next exit past Milford)

**Milford** 48380

❑    Phone: (248) 685-1561 or (800) 477-3178

**Web: www.metroparks.com/parks/pk_kensington.php#**

❑    Hours: Daily 6:00am-10:00pm

❑    Admission: $4.00 per vehicle, rides extra $2.00-$3.00.

Spanning over 4,000 acres (including the 1200 acre Lake Kent), this park offers family fun year-round. Some of the educational attractions include the Farm Center (discover and touch numerous animals) and the Nature Center (with wildlife exhibits and nature trails). For a break from the action, step aboard the Island Queen paddlewheel boat for a scenic trip around the lake (summer afternoons). Speaking of Lake Kent, it offers great fishing (you can even bring your own boat or use rentals including sailboats which are available) and 2 beaches in the summertime. Golfing is also available on the 18-hole course of the south side of the lake. Winter brings sled riding, tobogganing, cross-country skiing, and sleigh rides (minimum snow base of 4-6 inches required) to the park.

## PROUD LAKE RECREATION AREA
**Milford** - *3500 Wixom Road (I-96 exit Wixom Road north), 48382.* **Web: *www.michigandnr.com/parksandtrails/parklist.asp.*** *Phone: (248) 685-2433. Admission: $6.00-$8.00 per vehicle.* Including part of the upper Huron River, features include hiking trails, beaches and swimming, boating and canoeing, camping, and winter sports. It is also a great place to be (beginning the last weekend of April) when the site releases large batches of trout for fishing.

## RIVER RAISIN BATTLEFIELD VISITOR'S CENTER
**Monroe** - *1403 East Elm Street (I-75, exit 14), 48161.* **Web: *www.co.monroe.mi.us/monroe/default.aspx?PageId=107.*** *Phone: (734) 243-7136 or (743) 243-7137. Hours: Friday-Tuesday 10:00am-5:00pm (Memorial Day - Labor Day). Weekends only 1:00-5:00pm (Rest of the Year). Admission: FREE (donations accepted).* An important stop for interesting regional history, this visitor's center focuses on the battle (during the War of 1812) that

was the worst defeat for the Americans. The British and Chief Tecumseh's Indians killed over 800 settlers during this battle. A 10 minute presentation (with fiber optic maps, mannequins, and dioramas) summarizes the importance of who was in control of the Great Lakes.

## STERLING STATE PARK

**Monroe** - *2800 State Park Road (off I-75), 48161. Phone: (734) 289-2715. Web: www.michigandnr.com/parksandtrails/parklist.asp. Admission: $6.00-$8.00 per vehicle.* Camping, hiking trails, boating, fishing and swimming. Boat Rentals Memorial Day - Labor Day. Row boats, canoes, paddle boats.

## METRO BEACH METROPARK

**Mount Clemens** - *Metropolitan Parkway, 48043. Web: www.metroparks.com/parks/pk_metro_beach.php#. Phone: (586) 463-4581 or (800) 477-3172. Hours: Monday-Friday 8:00am-8:00pm. Weekends & Holidays 8:00am-Dusk. Admission: $4.00 per vehicle. Some additional activity fees.* A lakeside summer beach retreat (with a boardwalk over a mile long) that has several unique attractions including: The Tot Lot (a place for kids as young as 3 can ride their bikes without running over someone), Educational Nature Programs, Spray Zone and a heated pool. Also: VOYAGEUR CANOE Passengers help paddle a 34-foot (20-passenger) Montreal Canoe that makes trips daily from the North Marina. Advance registration required for individuals and groups. TRACKLESS TRAIN Shuttle service to Huron Point picnic and shore fishing areas, weekends and holidays.

## MAYBURY STATE PARK

**Northville** - *20145 Beck Road (I-96 to I-275 north, west on Eight Mile Road), 48167. Phone: (248) 349-8390. Web: www.michigandnr.com/parksandtrails/parklist.asp. Admission: $6.00-$8.00 per vehicle.* Mostly forest, features include horseback riding, cross-country skiing, hiking trails, bike trails, fishing, winter sports, and a visitors center and living farm featuring a petting area for kids. The Farm represents a small family farm where general farming practices are demonstrated. Maybury Farm is open all year Summer Hours: 10:00am-7:00pm, Winter Hours: 10:00am-5:00pm. Guided Tours by Reservation Phone: (248) 349-3858.

### HAYES STATE PARK

**Onstead** - *1220 Wampler's Lake Road (US-12 west to M-124), 49265. Web: www.michigandnr.com/parksandtrails/parklist.asp. Phone: (517) 467-7401. Admission: $6.00-$8.00 per vehicle.* W.J. Hayes State Park, in the heart of the Irish Hills, is bordered by a group of inland lakes frequented by anglers and boaters. Camping, boating, fishing, swimming and winter sports are offered.

### LAKE HUDSON RECREATION AREA

**Onstead** - *1220 Wampler's Lake Road (M-156 SE), 49265. Web: www.michigandnr.com/parksandtrails/parklist.asp. Phone: (517) 445-2265 Admission: $6.00-$8.00 per vehicle.* Nearly 2,700 acres of recreational opportunities around Lake Hudson. The park, which lies in southeast Michigan, offers premier muskie fishing and hunting. A new beach area provides an excellent place for sunbathing and swimming. Camping, hiking, boating, fishing, swimming and winter sports.

### ORTONVILLE RECREATION AREA

**Ortonville** - *5779 Hadley Road, 48462. Phone: (248) 627-3828 Web: www.michigandnr.com/parksandtrails/parklist.asp.* Camping, cabins, hiking trails, boating, fishing, swimming and winter sports.

### LAKELANDS TRAIL STATE PARK

**Pinckney** - *8555 Silver Hill, Rt. 1, 48169. Phone: (734) 426-4913. Web: www.michigandnr.com/parksandtrails/parklist.asp. Admission: $6.00-$8.00 per vehicle.* A 13-mile gravel trail connects Pinckney and Stockbridge. Along the way, you'll pass through rolling farmland and wooded areas that offer spectacular views. The Pinckney trailhead is a quarter mile north of M-36 on D-19 in Pinckney. The Stockbridge trailhead is on M-52 in Stockbridge.

## PINCKNEY RECREATION AREA

**Pinckney** - *8555 Silver Hill (I-94 exit 159, North), 48169. Phone: (734) 426-4913. www.michigandnr.com/parksandtrails/parklist.asp. Admission: $6.00-$8.00 per vehicle.* Camping, hiking (Lakelands trail is popular), boating, fishing, swimming, bicycle trails and winter sports.

## PLYMOUTH HISTORICAL MUSEUM

**Plymouth** - *155 South Main Street (one block north of Kellogg Park), 48170. Web: www.plymouthhistory.org. Phone: (734) 455-8940. Hours: Wednesday, Thursday, Saturday, Sunday 1:00-4:00 pm. Admission: $3.00 adult, $1.00 student (5-17), $7.00 family.* A kid-friendly museum with exhibits that include a scavenger hunt where "every child wins a prize". Experience the changes in this community from forests to fields to factories. In addition visitors can now see the newly expanded Daisy Air Rifle Exhibit complete with the original flooring from the factory, a complete collection of BB guns and toys made here in Plymouth and learn about the other BB gun companies located here which made Plymouth the Air Rifle Capital of the World! See the "Images of Abraham Lincoln" exhibit that features Lincoln in 10 phases of life (from boy to hero), wax figures of Abraham & Mary Todd Lincoln, and even displays a lock of Lincoln's actual hair!

## WOLCOTT MILL METROPARK

**Ray Township** - *(M-53, take the 26 Mile Road exit east to Romeo Plank Road north to 29 Mile Road), 48096. Phone: (586) 749-5997 or (800) 477-3175. www.metroparks.com/parks/pk_wolcott_mill.php. Hours: Weekdays 9:00am - 5:00pm, Weekends 9:00am - 7:00pm (May - October). Closes at 5:00pm (November - April). Restricted winter hours. Admission: $4.00 per vehicle. Hayrides extra.* A gristmill is always a fun experience (really, explain it to the kids like it is a giant "mousetrap" game inside - full of large gears and rubberbands, etc.). See the mid-1800's era gristmill grind wheat into flour on the huge millstones. (It's interesting to note that in a hundred years, most mills would only wear out maybe one set of millstones). Also featured is the Farm Learning Center (on Wolcott Road) that teaches the methods and importance of farming today. See cow milking, sheep demonstrations, and experimental vegetable plots.

## MCCOURTIE PARK

**Somerset Center** - *(US 12 and US 127 - 11/2 miles west - enter from South Jackson Road), 49282. Open dawn to dusk. Picnic facilities, ballfields.* Walk over 17 concrete bridges (each a different style), visit the underground apartments and garages, see the giant birdhouse and their tree chimneys. All of this concrete! Until you get up close, it will fool you - it looks like wood! Herb McCourtie, a concrete baron, left the park grounds to his hometown. It's unique enough to definitely write home about!

## CROSSWINDS MARSH WETLAND INTERPRETIVE PRESERVE

**Sumpter Township** - *(I-94 to exit 8 - go west), 48111.* **Web: www.waynecounty.com/parks/cwinds_ip.htm**. *Phone: (734) 261-1990. Free admission (small fee for programs).* Over 100 species of birds (binocular rentals available for $1.00) can be viewed at this 1000 acre artificially created wetland - one of the largest in the country. Learn more about the plants and wildlife that were moved to this area by taking a 2 mile canoe trip that has interpretive markers to describe what you are seeing. (Canoe rentals are available for $5.00 per hour).

# COE RAIL SCENIC TRAIN

840 North Pontiac Trail (I-96 - Wixom Road Exit - North)

**Walled Lake** 48390

❑　Phone: (248) 960-9440
　　**Web: www.michiganstarclipper.com/scenictr.html**
❑　Admission: Averages $10.00 per person.
❑　Tours: Train departs Sundays at 1:00 and 2:30pm. One hour long. (late April-October).

Train rides thru scenic countryside of Walled Lake and West Bloomfield in old-fashioned cars.

## *PONTIAC LAKE RECREATION AREA*

**Waterford** - *7800 Gale Road (off M-59), 48327. Phone: (248) 666-1020. www.michigandnr.com/parksandtrails/parklist.asp. Admission: $6.00-$8.00 per vehicle.* Archery ranges and horse trails/rentals make this park unique. Camping, hiking trails, boating, fishing, swimming, bicycle trails and winter sports.

## *DODGE NO. 4 STATE PARK*

**Waterford** - *4250 Parkway Drive (off M-59 west to Cass Elizabeth Road), 48328. Phone: (248) 682-7323.* **Web:** *www.michigandnr.com/parksandtrails/parklist.asp. Admission: $6.00-$8.00 per vehicle.* A white sandy beach and a one-mile shoreline on Cass Lake makes Dodge #4 State Park an excellent location for summer and winter water activities. Camping, fishing, boating, swimming and winter sports.

## *FRIDGE, (THE)*

**Waterford** - *Scott Lake Road (I-75 to Dixie Highway Exit - South), 48328. Phone: In season: (248) 975-4440. Off season: (248) 858-0906. www.co.oakland.mi.us/parksrec/ppark/fridge.html. Hours: Wednesday-Friday 4:00-9:30pm. Saturday 10:00am-10:00pm. Sunday Noon-8:00pm. (All times are weather permitting). Closed Christmas Eve and Day. (mid-December to mid-March). Admission: $4.00-$9.00. No riders under 30" tall permitted, and riders under age 10 must be accompanied by an adult.* Drop 55 feet (rather quickly) and then travel over 1000 feet as you and 3 close friends discover the thrill of tobogganing. The park has 2 runs, over 200 toboggans, and even a place to warm up with a fireplace and food. In the summer you'll find a tennis courts, a 5-story raft ride, wave pool, and BMX bicycle course.

## *DRAYTON PLAINS NATURE CENTER*

**Waterford** - *2125 Denby Drive (near Dixie Hwy. & M-59, Turn onto Edmore off of Hatchery Road). 48329. Phone: (248) 674-2119.* **Web:** *www.draytonplainsnaturecenter.org. Hours: Grounds open 8:00am-9:00pm (April -October). Only open until 6:00pm rest of year. Interpretive Center open Tuesday - Friday 11:00am - 2:00pm and Weekends Noon - 4:00pm. FREE*

*Admission.* 137 acres of trails along the Clinton River plus a nice Interpretive Center. In the center are displays of mounted animals in re-created scenes of their natural habitats.

## HIGHLAND RECREATION AREA

**White Lake** - *5200 East Highland Road (off M-59 East), 48363. Web: www.michigandnr.com/parksandtrails/parklist.asp. Phone: (248) 889-3750.* Camping, hiking, boating, fishing, swimming and winter sports. Horse rentals and trails too.

## ALPINE VALLEY SKI AREA

**White Lake** - *6775 East Highland Road (I-96 - Milford Road exit to M-59 West), 48383. Phone: (248) 887-4183. Web: www.skialpinevalley.com.* You'll have a real "Alpine" feeling since this resort offers 25 runs (some of which have many trees and are steep). Rental equipment: Skis (also shaped skis to learn easier) and snowboards.

## ROLLING HILLS COUNTY PARK

**Ypsilanti** - *7660 Stoney Creek Road, 48197. Phone: (734) 482-3866.* Summers: Wave pool, water slide, zero-depth pool, waterfall, picnic area, sports fields, fishing pond, grassy sunbathing area, sandy beach, 9-hole Frisbee golf course, tube rentals. Winter: Dual toboggan chutes, ice skating, and cross-county skiing.

# *SUGGESTED LODGING AND DINING*

**HOLIDAY INN EXPRESS HOTEL & SUITES**, **Dearborn (Allen Park)**, 3600 Enterprises Drive (off I-94). (313) 323-3500 or **www.dialinn.com**. The Family Suites have bunk beds w/ Redwing décor and the continental breakfast is massive. The indoor pool area is clean and kid-friendly, too.

**BEST WESTERN GREENFIELD INN**. 3000 Enterprise Drive, **Dearborn (Allen Park)**. (I-94 exit 206 east). Phone: (313) 271-1600 or **www.bestwestern.com**. Amenities: Spacious rooms (some w/ frig), large heated indoor pool & jacuzzi, fitness center, coffee makers, cookies at night, in-room VCRs, and Special price tickets available to The Henry Ford/Greenfield Village.

**HOLIDAY INN WEST HOLIDOME**. **Lansing**. 7501 W. Saginaw Hwy, 48917 (I-96 exit 93B). (517) 627-3211. Fun, clean Holidome for family fun. The pool temperature is just right and there are many "little tykes" playthings plus the arcade and ping pong games for older children. We liked having the TGIFridays restaurant right on the premises with their popular food and kids menu (even for breakfast).

**HOCKEYTOWN CAFÉ**. **Detroit**. Downtown (2301 Woodward, 313-965-9500, next to Fox Theatre) near all the sporting action is a good stop for food and sports themed meals. The new Hockeytown Cafe features new décor and new menu. The new decor is highlighted by custom motorcycles themed after the Detroit Red Wings. You're greeted by the 1962 Zamboni *(ice resurfacing machine)* and while you're waiting on your food, take a stroll around and gander at the Statues, The Walk of Fame, or the Ring of Honor. Look for your favorite player's showcase. Both the outdoor video screen and televisions throughout the Hockeytown Café carry the live in-arena video and audio of Red Wings games directly on fiber optics from Joe Louis Arena. The kids meals are around the $5.00 range. The adult entrees were delicious and a great value. Ample, well-lit parking nearby in lots or garages. Many "kid-friendly" shows next door at Fox Theatre, too.

**THE BEACH GRILL** - **Detroit (St. Clair Shores)**. (Jefferson Beach Marina Complex) - 24420 Jefferson (between. 9 & 10 mile). (586) 771-4455. Moderately priced meal and enjoy spectacular views of all the Great Lakes boats. Indoor/Outdoor dining. Trendy...yet family friendly. Kids menu $3.00-6.00. Open daily for lunch and dinner.

**CLARA'S LANSING STATION RESTAURANT**. **Lansing**. 637 E. Michigan Avenue. (517) 372-7120 or **www.claras.com**. Located in the historic Michigan Central Railroad Station, this place has the look and feel of a Victorian era station. Trains still pass by while you eat...and maybe you'll get lucky enough to eat on the platform for a great view. Daily lunch and dinner with moderate pricing. Children's Menu with basic American food fare priced between $3.00-$4.00. Nearby Olds Park (Lugnuts) and Impression 5 Museum.

# Chapter 6
## *South West Area*

# Our Favorites...

* S.S. Kewatin - Douglas

* Deer Forest - Coloma

* Kalamazoo Nature Center - Kalamazoo

* Kellogg's Cereal City - Battle Creek

* Saugatuck Dune Rides - Saugatuck

*Breakfast Buddies*

## *WHITEHOUSE NATURE CENTER*

**Albion** - *1381 East Erie Street (one-quarter mile southeast of the Albion College campus off Hannah St., on the North Branch of the Kalamazoo River), 49224. Phone: (517) 629-0582. **Web:** www.albion.edu/naturecenter/trails.asp. Hours: Monday-Friday 9:30am-4:30pm. Weekends, 10:30am-4:30pm. Closed major and college holidays. Free Admission.* A 135 acre outdoor facility for education that features 6 nature trails and 168 species of birds. Most of the trails are less than one mile long and each features different opportunities. Includes an observation room with live exhibits.

## *FORT CUSTER RECREATION AREA*

**Augusta** - *5163 West Fort Custer Drive (M-96 West), 49012. **Web:** www.michigandnr.com/parksandtrails/parklist.asp. Phone: (269) 731-4200. Admission: $6.00-$8.00 per vehicle.* Area comprises 2,988 acres located between Battle Creek and Kalamazoo. The terrain is typical of southern Michigan farm country, with second growth forests and remnant areas of prairie. The area features three lakes, the Kalamazoo River, and an excellent trail system. Camping, hiking, boating, fishing, swimming, bicycle trails, winter sports.

## *KELLOGG BIOLOGICAL STATION*

(13 miles northwest on SR89, between 40th and E. Gull Lake Drive)

### **Augusta** 49012

❑    Web: www.kbs.msu.edu/

KBS is Michigan State University's largest off-campus education complex and one of North America's premier inland field stations. The 4,065-acre station includes Kellogg Bird Sanctuary, Kellogg Farm, the Kellogg Biological Laboratories.

BIRD SANCTUARY: On East C Avenue. (269) 671-2510 or **www.kbs.msu.edu/bird_sanctuary/index.htm**. An MSU experimental facility of birds of prey, wild geese, ducks, swans, pheasants and peacocks. There are displays and observation decks. Several endangered species, like the genetically endangered red jungle fowl and Reeves' pheasant are on display, as well as the rare sharp-tailed grouse and greater prairie chicken (which is no longer found in Michigan). Hours: Daily 9:00am-7:00pm (May-October). Daily 9:00am-5:00pm (rest of year). Admission: $1.00-$4.00.

DAIRY CENTER: open to the public for self-guided tours every day of the year from 8:00 a.m. until sunset with guided group tours available through the Volunteer Program. Gather and watch in the Feed Center or Milking Parlor. 10461 North 40th Street, Hickory Corners. **www.kbs.msu.edu/Research_Facilities/Farm/Index.htm**. (269) 671-2507.

## BINDER PARK ZOO

7400 Division Drive (I-94 to exit 100 - go south)

**Battle Creek** 49014

❑     Phone: (269) 979-1351, **Web: www.binderparkzoo.org**
❑     Hours: Monday-Friday 9:00am-5:00pm, Saturday & Holidays 9:00am-6:00pm, Sunday 11:00am-6:00pm (mid-April to mid-October).
❑     Admission: $7.75-$9.75 (age 2+).
❑     Miscellaneous: Gift shop with unique animal items.

Natural settings offer over 250 animals in 80 exhibits that you can see while strolling along elevated wooden boardwalks. See exhibits like a Chinese Red Panda, and a Mexican Grey Wolf, interact with insects, and have fun learning at the Conservation Stations (a hands-on exhibit). The hands-on playground at the children's zoo is said to have the world's largest and most accurate dinosaur replicas, a petting zoo, and miniature railroad. Get nose-to-nose with one of the largest giraffe herds on an African Savanna.

## FULL BLAST

35 Hamblin Ave. (I-94 to I-194/M-66 - north), **Battle Creek**  49017

❑     Phone: (269) 966-3667 **Web: www.fullblast.org**
❑     Hours: Varies by activity and season but basically 10:00am-7:00pm. Afternoons only school days.
❑     Admission: $3.00-$7.00 per activity or day pass of around $16.00 to everything.

A family fun attraction with something for everyone. Attractions include a skateboard park, indoor and outdoor waterparks (with 2 –

100 ft. waterslides, a river float, bubble beach), 3 basketball courts, full-service health club, café and food court, and teen nightclub. Imagination Station (indoor)/Adventure Land (outdoor) - a playground with slides, climbing nets, and endless tunnels (Guest must be 54" or shorter to play) in playgrounds).

## *KELLOGG'S CEREAL CITY USA*

171 West Michigan Avenue (I-94 exit 98B to I-194/M 66 north. On
the riverfront.), **Battle Creek** 49017

- ❑   Phone: (269) 962-6230, **Web: www.kelloggscerealcity.com**
- ❑   Hours: Monday-Saturday 9:30am-5:00pm, Sunday 11:00am-
  5:00pm (Summer). Tuesday-Saturday 10:00am-4:00pm, Sunday
  12:00pm-5:00pm (April-May). Weekends only (January-March)
- ❑   Admission: $4.95-$7.95 per person (age 3+).
- ❑   Miscellaneous: Red Onion Grill - a 1930's style diner serves
  sandwiches. The Factory Store. Half of the facility is for older
  kids (in all of us) and another half is for younger kids.

Flakes started as an experiment for a new healthy breakfast food by Dr. Kellogg in the late 1800's. Within a couple of years, almost 40 different cereal companies had started in the Battle Creek area - including POST (one of the only surviving still). You'll learn this and more in the theater presentation on the first floor. Adults will find some of their marketing strategies unique - like asking people to stop eating their flakes because they were in short supply. As you go upstairs, don't be surprised to " bump" into Tony the Tiger or Snap, Crackle & Pop (we have video tape of big hugs from our kids to these characters)! The simulated working production line tour is where you can see, smell and taste a warm sample of fresh flakes being made. This is narrated by a "kernel of corn" hoping he becomes a "cereal flake" - so colorful and fun! Cereal City has hands-on interactives in a cobblestone lane setting. The "Tony" and "Tony Jr." is a soft play area where younger sets can climb up inside a cereal box and slide down as you're poured out of the box! There's a ball pit with gym, too. Before you leave, buy a box of special Corn Flakes with your photo on the front - a must souvenir for cereal lovers!

### LEILA ARBORETUM & KINGMAN MUSEUM OF NATURAL HISTORY

**Battle Creek** - *928 West Michigan Avenue (near 20th St), 49017. Phone: Museum (269) 965-5117, Arboretum (269) 969-0270* **Web:** *www.kingmanmuseum.org. Hours: (Museum) Tuesday-Friday 9:00am-5:00pm, Saturday 1:00-5:00pm. (Arboretum) Daily Dawn to Dusk. Admission: (Museum) $5.00 adult, $4.00 senior (65+), $3.00 student (3-18). The arboretum admission is usually Free. Planetarium $2.00.* It now features a sunken garden, a visitor's center, a children's adventure garden, and large floral displays (depending on season). The Kingman Museum of Natural History (West Michigan at 20th) has 3 floors of exhibits including dinosaurs and a planetarium. One exhibit shows the remnants of a sabre-toothed tiger. Visitors can see actual bones of the tiger and view other skeletons as well.

### COOK ENERGY INFO CENTER AND DUNES

**Bridgman** - *1 Cook Place (I-94 exit 16 or 23, follow signs - off Red Arrow Highway), 49106. Phone: (800) 548-2555.* **Web:** *www.cookinfo.com. Admission: FREE. Tours: The Cook Energy Center is currently open to school groups only. All schools must schedule their tours in advance; no drop-in tours are available. 45 minute guided. Miscellaneous: Picnic areas.* Technology and nature together - sounds impossible. Nuclear power, electricity and future energy sources are explained. From your arrival in the Energy Center lobby, your group will be whisked off to Theater 1 for a private screening of Dr. Nate's nuclear energy video. You'll learn the secrets of nuclear energy and how we use it to make electricity at the Cook Nuclear Plant. Next you're off to Theater 2 to watch a 26-foot 3-D rotating exhibit rise from the floor, rotate, and flash as the intricate working of a nuclear energy plant are displayed. Hike dune trails along Lake Michigan shoreline including forests and wetlands. There are also energy video games and hands-on displays. Schedule a fun "Power Trip" with Dr. Nate for your class or group and learn how nuclear energy is produced and used.

## *BEAR CAVE*

**Buchanan** - *4085 Bearcave Road (US 12 to 4 miles North on Red Bud Trail), 49107. Phone: (269) 695-3050. Hours: Daily 10:00am-4:00pm (Memorial Day-Labor Day). Miscellaneous: Clubhouse, pool, Jacuzzi, fishing, game room, horseshoes, shuffleboard, boat ramp, playground, boating and canoeing. Open May through September.* One of the few caves in Michigan that is accessible to the public, Bear Cave (150-feet long) is accessed by a narrow, winding stairway. The temperature is a constant 58 degrees F. so be sure to dress appropriately. A taped narration explains the sights of stalactites, flowstone, and petrified leaves. A warning though...the cave does contain bats. However, if you don't bother them, they usually won't bother you!

## *DEER FOREST*

Paw Paw Lake Road, 6800 Indian Lane (I-94 exit 39 north, follow signs), **Coloma** 49038

- ❑    Phone: (269) 468-4961, **Web: www.deerforest.com**
- ❑    Hours: Daily 10:00am-7:00pm (Memorial Weekend-Labor Day).
- ❑    Admission: $8.00-$12.00 (age 4+).
- ❑    Miscellaneous: Gift shop. Picnic areas. "Wild Child Play Habitat". Mini-golf. Gold panning. Kid's entertainment like magicians. Mostly in the woods and shaded.

Their slogan, "More fun than a zoo" is true, mostly because it's designed as an Animal and an Amusement Park. Fun and different animals to pet are baby zebras and mini-horses (the size of dogs) or sit between the humps of a camel. Most every animal here is tame enough to pet (making it different than a zoo). You can also ride ponies and camels, a treetop Ferris wheel, a carrousel or mini-train. Our favorite part had to be Storybook Lane, a large park within the park, where you meander around the lane. Each setting illustrates a different Nursery Rhyme scene like "3 Men in a Tub" (in a pond with real frogs and small fish) or "Baa Baa Black Sheep" (with what else but, black sheep). Deer Forest's Storybook Lane has a wonderful history. Who can forget the magic of getting your first elephant key, and bringing it to the Storybook Lane, then keeping and treasuring it forever? Today still, your children's faces will light up as they turn the elephant key, and listen to the many fairy-tale stories and children's songs (extra $2.50 for key, great souvenir). To get your money's worth, be sure to spend several hours here and plan a picnic or buy at the snack bar. Also, lots of photo ops everywhere.

## SS KEEWATIN

CR A2 (Blue Star Highway & Union Street) (Kalamazoo River near bridge at Harbour Village, off I-196 & US 31), **Douglas** 49406

❑     Phone: (269) 857-7235
        **Web: www.keewatinmaritimemuseum.com**
❑     Hours: Daily 10:30am-4:30pm (Summers only).
❑     Admission: Average $5.00 per person (ages 6+).
❑     Miscellaneous: Extensive nautical gift shop and museum. To keep the kids curious, tell them to look for the captain's boots he left on the ship (Note: you'll find them towards the very end of the tour!)

This visit sure was nostalgic. As we approached the large vessel (350 feet long), Michele remembered the same eerie feeling it gave her as a child. It went out of service in 1965 and was brought here as a museum in 1967. I was about 10-12 years old when I first visited. Now, with my children and husband in tow, we escaped back to the time of luxury liners, elegant dining rooms, handsome staterooms, and the grand ballroom. Occasionally, pictures from the movie "Titanic" appeared on the walls and with good reason. If you liked the movie, or just the romance of the grandiose "floating hotel" - Keewatin (Key-way-tin) will fill your dreams. However, the ship is not fully restored, and is a mix of pristine wood and etched Italian glass mixed with the smell and look of old upholstery and worn paint. Well, back to reality - your kids will love that they get to go inside the "really huge boat" and even get to climb up to the top deck and turn the ship's wheel.

## MUSEUM AT SOUTHWESTERN MICHIGAN COLLEGE

**Dowagiac** - *58900 Cherry Grove Road (east on SR62 from SR51), 49047. Phone: (269) 782-1374.* **Web: www.smc.cc.mi.us/museum.** *Hours: Tuesday-Saturday, 10:00am-5:00pm. Open until 8:00pm* *on Wednesdays. Closed on national, state and college holidays.* An interactive adventure in local history and an exciting exploration in science and technology. Cass County history is explored through displays on science, agriculture, industry (Heddon lures & Roand Oak Stoves), American Indians, the Underground Railroad. Try on vintage-style clothing of the 19$^{th}$ century, travel thru an archeological time tunnel or solve mysteries of the past by reconstructing pottery from shards. Now, put your energy and curiosity to use in two galleries of sensory stimulation exploration of Science and Technology. Displays of light & minerals, air & motion, generating light, and producing energy. A walk-in camera obscura shows the earliest photographic techniques and a pedal-powered electrical generator awaits the visitor's muscle power.

## *CHARLTON PARK VILLAGE & MUSEUM*

2545 South Charlton Park Road (2 miles South on SR 37 then 4 miles East on SR79 - follow signs), **Hastings** 49058

- ❑ Phone: (989) 945-3775, **Web: www.charltonpark.org**
- ❑ Hours: Tuesday-Sunday 9:00am-4:30pm. (Memorial Day-Labor Day), plus festivals.
- ❑ Admission: $2.00-$4.00 (age 5+). Special events can have various admission fees and are the best time to visit (many re-enactors): Civil War Muster or Steam Engine Show (July) & Pow Wow (September).

A very authentic recreation of an 1890's rural Michigan town, this village offers 25 buildings that include a schoolhouse, a blacksmith shop, an 1880's doctor's home, a general store, an 1885 church, a print shop, a cabin and a wigwam. Also find a beach, boat launch, and playground in the recreational part of the park complex.

## *GILMORE CAR MUSEUM*

**Hickory Corners** - *6865 Hickory Road (M43 at Hickory Road), 49060. **Web: www.gilmorecarmuseum.org**. Phone: (269) 671-5089. Hours: Daily 9:00am-5:00pm (early May - last weekend in October). Admission: $6.00-$8.00 (age 7+).* Have you ever had a dream about finding that "priceless" antique car in someone's barn? See more than 130 unique and rare cars all displayed in antique barns. A few cars that you will see include Cadillacs, Packards, and even a steam powered car. Also, you'll find a reproduction of the Wright Brother's plane and a narrow gauge train. For the "tikes" they have antique pedal cars.

## K-WINGS HOCKEY

**Kalamazoo** - *3600 Vanrick Drive (I-94 - Sprinkle Road exit - Wings Stadium), 49001. Phone: (269) 345-5101 tickets or (269) 345-9772 office. Web: www.kwings.com*. You'll experience hard-hitting, fast-paced action, great music, humorous on-ice promotions, contests, and the antics of Slappy, the K-Wings zany mascot. An UHL affiliate team (October - April). $5.00-$15.00. Public skating and rentals at rink, too.

## ECHO VALLEY

**Kalamazoo** - *8495 East H Avenue, 49004. Phone: (269) 349-3291 Web: www.echovalleyfun.com. Hours: Friday 6:00-10:00pm. Saturday 10:00am-10:00pm. Sunday Noon - 7:00pm. (mid-December to early March). Admission: (Toboggans) $10.00. All day passes $15.00. (Inner Tubing) $10.00. (Ice Skating) $5.00. Miscellaneous: Lodge and snack bar. Outdoor ice skating rink. Parents & Chaperones who prefer to observe all the fun rather than participate may enter Echo Valley at no cost.* Aaah…the feeling of that sled racing down a fresh snow covered hill…and the air getting colder on my face…is a childhood memory that I will never forget. Relive those memories and introduce your kids to the fun of tubing and tobogganing that makes winter a blast. Old wood toboggans have been replaced with super-fast custom made sleds molded from a single piece of polyethylene. The toboggans are equipped with padded seats and Teflon runners. Eight icy and fast tracks await you as you fly down a hill of over 120 feet, at speeds of up to 60 miles per hour. The best part of all is that at this resort there is a tow rope to pull the toboggans back up the hill.

## *KALAMAZOO NATURE CENTER*

7000 N. Westnedge Ave. (I-94 to US131 exit 44 E.), **Kalamazoo** 49004

- ❑ Phone: (269) 381-1574, **Web: www.naturecenter.org**
- ❑ Hours: Monday-Saturday 9:00am-5:00pm, Sunday & most holidays 1:00-5:00pm. (Extended summer hours). Closed winter holidays.
- ❑ Admission: $5.50 adult, $4.00 senior (55+), $3.50 child (4-13).
- ❑ Miscellaneous: Nature trails (one is wheelchair and stroller accessible). Gift shop - large variety of Insect Inside Candy.

When you enter, either walk over to the Tropical Rainforest (3 stories) environment that's home to parrots, iguanas, tropical plants and exotic fish or walk through Bugs in our Lives and Nature Up Close. You'll walk through giant tree trunks and discover nature 10 times the size of life. Imagine 8 foot tall flowers and watch out for that huge frog - it's like the movie Bugs Life! We especially liked the pollen exhibit where the kids can try to help bees pollinate flowers. It's a clever demo and we learned bees pollinate by accident. Explore a bughouse kitchen inside and out to find unwanted—and beneficial—bugs crawling around inside. The Expedition Station is outstanding with a collection of stuffed birds and real bones - all hands-on. Visit the Sun/Rain Room for a visual experience with the enchanting "Crystal Rain...Glass in Nature" exhibit. See glass as "crystal rain" glitters, reflects, and delights in its natural surrounding. Outside, walk through 1000 acres of dense hardwood forest and check out the Butterfly House, Hummingbird Garden or Delano Pioneer Homestead - early life in Michigan.

## *KALAMAZOO SYMPHONY ORCHESTRA*

**Kalamazoo** - *126 East South Street (Miller Auditorium), 49007. Phone: (269) 349-7759. Tickets: (800) 228-9858.* **Web: www.kazoosymphony.com** *or* **www.kjso.org**. The season includes family concerts and FREE summer outdoor concerts. Look for the Family Discovery Concert and the Crazy Classics Concert. The youth symphony provides an orchestral experience of the highest quality for talented young musicians in southwest Michigan. Players are drawn from the Kalamazoo metropolitan area and surrounding communities.

## KALAMAZOO VALLEY MUSEUM

230 North Rose Street (I-94 Westnedge Ave. exit 76 north to M-43
east), **Kalamazoo** 49007

- ❏ Phone: (269) 373-7990, **Web: http://kvm.kvcc.edu/**
- ❏ Hours: Monday-Saturday 9:00am-5:00pm, Sunday 1:00-5:00pm.
  School-year Saturdays 5:00-9:00pm also. Closed some major
  holidays.
- ❏ Admission: FREE
- ❏ Miscellaneous: Digistar Planetarium. Challenger Mini-Mission
  (5th graders and up as a group actually simulate an astronaut
  mission using working equipment!). $3.00-$5.00 charge for
  Astronomy/Space related activities.

What an unexpected surprise! The Kalamazoo Valley should be
proud. It's interesting to learn that funds for the museum were
raised by the community with the museum artifacts found mostly
by locals in their attics and basements. In an 1860's farm kitchen,
make a seed wreath or search for the lost town of Singapore or test
your spelling skills in a schoolhouse. Our favorite hands-on
displays were: the create your own sand dunes or tornadoes - can
you stop them?... and the Race Cars that show you it's easier to
work together than alone. What impressed us was that most
displays were actual hands-on, not just push buttons. It was also
interesting to learn about all of the products manufactured in the
area over the years. Every young kid loves the Children's
Landscape Play Area. Oops, almost forgot - check out their 2500
year old woman (mummy)!

## WOLF LAKE FISHERY INTERPRETIVE CENTER

34270 County Road 652 (US 131 exit 38, 6 miles west of
Kalamazoo on M43), **Kalamazoo (Mattawan)** 49071

- ❏ Phone: (269) 668-2876
  **Web: www.michigan.gov/dnr** (click on Fishing)
- ❏ Hours: Tuesday-Saturday 10:00am-6:00pm, Sunday 10:00am-
  5:00pm. (Call for Winter hours)
- ❏ Admission: Free

❑     Miscellaneous: Picnic Area. Trails.

If you've never been to a "fish farm" it's worth a trip. This one has a museum center with a stuffed sturgeon - it's big - the largest fish caught in the state - 87 inches long and 193 pounds! Learn about fish life cycles and habitats, as well as why they even have fisheries. There's a slide show of hatchery operations and occasional hatchery tours (several times, especially Saturdays in the spring and summer). The hatchery looks like a giant scientific engineering lab with all the pipes, basins and valves. Outside, there are display ponds with steelhead, grayling, sturgeon and Chinook salmon - you can feed the fish and watch them jump for food. Kids will love the fishing derbies (June-August). If you want them to have a positive fishing experience, they're almost guaranteed to catch here.

## *KALAMAZOO AIR ZOO*

3101 East Milham Road (I-94 exit 78 to airport, corner of East Milham Avenue and Portage Road), **Kalamazoo (Portage)** 49002

❑     Phone: (269) 382-6555, **Web: www.airzoo.org**

❑     Hours: Generally Monday-Saturday 10:00am-5:00pm (later in warmer months). Sunday Noon-6:00pm.

❑     Admission: $19.50 adult, $17.50 senior (60+), $15.50 child (6-15). Active and retired military receive a 20% discount for family. Prices include all rides, theaters, simulators and admission to both the Air Zoo and the Flight Education Research Center.

❑     Miscellaneous: Kids Korner - Designed for the littlest aviator, this play area is suitable for children from one to five years of age. This area features four arcade-style rides along with various aviation-related toddler toys. Gift shop. Theater (old war movies)

The new 106,000-square-foot Air Zoo features aircraft exhibits, flight simulators and indoor amusement rides. "It's a land of lions and tigers and bears" – it's an Air Zoo! Enter the world of imaginative and colorful aircraft with names like Tin Goose... Gooney Bird... Flying Tiger and the "cats", Wildcat... Hellcat... Bearcat... Tigercat...and Tomcat. What a great way to intrigue those little guys who don't find aircraft museums amusing...until now. Let your kids try to count the number of different "species" represented. "Would-be aviators" can try a virtual reality ride as a family in a flight simulator (tilt, turns, even engine and wind noise) or cockpit cutaways where you can press, pull and push levers and buttons. Some productions are in a 4-D theatre.

MICHIGAN SPACE AND SCIENCE CENTER - *(due to open sometime in late 2006 or 2007)*. Inside see satellites (something you don't see at many museums), spacesuits, a moon rock, a lunar surveyor, and black holes. Be sure to check out these, too: the plans call for over 75 interactives versus the 10 that were in the old building. It will be a full-fledged science center based on spaceflight. It will have all of the old artifacts and exhibits, including the Mars rover, Space Capsule (climb in), plus many new ones. Get to "kid-power" a rocket and learn why an airplane can't fly in space! The centerpiece will be The Apollo 9 capsule, flown in earth orbit by Jackson area natives James McDivitt, David Scott and Russell Schweickert.

## CORNWELL'S TURKEYVILLE USA

**Marshall** - *18935 15 ½ Mile Road (I-94 to I-69 exit 42), 49068. Phone: (269) 781-4293 or (800) 28-4315. www.turkeyville.com. Hours: Daily 11:00am-8:00pm. (April-October) 11:00am-7:00pm (November-March).* You're invited to the County Fair by Grandma and Grandpa Cornwell where tradition starts with farm-raised, preservative-free turkey. Choose from fun menu items (all contain turkey!) like "Sloppy Tom" barbecue sandwich or "Buttered Tom" cold sandwich. Also Ice Cream Parlour, General Store and Country Junction bakery for dessert. Dinner Theatre with productions like "South Pacific" and "Christmas Memories". Call or visit website for schedule. If your kids need to use restrooms, make sure they know the difference between "Toms" and "Hens".

## YANKEE SPRINGS RECREATION AREA

**Middleville** - *2104 Gun Lake Road (US-131, exit 61. East on A-42), 49333. www.michigandnr.com/parksandtrails/parklist.asp. Phone: (269) 795-9081. Admission: $6.00-$8.00 per vehicle.* Yankee Springs Recreation Area was once the hunting grounds of the Algonquin Indians and the famous Chieftain, Chief Noonday. The site of Yankee Springs was established in 1835 and the village was made famous by Yankee Bill Lewis who owned and operated a hotel along the stagecoach run from Kalamazoo to Grand Rapids. Camping/cabins, hiking trails, boating, fishing, swimming, bicycle trails, and winter sports.

## BITTERSWEET SKI AREA

**Otsego** - *600 River Road. 49078. Phone: (269) 694-2032.* **Web:** *www.skibittersweet.com. Hours: Daily (December-March).* 16 runs. Night skiing, lessons, rentals. Food service available.

## MOUNT BALDHEAD

**Saugatuck** - *(by the river near Oval Beach), 49453.* Climb the 279 steps and you'll be rewarded with a great view this huge dune and Lake Michigan.

# SAUGATUCK DUNE RIDES

Blue Star Highway (A2) (I-196 exit 41southwest)

### Saugatuck 49453

❑   Phone: (269) 857-2253, **Web: www.saugatuckduneride.com**
❑   Hours: Monday-Saturday 10:00am-5:30pm, Sunday Noon-5:30pm (May-September). Open until 7:30 (July & August). Weekends only (October)
❑   Admission: $14.50 adult, $9.50 child (3-10).
❑   Tours last 35 minutes.

A calm, relaxing dune ride - NOT! An amusement thrill ride is more like it! The scenic ride on 20-passenger dune schooners (with airplane tires for "flying") goes over dunes between Lake Michigan and Goshorn Lake. On a clear day, you'll get a view of the coastline from a tall peak, speed through woodlands and maybe get a view of the lost city of Singapore - an old lumber town left as a ghost town. The trip is well worth the money and very entertaining. Our driver was hilarious and there were dozens of comical signs along the way like "Bridge Out" or "Men Working". Meet the family of beech trees and the tree shaped just like the number four. Ladies, be prepared for a new hairdo by the end of your trip. They only go 35 mph but it's enough to give you butterflies every now and then. It may frighten small pre-school children - unless they love kiddie roller coasters.

## STAR OF SAUGATUCK

**Saugatuck** - *716 Water Street (off I-196), 49453. Phone: (269) 857-4261. Web: www.saugatuckboatcruises.com. Hours: Leaves daily, every 2 hours beginning at 11:00am. Last trip departs at 8:00pm. (Memorial Day - Labor Day). Weekends in October. Admission: $8.00-$14.00 (age 3+).* A 90 minute scenic cruise on the Kalamazoo River. One of the many sights you'll see is "Singapore", the lumbering ghost town buried under the dunes. The 67 foot paddlewheeler offers 2 decks, live narration, and can seat 150+ passengers per trip.

## GRAND MERE STATE PARK

**Sawyer** - *12032 Red Arrow Highway (I-94, exit 22 west), 49125. Web: www.michigandnr.com/parksandtrails/parklist.asp. Phone: (269) 426-4013. Admission: $6.00-$8.00 per vehicle.* Great sand dunes and over a mile of shoreline on Lake Michigan. Natural area behind dunes with 3 lakes. No camping. Warren Dunes State Park is also here (see separate listing below).

## WARREN DUNES STATE PARK

**Sawyer** - *12032 Red Arrow Highway (I-94 exit 16 south), 49125. Web: www.michigandnr.com/parksandtrails/parklist.asp. Phone: (269) 426-4013. Admission: $6.00-$8.00 per vehicle.* The highlight is obvious - over 2 miles of Lake Michigan shoreline complete with sandy/grassy dunes. The dunes are always changing, so each visitor is greeted by a different formation on each visit. If it's a windy day, you can almost hear the sand sing (or some say, squeak). The park has 2½ miles of shoreline, 6 miles of hiking trails and is open year-round. Also featured are hundreds of modern campsites, cabins, hiking, swimming and winter sports. Grand Mere State Park is also here and administered by Warren Dunes.

## DR. LIBERTY HYDE BAILEY MUSEUM

**South Haven** - *903 Bailey Avenue (off Blue Star Hwy. & Aylworth Avenue on Bailey Avenue), 49090. Phone: (269) 637-3251 or (269) 637-3141. Web: http://lhbm.south-haven.com/. Hours: Thursday-Monday 1:00-5:00pm. Weekends only (January & February).*

*Donations accepted.* The Museum marks the birthplace of world-famous botanist and horticulturist, Liberty Hyde Bailey. He designed the first horticultural laboratory building at Michigan Agricultural College (now Michigan State). You'll find lots of Bailey family artifacts.

## KAL-HAVEN TRAIL STATE PARK

**South Haven** - *23960 Ruggles Road (I-96, exit 22 west), 49090. Web: www.michigandnr.com/parksandtrails/parklist.asp. Phone: (269) 637-2788.* Journey onto the 34-mile crushed limestone path connecting South Haven and Kalamazoo. The trail wanders past farm lands, through wooded areas, and over streams and rivers. Along the way, see a camelback and covered bridge.

## MICHIGAN MARITIME MUSEUM

260 Dyckman Avenue (I-196 exit 20 west on the banks of the Black River), **South Haven** 49090

- ❑ Phone: (269) 637-8078 or (800) 747-3810.
  **Web: www.michiganmaritimemuseum.org**
- ❑ Hours: Monday-Saturday 10.00am-5:00pm. Sunday Noon-5:00 pm. Closed Tuesday Labor Day-Memorial Day. Closed Christmas and Easter.
- ❑ Admission: $6.00 adult, $5.00child (5-12), $22.00 family. Includes Museum and Tall Ship boarding.
- ❑ Miscellaneous: Boardwalk, museum shop.

This Great Lakes maritime history showcase tells stories of vessels that passed through these waters and the people who built them. They have displays featuring lumber ships, luxury steamboats, Native Americans, fur traders, and settlers. A kids' favorite is the US Lifesaving Service and Coast Guard Exhibit. See actual full-size rescue boats and stations. The Boat Shed allows visitors to see and ask questions about actual boats being constructed. The replica of Friends Good Will, a 19th Century sloop that served both American and British Navies in the War of 1812, is used as a floating classroom and tourist attraction. The ship was built in Detroit in 1811 as a merchant vessel, but later commandeered to haul military supplies in the War of 1812. It was later captured by the Royal British Navy and recaptured by the Americans. The 56-foot replica sloop is licensed to carry 28 passengers and a crew of four. The ship helps teach students about Great Lakes history and passes on skills such as sailing, navigating and many traditional maritime skills.

## VAN BUREN STATE PARK

**South Haven** - *23960 Ruggels Road (south of town on Blue Star Highway to entrance), 49090. Phone: (269) 637-2788. Web: www.michigandnr.com/parksandtrails/parklist.asp. Admission: $6.00-$8.00 per vehicle.* Their main attraction is the large, duned beach and swimming. A couple hundred campsites and hiking trails, too.

## CURIOSITY KIDS' MUSEUM

415 Lake Blvd. (I-94 exit 27 north, downtown)

**St. Joseph** 49085

- ❏ Phone: (269) 983-CKID, **Web: www.curiouskidsmuseum.org**
- ❏ Hours: Wednesday-Saturday 10:00am-5:00pm, Sunday Noon-5:00pm. (Extended summer hours - open Mondays and Tuesday also). Closed major holidays and two weeks in September.
- ❏ Admission: $4.00 general (age 1+). Summer rate $5.00 (June-August).

This fun place has hands-on learning and curiosity building exhibits. From Geo Kids & the Global Child to Dinomania, a TV studio or Bubbles…each exhibit has costumes to wear that match the type of activity. Serve customers in a diner or pick apples from trees, then process them and sell apple products at the market. A really cool room-sized space exhibit features a rocket with a NASA blast-off launch game, a mars rover table with mars surface, virtual planets to visit, a moon surface with extending arm for rock pickup, rocket propulsion blast off, and a mission control center to other areas of the museum. The "Ship" exhibit lets kids try their hand at navigating Great Lakes waters as a captain or pirate. Use coast guard signal flags, machines to load gear, and even build your own fish computer game. What fun!

## *SILVER BEACH COUNTY PARK*

410 Vine Street & Lake Street (St. Joseph Train Station below the bluff) **St. Joseph** 49085

❑    Phone: (269) 985-9000 restaurant or (269) 982-0533  beach

**Web: www.berriencounty.org/parks/**

Silver Beach is below the bluff in downtown St. Joseph on Lake Street. It has a large parking lot, men's and women's bathhouses, park office and visitors' center, bike racks, playground equipment, volleyball nets and 1600-foot beach for swimmers (lifeguard on duty during the summer). Vehicle fee is $5.00-$7.00. Park opens at 5:00am. One of the cleanest family beaches you'll visit.

**SILVER  BEACH  PIZZA**: outside dining, smoke-free inside dining.  410 Vine Street, St. Joseph (269) 983-4743. Daily, Lunch and Dinner. Moderate pricing. Very casual. Located in the train depot 200 yards from Silver Beach. In a historic, and still used, railroad station. Kids love waving at the conductors as they toot their whistles when the trains go by.

## *THREE OAKS SPOKES BICYCLE MUSEUM*

One Oak St. & South Central (old train station), **Three Oaks** 49128

❑    Phone: (269) 756-3361 or (888) 877-2068

**Web: www.applecidercentury.com/museum.htm**

❑    Hours: Daily 9:00am-5:00pm (call ahead on weekdays).

More than two dozen exhibits including an 1860's "boneshaker" to a "monster cruiser" (36 inch balloon tires). It's home to several antique and classic bicycles, information on the history of cycling, history of the city of Three Oaks, and railroad equipment, including a replica of the telegraph room that formerly occupied the train station. The tracks alongside the museum are still in service for Amtrak passenger trains. Available at the museum are maps of 12 area bike routes.

# Chapter 7
## *Upper East Area*

# Our Favorites...

* Pictured Rocks - Munising

* Great Lakes Shipwreck Museum - Paradise

* Tahquamenon Falls - Paradise

* Museum of Ojibwa Culture - St. Ignace

* Soo Locks & Boat Tours - Sault Ste. Marie

*Huge Freighters At Work...*

## *DELTA COUNTY HISTORICAL MUSEUM AND LIGHTHOUSE*

(Ludington Park, the east end of Ludington Street)

**Escanaba** 49829

❑     Phone: (906) 786-3428 or (906) 786-3763
      **Web: www.cr.nps.gov/maritime/light/escanaba.htm**
❑     Hours: Daily 11:00am-7:00pm (June-Labor Day).
❑     Admission: $1.00 for lighthouse entrance, otherwise free.

Chronicles the development of the Upper Peninsula and Delta County, especially logging, railroads and shipping industries. An unusual display of a 1905 motor launch powered by only a one-cylinder engine is there also. Most folks make a point to go nearby to the restored 1867 Sandpoint Lighthouse. The keeper's house is furnished in period with winding stairs leading to the lighthouse tower's observation deck.

## *HIAWATHA NATIONAL FOREST*

2727 North Lincoln Road (shorelines on lakes Huron, Michigan and Superior), **Escanaba** 49829

❑     Phone: (906) 786-4062, **Web: www.fs.fed.us/r9/hiawatha**
❑     Hours: Daily, open 24 hours.
❑     Miscellaneous: Point Iroquois Lighthouse & Maritime Museum, Sault Ste. Marie (906-437-5272).

The forest manages two uninhabited islands, Round and Government Islands which are accessible by boat. Boating and other outdoor activities are allowed on Government Island. On the northern tip of the forest is the Grand Island National Recreation Area and Pictured Rocks National Lakeshore. Fishing for bass, pike, trout and walleye are good. Cross-country skiing and snowmobiling, camping, canoeing, hiking or bicycling trails, and swimming are available. There is a visitor's center (Munising, open business hours, daily) and cabin rentals too. Near Munising are the Bay Furnace ruins, the remains of an 1870's iron furnace.

## FAYETTE STATE HISTORIC PARK (GHOST TOWN)

13700  13.25 Lane (US-2 to M-183 south), **Garden** 49835

❑     Phone: (906) 644-2603

     **Web: www.sos.state.mi.us/history/museum/musefaye/index.html**

❑     Hours: Daily 9:00am-5:00pm (mid-May to mid-October). Longer
     evening hours in the summer.

❑     Admission: $6.00-$8.00 per vehicle.

Travel back in time over 100 years as you walk around a preserved
industrial community. The Visitor's Center has a scale model of
the city when it was buzzing and info on hiking trails around the
complex. See docks where schooners tramped and mostly
reconstructed iron furnaces and kilns along with support buildings
for the then, booming, industry. Best to visit for guided tours in the
summertime. Camping, boating, fishing, swimming, and winter
sports are also available.

## MICHIHISTRIGAN MINI-GOLF

US 2 (Halfway between SR 77 and SR 117), **Gould City** 49838

❑     Phone: (800) 924-8873

❑     Hours: (Late May - late September)

❑     Admission: $4.00/round.

Locals and visitors stay at cabins and campgrounds on the
premises plus eat at the restaurant full of Michigan pride. By
accident, the owners "threw" clay creating forms looking like the
Upper and Lower Peninsula of Michigan. Using aerial photos of
the state, they built a scale model of Michigan covering many
acres. Each hole is a different important town. After 18 holes, fish
the stocked "Great Lakes" around the course. Snowmobile in the
winter right from your cabin. This is one-of-a-kind!

## INDIAN LAKE STATE PARK

**Manistique** - *CR-442 West, 49854. Phone: (906) 341-2355. **Web:**
www.michigandnr.com/parksandtrails/parklist.asp.     Admission:
$6.00-$8.00 per vehicle.* Located on Indian Lake, the 4th largest
inland lake in the Upper Peninsula. It is 6 miles long and 3 miles

wide. The lake was once called M'O'Nistique Lake. According to surveyor records dated 1850, Native Americans lived in log cabins near the outlet of the Lake. Camping/cabins, hiking, boating, fishing, swimming, bicycle trails, and winter sports.

### PALMS BOOK STATE PARK (BIG SPRING)

**Manistique -** *(US 2 to M-149), 49854. Phone: (906) 341-2355. Web: www.michigandnr.com/parksandtrails/parklist.asp. Admission: $6.00-$8.00 per vehicle.* Beaching and boating are the only activities offered (no fishing or camping) but most come to board rafts and float across the wide spring. In the middle of the spring, look below at the huge trout being swished around by the hot springs flowing out from below - and yet the water is kept at 45 degrees constantly. The American Indians call this area "kitch-iti-kipi" or "Mirror of Heaven".

# GRAND ISLAND SHIPWRECK TOURS

### 1204 Commercial Street (M-28 west of town - watch for signs)

### Munising 49862

- ❑  Phone: (906) 387-4477, **Web: www.shipwrecktours.com**
- ❑  Admission: $25.00 adult, $11.00 child (6-12).
- ❑  Tours: (2 hours) @ 10:00am & 1:00pm (June, September, October). 10:00am, 1:00 & 4:00pm (July & August). Weather permitting.

When you realize that there are over 5000 shipwrecks on the bottom of the Great Lakes...it makes you probably wonder...why are you about to get on a boat? Don't worry, today you can safely voyage (and see) the underwater world of Lake Superior. Board Michigan's only glass-bottomed boat for your chance to see 3 of these wrecks. The clarity of the water is amazing and you will actually see an intact 136', 1860's cargo ship...right under your boat! It's a great idea to visit their website for the complete story (and photographs) of each boat that you will see. Also pass by the South Lighthouse and an original settlement on Grand Island.

## *PICTURED ROCKS CRUISES*

(Boats depart from Munising's harbor - downtown)

**Munising 49862**

- ❏  Phone: (906) 387-2379,  **Web: www.picturedrocks.com**
- ❏  Admission: $29.00 adult, $12.00 child (6-12).
- ❏  Tours: Departure times can vary - generally there are 2-7 trips per day (weather permitting). Call or visit website for schedule. (Memorial Day weekend - mid-October)

A picturesque 37-mile (3-hour) tour that takes you as close to the rocks as you can safely get (you can almost touch them). See colorful and majestic formations along Lake Superior's shore, some are sharp pointed and rise over 200 ft. high. The cruise passes points such as Lovers Leap, Grand Portal, Miners Castle and Indian Head. These rock sculptures are described with legend and lore by your captain.

## *PICTURED ROCKS NATIONAL LAKESHORE*

M-28 and CR-H58, **Munising** 49862

- ❏  Phone: (906) 387-3700,  **Web: www.nps.gov/piro**
- ❏  Hours: (Visitor Center) Monday-Saturday, 9:00am-4:30pm. (year-round). Daily with longer hours (mid-May through October)
- ❏  Miscellaneous: Camping, hiking trails, boating, fishing, swimming, winter sports. Michigan Great Outdoor Culture Tour mini-dramas and special talks/tours (summer).

Tens of thousands of acres of wilderness along over 40 miles of Lake Superior where ice-carved rocks resemble familiar shapes. Look for parts of ships or castle turrets. The rocks are also multi-colored from the minerals that seep into the soil. There are several awe-inspiring platform stops (some 200 foot cliffs) like Miners' Castle or Grand Sable Dunes. Rough camping and rugged backpack hiking is popular for those accustomed to it. There's also a Maritime Museum and Au Sable Light Station in the area.

# *GARLYN ZOOLOGICAL PARK*
US 2 (40 minutes west of the Big Mac bridge)
**Naubinway** 49762

- ❑   Phone: (906) 477-1085, **Web: www.garlynzoo.com**
- ❑   Hours: Daily 11:00am-7:00pm (April-October). Saturday & Sunday Only 11:00am-5:00pm (November & March).
- ❑   Admission: $8.00 adult, $7.00 child (4-16), $27.00 family.
- ❑   Miscellaneous: Gift shop

The UP's biggest collection of animals (25+ species) that includes - black bears, white-tail deer, camels, wallabies, reindeer, llamas, cougar and coyote. Grain can be purchased to hand feed many of the animals.

## *MUSKALLONGE LAKE STATE PARK*
**Newberry** - *(CR-407), 49868. Phone: (906) 658-3338. Web: www.michigandnr.com/parksandtrails/parklist.asp. Admission: $6.00-$8.00 per vehicle.* The 217-acre park is situated between the shores of Lake Superior and Muskallonge Lake and the area is well known for its forests, lakes, and streams. Camping, hiking, boating, fishing and swimming.

## *OSWALDS BEAR RANCH*
**Newberry** - *Highway 37 (four miles north on M- 123 to Deer Park Road (H-37), 49868. Phone: (906) 293-3147. Web: www.exploringthenorth.com/oswald/bear.html. Hours: Daily 10:00am-6:00pm (Memorial Day weekend-September). Admission: $10.00 per carload.* Like any proud father, Newberry resident Dean Oswald enjoys sharing the accomplishments of his 23 grown North American Black Bears with visitors. The bears roam freely within their three well maintained natural habitats. Sleeping areas, or "dens", are provided for the animals, as well as plenty of climbable trees and swimming pools. Visitors are able to walk around the entire perimeter of the habitat to view the bears in all areas. While strolling the grounds, Oswald will point to each and list their different personalities, names and even their weight. This is not a drive-thru, it's a walkabout.

## *GREAT LAKES SHIPWRECK MUSEUM*

110 Whitefish Point Road (M-123 north to Whitefish Point Rd. for 11 miles), **Paradise** 49768

❑ Phone: (906) 492-3747 or (877) SHIPWRECK
   **Web: www.shipwreckmuseum.com**

❑ Hours: Daily 10:00am-6:00pm.

❑ Admission: $10.00 adult, $7.50 child (12 & under), $26.00 family.

❑ Miscellaneous: Overnight Accommodations: Relax in comfort in the adaptively restored 1923 Coast Guard Lifeboat Station Crews Quarters offering five themed rooms with queen size beds, a private bath, TV/VCR, and data ports with satellite technology, yet retain all the historic charm of a by-gone era. $125-$150 per room (2 persons to a room).

The working lighthouse and restored keeper's quarters are the oldest on Lake Superior since 1849 and a crucial point on the Lake. Gordon Lightfoot's ballad, "The Wreck of the Edmund Fitzgerald", plays as you view the actual bell recovered from the ship! Displays of ships claimed by Lake Superior's storms include the Invincible 1816, the Independence (story of sailor "The Man Who Never Smiled Again" survivor), and the Edmund Fitzgerald in the 1970's (29 sailors aboard, all perished). See the short film on the history of the Edmund Fitzgerald and the raising of the bell honoring a request by surviving family members to establish a permanent memorial. Also, take the time to tour the Lighthouse Keeper's home to discover how a family survived with little contact with the nearby community. To add to what is already an extremely emotional visit, take a reflective walk out on to the boardwalk and beach of Whitefish Point - the "Graveyard of the Great Lakes" as you watch large freighters fight the turbulent waters. Please make the trip to Whitefish Point to see this...we were very "moved" by this visit!

## *TAHQUAMENON FALLS STATE PARK*

41382 West M-123 (Off SR 123 heading north, then west 5-12 miles. Watch for entrance signs), **Paradise** 49768

❏    Phone: (906) 492-3415 or (800) 44-PARKS
     **Web: www.michigandnr.com/parksandtrails/parklist.asp**
❏    Hours: Daily, Dawn to Dusk.
❏    Admission: $6.00-$8.00 per vehicle.
❏    Miscellaneous: Modern camping near falls or on river. Picnicking. Hiking trails. Fishing. Canoeing. Snowmobiling, snowshoeing, cross-country skiing. Gift shop, snack bar & Camp 33 Gift Shop and Pub at Upper Falls.

This is the land of Longfellow's Hiawatha - "by the rushing Tahquamenaw" Hiawatha built his canoe. On the hiking trails, moose, balk eagles, black bear, coyotes, otter, deer, fox, porcupine, beaver and mink may be occasionally spotted. The short 4/10 of a mile walk out to the Upper Falls reveals one of the largest waterfalls east of the Mississippi. Nearly 50 feet tall and more than 200 feet across, its amber color is a pleasing site. The amber color of the water is not from mud or rust - discover what causes it. The Lower Falls are four miles downstream. They are a series of five smaller falls and rapids cascading around an island. For the best photo-ops, we suggest wide angle lens (or purchase great postcards at the gift shop). May we suggest a stop for a bite to eat at Tahquamenon Pub. The replica 1950 logging camp has two focal points - the beautifully displayed animal skins and the warm fireplace. This is a great place to try UP specialties like whitefish or pasties (pronounced "pass-tees" - so you'll sound like a local!).

## *MUSEUM SHIP VALLEY CAMP*

501 East Water Street (east of the locks - waterfront)

**Sault Ste. Marie** 49783

❏    Phone: (906) 632-3658 or (888) 744-7867
     **Web: www.thevalleycamp.com**
❏    Hours: Daily 10:00am-5:00pm (mid-May to mid-October). Extended hours July -September.
❏    Admission: $9.00 adult, $4.50 child (6-16).

Museum Ship Valley Camp (*cont.*)

Walk-in tours are offered of the 1917 steam powered freighter containing the world's largest Great Lakes maritime museum. Many come to see the Edmund Fitzgerald Exhibit - two lifeboats from the actual boat along with multimedia shows of the tragic event. Several mechanical (dormant) parts of the ship are touchable. A long aquarium is along one wall with marine life found in the area. After seeing the large freighters and their crew go through the locks, kids will love to see an actual ship's pilot house, dining rooms and crew's quarters.

## *RIVER OF HISTORY MUSEUM*

209 East Portage Avenue (1<sup>st</sup> floor of restored Federal Building)

### Sault Ste. Marie 49783

- ❑    Phone: (906) 632-1999
- ❑    Hours: Monday-Saturday 10:00am-5:00pm. Sunday Noon-
      5:00pm (mid-May to mid-October).
- ❑    Admission: $3.00-$5.00 (age 8+).

St. Mary's River history through exhibit galleries of sight and sound. Join the River as she tells her story of the events she has witnessed, people she has met, and changes wrought along her shores and waters. Follow Chippewa Indians to French fur traders to modern industry. The sound of locks and canals being built is one of the audio enhanced exhibits.

## *SOO LOCKS PARK*

Downtown. Portage Avenue (Within view of International Bridge. Follow signs off I-75), **Sault Ste. Marie** 49783

- ❑    Phone: (906) 632-2394
      **Web: www.soolocksvisitorscenter.com**
- ❑    Hours: Daily 10:00am-6:00pm (early-May – mid-October).
- ❑    Admission: FREE
- ❑    Miscellaneous:  Run by the US Army Corp of Engineers. To
      view live pictures of the Soo Locks Visit on their website.
      Theater showing film on history of operations.

The highlights at Soo Locks Park are:

OBSERVATION PLATFORM - 2$^{nd}$ level or Riverside view of the locks. It's unbelievable how actual freight ships move precisely into concrete locks and then are lowered or raised to the level of the next part of the lake. How do they do it? (Learn how…and they do not use pumps). Now the longest in the world, they are still the largest waterway traffic system on earth. A public address system lets visitors know which vessels are coming through the locks and what their size, cargo, nationality and destination are.

WORKING MODEL OF A LOCK (with real water moving a model boat) is inside the museum building and best to watch before outdoor viewing.

Dress appropriately for weather outside because you'll want to watch the large freighters rise up in the water before your eyes!

## *SOO LOCKS BOAT TOURS*

Dock #1: 1157 E. Portage Ave; Dock #2: 515 E. Portage Ave.

**Sault Ste. Marie** 49783

❑     Phone: (906) 632-6301 or (800) 432-6301
      **Web: www.soolocks.com**
❑     Hours: Daily 9:00am 4:30pm (mid-May to mid-October). Later
      hours on summer weekends.
❑     Admission: $19.00 adult, $9.00 child (4-12).

While watching the ships go through the locks and enjoying the park is fun, it's much more thrilling to actually go THROUGH the locks on a ship. On the Soo Locks Tour, you'll be in for a two-hour live narrated excursion that will actually take you through the Locks, right alongside the big freighters. Your tour boat will ride the water as it is raised twenty-one feet, straight up, to the level of Lake Superior. You will then cruise under the International Bridge and railroad bridge before crossing into Canadian waters where you'll see one of Canada's largest steel plants in operation. You will return to the lower harbor through the historic "newly restored" Canadian Lock and cruise past the St. Mary's Rapids.

## TOWER OF HISTORY
### 326 East Portage Avenue (east of the locks)
### Sault Ste. Marie 49783

- ❑   Phone: (906) 632-3658 or (888) 744-7867
  **Web: www.towerofhistory.com**
- ❑   Hours: Daily 10:00am-6:00pm.
- ❑   Admission: $4.00 adult, $2.75 child (6-16).

A 21-story tower offering a panoramic view of the Soo Locks, the St. Mary's River Rapids, and many historical homes. The tower museum has Native American artifacts and a video show depicting the history of the Great Lakes and Sault Ste. Marie. You ride to the top by elevator.

### SENEY NATIONAL WILDLIFE REFUGE

**Seney** - *(M-77, 5 miles south of Seney), 49883. Phone: (906) 586-9851.* **Web: www.exploringthenorth.com/seney/seney.html**. *Hours: Daily 9:00am-5:00pm (mid-May - mid-October). Admission: FREE.* Take the family on a driving journey (7 miles, self-guided, starts at Visitor's Center parking lot) that allows the chance to see wildlife such as: nesting loons, cranes, swans, Canadian geese, bald eagles, deer, and others. An orientation slide show is shown every half hour. This show introduces viewers to the variety of wildlife found on the Refuge, as well as management techniques. The center is complete with a natural history book store and children's touch table. Over 70 miles of trails are also available for your hiking adventures.

## TOONERVILLE TROLLEY & RIVERBOAT RIDE
### Soo Junction Road (North off M-28 - Watch for signs to CR-38)

### Soo Junction 49868

- ❑   Phone: (906) 876-2311 or (888) 778-7246
  **Web: www.destinationmichigan.com/toonerville-trolley.html**
- ❑   Hours: Times vary - call ahead for schedule (mid-June - early October). Train only excursions Tuesday-Saturday (mid-June-August only)

❑    Admission: (Train & Riverboat - 6 ½ hours) $31.50 adult, $15.00 child (6-15). (Train only - 1 ¾ hours) $12.50 adult, $6.25 child (6-15). Kids 5 and under are FREE. Ask about kids FREE family days (train only).

Nearly a day (a 6½ hour tour) awaits you as you journey to see Michigan's largest falls (50' high), The Tahquamenon Falls (see separate listing). Start with a 5 mile, 35 minute narrow gauge rail trip, and then connect with a narrated 21-mile riverboat cruise with lots of chances to see area wildlife. Once the boat docks, take a short walking trip to see the falls. What's really neat is that the falls are undisturbed and really do look like Niagara Falls might have looked to early settlers (smaller, but still very coool!). The train only tour does not go to the Falls.

## *CASTLE ROCK*

Castle Rock Road (I-75 to exit 348), **St. Ignace** 49781

❑    Phone: (906) 643-8268

**Web: www.stignace.com/attractions/castlerock/**

❑    Hours: Daily 9:00am-9:00pm. (early May to mid-October)

See and climb (189 steps) the legendary Castle Rock (a limestone "sea stack" - nearly 200 feet tall) that Native Americans once used as a lookout. Be sure to check out Paul Bunyan and Babe! A great piece of history and what a view for a half dollar! There are lots of Native American gifts in the shop below. This is a difficult climb, aerobically, so take your time and don't plan on carrying the kids up…everyone will have to climb the stairs on their own (you'll feel like "Rocky" when you reach the top)! Don't worry, the walk down is much easier.

## *DEER RANCH*

**St. Ignace** - *1510 US Highway 2 West (US 2, 4 miles west of Big Mac Bridge), 49781. Phone: (906) 643-7760. **Web:** www.deerranch.com/main.cgi. Admission: $4.00 (age 4+).* Gift Shop featuring Deer skin products including many sizes of moccasins. They have a nature trail where you can feed and photograph native Michigan Whitetail Deer and fawns. (May-November)

## *MUSEUM OF OJIBWA CULTURE*

500-566 North State Street (at the north end of the boardwalk, downtown, across from waterfront), **St. Ignace** 49781

❑    Phone: (906) 643-9161

      **Web: www.stignace.com/attractions/ojibwa**

❑    Hours: Daily 11:00am-5:00pm (Memorial weekend - late June and Labor Day-early October). Daily 10:00am-8:00pm, except Sunday open at Noon (Late June-Labor Day).

❑    Admission: $1.00-$2.00 general, $5.00 family.

❑    Miscellaneous: Native American Museum Store. Marquette Mission Park adjacent is supposed site of grave of missionary Father Marquette and also site of archeological discoveries.

The museum is housed in Father Marquette's French Jesuit Mission Church and dedicated to his focus on Ojibwa Indians, the first inhabitants of this region. Learn traditions of the peoples through an 8-minute video presentation that relates the importance of the Ojibwa family, dioramas of an Ojibwa family network, and frequent demonstrations by Native American interpreters (esp. outside in the giant long house or the realistic teepee with weaved bark mats). There is a "kid-sized" longhouse indoors where kids can play, then walk diagonally over to the Interactive Kids Area: felt play, dark boxes, color drawings of Ojibwa symbols or make a paper canoe or scroll stories. The easy to understand descriptions with every display or activity really help you understand their way of life…they often relate it to our modern way of life.

### *MYSTERY SPOT*

**St. Ignace** - *150 Martin Lake Road (US-2 West, 5 miles west of Mackinac Bridge), 49781. Phone: (906) 643-8322. **Web:** www.stignace.com/attractions/mysteryspot/. Hours: Daily 8:00am-9:00pm (mid June - Labor Day). Daily 9:00am-7:00pm (after Labor Day - late October & mid-May to mid-June). Admission: Average $4.00 (age 5+).* O.K. - Illusion or reality? Reality or illusion? That's up for you to decide, but one thing's for sure…you'll sure have fun doing it. See the laws of physics as we know them…and why they don't apply to the "Mystery Spot". The kids will love this science lesson. There's also mini-golf and a maze on the premises.

## *STRAITS STATE PARK*

**St. Ignace** - *720 Church Street (I-75, exit onto US-2 East), 49781.*
*Web: www.michigandnr.com/parksandtrails/Parklist.asp. Phone:*
*(906) 643-8620. Season: March thru October. Admission: $6.00-*
*$8.00 per vehicle.* Great views from an observation platform of the
Mackinac Bridge and the Straits of Mackinac. Camping/mini-
cabins, picnicking, boating, fishing, swimming and winter sports.
A visitor's center highlights Father Marquette exploration in the
area. The Father Marquette National Memorial tells the story of
that 17th-century missionary-explorer and the meeting of French and
Native American cultures deep in the North American wilderness.
Explore the National Memorial and an outdoor interpretive trail.

## *TOTEM VILLAGE*

**St. Ignace** - *1230 US Highway 2 West (US 2, 2 miles west of Big Mac*
*Bridge), 49781. Phone: (989) 643-8888. Hours: Open daily May-*
*October.* They've set this place up for picture taking. For example,
pose your family beside a teepee or next to a giant totem pole. The
focus is on scientifically studied lifestyles of the Indian culture and
significant contributions of Upper Peninsula people. There's a model
of the first American Lake Superior sailing ship, a replica of Fort Fond
du Lac, a Scale model of the first Soo Locks, a trading post, an old-
time sugar camp and live bobcats, foxes & reindeer.

# Chapter 8
# *Upper West Area*

# Our Favorites...

* Copper Harbor Lighthouse

* Copper & Iron Mines

* Michigan Iron Industry

* National & State Parks

* U.P. Children's Museum - Marquette

*A Giant "Copper Rock"*

### *BARAGA STATE PARK*

**Baraga** - *1300 US-41 South, 49908. Phone: (906) 353-6558. Web: www.michigandnr.com/parksandtrails/parklist.asp. Admission: $6.00-$8.00 per vehicle.* Along the Keweenaw Bay offers modern and rough camping, beach with swimming (water doesn't get much above 50 degrees though), boating, fishing, and hiking.

### *BRIMLEY STATE PARK*

**Brimley** - *9200 West 6 Mile Road (I-75, take M-28 west to M-221), 49715. www.michigandnr.com/parksandtrails/parklist.asp. Phone: (906) 248-3422. Admission: $6.00-$8.00 per vehicle.* Brimley State Park provides recreational opportunities along the beautiful shore of Lake Superior's Keewenaw Bay. Available for camping, boating, fishing and swimming.

## *COPPERTOWN USA MUSEUM*

109 Red Jacket Road (2 blocks west of US-41)

**Calumet** 49913

❑  Phone: (906) 337-4354
   **Web: http://uppermichigan.com/coppertown/main.html**
❑  Hours: Monday-Saturday 10:00am-5:00pm (mid-June to mid-October). Sunday 12:30-4:00pm (in July & August).
❑  Admission: $1.00-$3.00 per person.

Michigan's Copper Industry began thousands of years ago when ancient miners chipped away at exposed veins of pure copper with huge hammerstones. Tools and techniques of mining advanced considerably in the centuries that followed and Coppertown's Mining Museum traces the evolution of miners. More than a copper museum, but rather a Visitor's Center (even includes a walk-in, simulated copper mine) for the Keweenaw Peninsula. See how copper mining has evolved from the early Native Americans who mined with stone hammers to the techniques used during the "Copper Rush". Exhibits include: Early Miners, Two Man Drill, Foundry - Casting Metal Products, The Hospital, Sheffield Pump Car and Loading Ore Cars.

## IRON COUNTY MUSEUM

Museum Drive (off M-189 to CR-424), **Caspian** 49915

❑  Phone: (906) 265-2617 **Web: www.ironcountymuseum.com**

❑  Hours: Monday-Saturday & Holidays 9:00am-5:00pm, Sunday
1:00-5:00pm (mid-May to October).

❑  Admission: $2.50-$5.00 (ages 5+).

A historic, educational site that has 20 buildings including pioneers' cabins, a logging camp, train depot, and schoolhouse. The community was built here because of the Caspian Mine (during its peak production, it was the area's largest producer of iron ore). The Headframe, or hoisting building, one of the earliest of its type, has been placed on The National Register of Historic Places. The very rare exhibit is the Monigal Miniature lumber camp, over 80 feet long and reputed to be the "largest in the world." The Mining Halls contain early mining tools and equipment, several glass dioramas showing underground ore bodies, tramming tunnels and mine levels, a memorial to the 562 miners killed, and the development of unions. One of the homes featured was the home of Carrie Jacobs-Bond who was a nationally known composer of the 19<sup>th</sup> Century. Composing over 200 songs, her hits included "I Love You Truly" and "Perfect Day". This success allowed her to become the first female composer to earn a million dollars.

## LAUGHING WHITEFISH FALLS SCENIC SITE

**Cedar River** - *N7670 Highway, M-35, 49813. Phone: (906) 863-9747. Web: www.michigandnr.com/parksandtrails/parklist.asp.* One of the Upper Peninsula's many impressive waterfalls. Picnic area, foot trails, and 3 observation decks overlooking the falls. No camping or services.

## WELLS STATE PARK

**Cedar River** - *N7670 Highway M-35, 49813. Phone: (906) 863-9747. Web: www.michigandnr.com/parksandtrails/parklist.asp. Admission: $6.00-$8.00 per vehicle.* J.W. Wells State Park is located on Green Bay approximately 30 miles south of Escanaba, 25 miles north of Menominee or one mile south of Cedar River. Its

678 acres include a 3 mile shoreline with a beautiful sandy beach for swimming, a large picnic area, campground and rustic cabins that are available to rent year round. There are seven miles of trails to hike in summer and cross-country ski in the winter. Also boating, fishing, and bicycle trails.

### CRAIG LAKE STATE PARK

**Champion** - *(8 miles West of Van Riper State Park - on US-41 / M-28), 49814. www.michigandnr.com/parksandtrails/parklist.asp. Phone: (906) 339-4461.* Craig Lake is a wilderness area (the most remote state park in the system) and access into the park is somewhat of an adventure. Only vehicles with high ground clearance are recommended due to the rocky conditions of the road. But if you're really into "getting away from it all" the park contains six lakes for fishing and a variety of wildlife such as black bear, deer, loons, beaver, and part of the Upper Peninsula moose herd.

### VAN RIPER STATE PARK

**Champion** - *SR 41 (west of town), 49814. Phone: (906) 339-4461. Web: www.michigandnr.com/parksandtrails/parklist.asp. Admission: $6.00-$8.00 per vehicle.* This 1,200 acre park contains one-half mile of frontage on the east end of Lake Michigamme with a fine sand beach. The water temperature is generally moderate - a pleasant change from Lake Superior temperatures. There is also one and one-half miles of frontage on the Peshekee River. Camping, boating, and swimming are here but most come hiking to look for Canadian moose imported to this park by helicopters. Cabins and winter sports are also available.

## COPPER HARBOR LIGHTHOUSE BOAT TOURS

(Copper Harbor Marina, ¼ mile west of Copper Harbor on M-26)

**Copper Harbor** 49918

❑ Phone: (906) 289-4966
   **Web: www.copperharborlighthouse.com**
❑ Admission: $14.00 adult, $9.00 child (12 and under). Children sitting on laps are FREE.

Copper Harbor Lighthouse Boat Tours (*cont.*)

❑   Tours: Narrated, 60-90 minutes. Daily every two hours 10:00am
    - 5:00pm and are subject to weather conditions. (Memorial Day
    to mid-October).

The only way to see the Copper Harbor Lighthouse (which is
actually a part of the Fort Wilkins State Park) is by boat tour.
Once ashore, short walking paths wind you among historic
signposts and shipwreck artifacts. Such items include the keel of
the first shipwreck on Lake Superior, the John Jacob Astor, which
was blown onto the rocky shores of Copper harbor in the fall of
1844 while attempting to deliver supplies to those who would
spend the winter here. You will then tour the original lightkeeper's
dwelling, the oldest remaining lighthouse structure on Lake
Superior, which preceded the 1866 building. Recently renovated
and made into a lighthouse museum, the dwelling features
maritime exhibits including a fourth order Fresnel lens. You can
ask questions or listen to stories from the staff historian while
enjoying interactive exhibits which tell of lighthouse construction
on the Great Lakes. The daily lives of these keepers become real
while walking among the period furnishings and hearing actual
stories of the people who worked in the United States Lighthouse
Service. During this narrated tour, you'll have the chance to not
only see the lighthouse, but also the first real attempts at creating a
copper mine shaft (dates back to the 1840's).

## *DELAWARE COPPER MINE TOUR*

### (12 miles south on US 41), **Copper Harbor** 49918

❑   Phone: (906) 289-4688
    **Web: www.copperharbor.org/site_files/del_mine.html**
❑   Admission: ~$8.00 adult/Half Price child (age 6+).
❑   Tours: Self-guided tours. Daily 10:00am - 5:00pm (September to
    mid-October). Guided tours depart every 20 minutes, Daily 10:00
    am - 6:00 pm. (June-August)

This mid-1800's copper mine offers a 45 minute underground
walking tour. The tour will take you down Shaft No. 1 to the first
level (at a depth of 110 ft.) where you'll see pure veins of copper

exposed. Above ground, take the walking trails to the mine ruins, sawmill, large antique engine display, and train collection featuring "G" scale and 7½" gauge. Stop by the zoo to visit the miniature deer or search the rock piles of souvenir copper. Dress for 45-50 degree F. temperatures.

## *FORT WILKINS HISTORIC STATE PARK*

US-41 East, **Copper Harbor** 49918

❑   Phone: (906) 289-4215

    **Web: www.michigandnr.com/parksandtrails/parklist.asp**

❑   Admission: $6.00-$8.00 per vehicle.

Today, Fort Wilkins is a well-preserved example of mid-19th century army life on the northern frontier. Through Fort Wilkins' exhibits, audiovisual programs and living history interpretation, visitors may explore the daily routine of military service, experience with soldiers' families the hardships of frontier isolation and discover the life ways of another era. Attractions include 19 restored buildings, costumed interpreters, copper mining sites, evening slide programs, camping and picnicking. The fort was built to protect copper miners from local tribes - completely made from wood. The site also includes the Copper Harbor Lighthouse with a restored 1848 lightkeeper's dwelling, 1866 lighthouse, 1933 steel light tower and interpretive trails (see separate listing). The lighthouse is reached by boat.

## *BEWABIC STATE PARK*

**Crystal Falls** - *1933 US-2 West, 49920. Phone: (906) 875-3324. Web: www.michigandnr.com/parksandtrails/parklist.asp. Admission: $6.00-$8.00 per vehicle.* Camping, hiking trails, boating, fishing, and swimming available. Home to virgin woodlands and a wood bridge to the island.

## ADVENTURE COPPER MINE

200 Adventure Road (12 miles east of Ontonagon, off SR38)

### Greenland 49929

- ❑ Phone: (906) 883-3371

  **Web: www.exploringthenorth.com/mine/venture.html**
- ❑ Hours: Daily 9:00am-6:00pm (Memorial Day weekend - end of color season).
- ❑ Tours: Guided one hour, ¼ mile tour. $10.00-$35.00 adult, $6.00-$19.00 child.
- ❑ Miscellaneous: Gift Shop with copper crafts. Camping with hookups. Snowmobiling area and underground tours. A jacket and walking shoes are recommended.

Put on your hard hat for the beginning of your tour ride to the mine entrance. Turn on the miner's light as you follow the path 300 feet underground walking through passages worked by miners over 100 years ago. You'll see large clusters of pure copper with silver threads and quartz and calcite crystals. Look down into open mine shafts that run hundreds of feet into the earth. The second half of your tour, you emerge from the depths of the mine onto an overlook bluff for a great view of the distant hills and valleys.

## MCCLAIN STATE PARK

**Hancock** - *M-203 West, 49930. Phone: (906) 482-0278.* **Web:** *www.michigandnr.com/parksandtrails/parklist.asp.    Admission: $6.00-$8.00 per vehicle.* The sunsets at McLain State Park are spectacular and the view of the lighthouse is magnificent. Camping/cabins, hiking, boating, fishing, swimming and winter sports.

## QUINCY MINE HOIST

201 Royce Road (along US-41 - part of Keeweenaw Peninsula National Park), **Hancock** 49930

- ❑ Phone: (906) 482-5569 or (906) 482-3101

  **Web: www.quincymine.com**
- ❑ Hours: Monday-Saturday 9:30am-5:00pm. Sunday 11:00am-5:00pm (Summer). Shorter hours (mid-May and early September).

- ❑ Admission: (Surface & Underground Tour) $12.50 adult, $7.50 child (6-13). (Surface & Tram Ride) $9.50 adult, $4.50 child (6-13). Senior discounts.
- ❑ Tours: Depart every half hour. Hard hats and warm coats are provided.
- ❑ Miscellaneous: Gift shop. As you can expect, this tour might not be suitable for younger children who don't like dark places, loud noises, etc.

The "hoist" is where all the ore was hauled to the surface, and what you will see is the world's largest. The shaft started in the mid-1800's and operated until the 1960's, eventually reaching a depth of over 10,000 feet! As you can imagine, at this depth it can get quite "hot" (with temperatures averaging over 90 degrees F.). On the outside, you can view the shafthouse which is over 150 feet tall and has hauled millions of pounds of copper to the surface. You can also travel over 2000 feet into the hill to view portions of the mine that were carved during the Civil War era.

## *ISLE ROYALE NATIONAL PARK*

800 East Lakeshore Drive (only accessible by boat or seaplane)

### Houghton 49931

- ❑ Phone: (906) 482-0984, **Web: www.isleroyale.com/isle.htm**
- ❑ Hours: (mid-April to October)
- ❑ Miscellaneous: Isle Royale Queen (906-289-4437) offers summertime boat trips (4 ½ hours) from Copper Harbor and the Ranger III leaves Houghton summer times (6 ½ hours). There's also a seaplane that floats over to the Isle.

The nation's only island national park is where roughed campers (no campfires permitted) or woodsy lodgers (only one on the entire island) gravitate. Backpacking hiking, canoeing, charter fishing trips or sightseeing trips are available. With 99 percent of the island still wilderness, many opt for marked trails like Greenstone, Minong, Mt. Franklin, Mt. Ojibwa, or the Rock Harbor Lighthouse. The trails are about 45 minutes in length along cliffs, paths of fir and wildflowers, and past many moose, wolves and beavers. Try to visit Siskiwit Lake's Ryan Island, the largest island on the largest freshwater lake in the world! For those of that would prefer to enjoy the beauty of Isle Royale in a more civilized manner, the Rock Harbor Lodge provides excellent accommodations. It is located along the picturesque shores of Lake Superior and has both American-plan rooms (meals and lodging inclusive) and charming light-housekeeping units. Other facilities and services available at the Rock Harbor Lodge include a dining-room, snack bar, gift shop, marina, rental boats, motors, and canoes, guided fishing, and sightseeing tours.

### MILLIE MINE BAT CAVE

**Iron Mountain** - *(Just off East A on Park), 49801. Phone: (906) 774-5480.* Batcave…hummm…must be Batman's home right? Well, not really, but this IS the second largest (known in the North America) home for hibernating bats! The mine is 350 feet deep that has several rooms with a consistent temperature of 40 degrees…just perfect for the furry little creatures. You'll find a walking path, benches, and informational plaques. The bats come in for the winter in September and leave in April (if you're not scared…these are wonderful viewing times). There is a "bat cage" preventing humans from entering the depths of the cave but still allowing bats the freedom to move in and out. FREE admission. Always open. Closed during snow months.

## IRON MOUNTAIN IRON MINE

### (US-2 - 9 miles east of Iron Mountain - Look for "Big John!")

### Iron Mountain (Vulcan) 49852

❑    Phone: (906) 563-8077
     **Web: www.ironmountainironmine.com**
❑    Hours: Daily 9:00am-5:00pm (June - mid-October). Tours are 45 minutes long.
❑    Admission: $6.00+ per person (age 6+).

"But Mom and Dad, why do we need a raincoat…it's not raining outside?". Well…you explain as you're buttoning up their raincoats... that it is probably raining INSIDE! Begin your journey by getting dressed properly for it with a raincoat and hardhat. Then you'll take a train ride through tunnels (over ½ mile long) into the mine on the same tracks that the miners used until 1945 (The mine actually produced over 22 million tons of iron ore). As you travel into the mine (over 400 feet deep), your kids will start to see the "rain" inside (the dripping water) and will be glad that they are dressed properly. Learn the drilling methods that were used like "Double Jack" or "Water Liner" and see demonstrations of both.

### BLACK RIVER NATIONAL FOREST SCENIC BYWAY

**Ironwood** - *County Road 513 (US 2/SR 28 to CR 513), 49938. Web: www.byways.org/browse/byways/10780/. Phone: (906) 667-0261.* See the Black River with several beautiful waterfalls. Five waterfalls are 20 to 40 feet high and are named for their characteristics like Sandstone (red rock riverbed), Gorge, and Conglomerate (rock ledges). Paved sidewalks and a kid-friendly swinging bridge, and a pass by Ski Flying Hill (only one in the states) where you might see ski flying (jumping) events (especially late January).

## OTTAWA NATIONAL FOREST

(Almost 1 million acres off US 2), **Ironwood** 49938

❑   Phone: (906) 932-1330 Visitor Center
    **Web: www.fs.fcd.us/r9/ottawa**
❑   Hours: Dawn to dusk.

More than 50,000 acres of the expanse are designated wilderness with barely untouched lakes and trees. With more than 35 waterfalls within the forest, many plan to take the marked trails to catch a view. The 500 lakes and 2000 miles of rivers provide good fishing for trout and salmon. When the ground freezes, many try snowmobiling, ice fishing and cross-country skiing. In Watersmeet there are two facilities - The J.W. Tourney Forest Nursery and Visitors Center (US-2 and US-45). Great Lakes tree seed and stock are supplied here, as well as, exhibits, audiovisual programs and naturalist-led group walks and talks. Camping, hiking, boating and swimming are also available. Lake Gogebic State Park is included as part of the forest.

# DA YOOPERS TOURIST TRAP

490 North Steel Street (US 41)

### Ishpeming 49849

- ❑ Phone: (906) 485-5595, **Web: www.dayoopers.com**
- ❑ Hours: Daily 9:00am-8:00pm (Memorial Day-September). Times vary rest of the year.
- ❑ Admission: FREE

The UP life is "unique" to say the least. When talking to locals, we often heard that one of the greatest things about living up here is that you have time for a hobby (since you can only work 6 months a year). Well, "Da Yoopers" actually started as a singing group that promoted the "uniqueness" of this life around the state. They have fun "poking fun" and you'll see and hear it all at the "tourist trap". Not only can you learn how to really talk like a Yooper... but where else will you ever see a snowmobile that was built for "summer" use, a chainsaw the size of an 18-wheeler (in the Guinness Book...world's largest, really), or the world's largest firing rifle? We agree, be sure to pick up some "Da Yoopers" music before you leave to really get the most from your UP adventure.

## TILDEN OPEN PIT MINE TOURS

**Ishpeming** - *(depart from Ishpeming Chamber of Commerce), 49849. Phone: (906) 486-4841. Admission: $9.00/person. Tours: (Reservations required). Tuesday-Saturday @ Noon (mid-June to mid-August). 3 hour tours. Miscellaneous: For safety reasons no dresses, skirts, open-toed shoes, or children under age 10 are permitted on this tour.* One thing you'll know for sure after completing this tour is that the iron industry in Michigan is still very much a thriving business. We suggest to go to the Michigan Iron Industry Museum (see separate listing) first to see how it WAS mined. Then, see this huge pit (that is over 500 feet deep!) where the iron ore is mined and refined by some of the largest mining equipment in the world. (We really think it would be fun if they painted "Tonka" on the sides of the equipment!)

### *US NATIONAL SKI HALL OF FAME AND MUSEUM*

**Ishpeming** - *(US 41 between Second and Third Streets), 49849. Phone: (906) 485-6323.* **Web: http://skihall.com/www/home.php.** *Hours: Monday-Saturday 10:00am-5:00pm. Admission: $1.00-$3.00 (age 10+).* Watch an 18 minute orientation tape, then explore the gallery of greats of American skiing. Also study the development of the sport through trophies, photos, old grooming equipment and a cable car.

## *HOUGHTON COUNTY HISTORICAL MUSEUM CAMPUS*

5500 State Route 26 (after crossing the Portage Lake Lift bridge, head north on M-26), **Lake Linden** 49945

❑   Phone: (906) 296-4121, **Web: www.habitant.org/houghton**
❑   Hours: Monday-Saturday 10:00am-4:30pm, Sunday Noon-4:00pm (June-September).
❑   Admission: $3.00-$5.00.

Eight historic buildings including themes of a Country Kitchen, Grandma's Room, Medicinal, Mining Room and Forestry Room. Kids will like trying to figure out what "bull ladle", "fanny", or "kibble" are. There's also a schoolhouse, log cabin, tool shop, church, railroad depot and Copperland sculptures.

### *LAKE GOGEBIC STATE PARK*

**Marenisco** - *N9995 State Highway M-64 (M-64 between US-2 and M-28), 49947.* **www.michigandnr.com/parksandtrails/parklist.asp.** *Phone: (906) 842-3341. Admission: $6.00-$8.00 per vehicle.* Enjoy shaded, waterfront camping on the shore of Lake Gogebic, the largest inland lake in the Upper Peninsula. Sandy beach, picnic area, boating, fishing.

### *MARQUETTE COUNTY HISTORICAL MUSEUM*

**Marquette** - *213 North Front Street, 49855. Phone: (906) 226-3571.* **Web: www.marquettecohistory.org.** *Hours: Monday-Friday 10:00am-5:00pm. Summer Saturdays. Closed holidays. Admission: $1.00-$3.00 (over 12).* A pioneer focus on mining and lumbering with changing exhibits of artifacts. Some of the highlights include a Native American diorama, a fur trading post, an antique gun collection, and fully furnished dollhouses. William Austin Burt, inventor, legislator, land surveyor and millwright, patented the Solar Compass in 1836. This compass was used to set meridian (north-south) lines in federal land surveys - helping to build many mills in the UP. Loads of rooms are filled with colorful artifacts and stories that bring local history to life…with ease.

## MARQUETTE MARITIME MUSEUM

(East Ridge and Lakeshore Blvd.), **Marquette** 49855

❑   Phone: (906) 226-2006, **Web: www.mqtmaritimemuseum.com**
❑   Hours: Daily 10:00am-5:00 pm (day after Memorial Day-
     September).
❑   Admission: General $3.00 (over 12 only).
❑   Tours: Nearby Marquette Harbor Lighthouse. The lighthouse is
     the oldest significant structure in the city and more importantly,
     the lighthouse is one of the most historic navigation beacons on
     Lake Superior and critical to the development of the Great Lakes
     iron ore trade. The Museum offers tours through the lighthouse
     and grounds.

Marquette and Lake Superior maritime heritage with antique charts, boats and models. It preserves the unique romance, glamour, and history of the days when topsail schooners, Mackinac boats, fur trading canoes, work-a-day fish tugs, lumber hookers, and mighty steam barges plied the lakes. Children love the hands-on exhibits and recreated dockside offices of a commercial fishing and passenger freight companies. Ever seen a fishing shanty kids?

## MARQUETTE MOUNTAIN SKI AREA

**Marquette** - *4501 County Road 553, 49855. Phone: (800) 944-SNOW.* **Web: www.marquettemountain.com**. 8 runs, rental equipment, babysitting, and lessons are available. Great children's programs for all skill levels. Also now offering, Ski-by-the-hour rates as low as $4.00/hour (2-hour minimum), and Sunday Family Days.

## PRESQUE ISLE PARK

**Marquette** - *Lakeshore Blvd, 49855. Phone: (906) 228-0461 or (800) 544-4321. Hours: Daily 7:00am-11:00pm.* A beautiful 300+ acre park that is located on a rock peninsula on Lake Superior. Some interesting trivia..."Presque Isle" means "almost an island". As you can imagine, the views are incredible with many lookouts, nature trails along bogs (in winter they are cross-country skiing or snowshoeing trails), and picnic facilities. An outdoor pool and waterslide (160') are also available (FREE admission) in the summer.

## UPPER PENINSULA CHILDREN'S MUSEUM

### 123 West Baraga Avenue, **Marquette** 49855

- ❑ Phone: (906) 226-3911, **Web: www.upcmkids.org**
- ❑ Hours: Monday-Wednesday & Saturday 10:00am-6:00pm. Thursday 10:00-7:30pm. Friday 10:00am-8:00pm. Sunday Noon-5:00pm.
- ❑ Admission: $4.50 adult, $3.50 child (2-17).

A very family friendly place that features exhibits that were suggested by local area kids. Some of the fun programs available (subject to change) include:

WHERE'S YOUR WATER? Crawl through the drain field and into an aquifer to explore life under a pond. Upon your return to the "real world", use microscopes and computers to examine water elements first hand. Touch tank. WONDER GROUND gives you a glimpse of the underground by digging. ALL ABOARD! RECYCLO-TORIUM, a fun filled creation station filled with different "stuff" to take apart, reassemble and just plain create. In the INCREDIBLE JOURNEY walk thru giant-size parts of the body.

## MICHIGAN IRON INDUSTRY MUSEUM
73 Forge Road (on Forge Road off County Road 492)
### Negaunee 49866
❑    Phone: (906) 475-7857, **Web: www.michigan.gov/hal**
❑    Hours: Daily 9:30am-4:30pm (May to mid-October).

The theme is set for this museum with the "step back in time" approach. Today, the museum tells the story of Michigan's three iron ranges and the people who worked them, through museum exhibits, audio visual programs, and outdoor interpretive trails. Walk on paths that wind you through a forest that gives you a sense of what the UP was like when it was still undeveloped. It's really neat to see how things in this region were changed (both below and above ground) by observing interesting time-line exhibits. The kids have several hands-on exhibits and also get to see a model of the Soo Locks and mining cars and other equipment.

## ONTONAGON COUNTY HISTORICAL MUSEUM
422 River Street, **Ontonagon** 49953
❑    Phone: (906) 884-6165
❑    Hours: Monday-Saturday 9:00am-5:00pm. Closed Saturdays (January-April).
❑    Admission: General $2.00 (over 16)
❑    Miscellaneous: Nearby is Bond Falls and Agate Falls (906) 842-3341…perfect for picnics.

County artifacts displays including photos, logging and mining equipment and Finnish items. Kids are amazed at the replica copper boulder found in 1843 and weighing over 3,700 pounds.

# PORCUPINE MOUNTAINS WILDERNESS STATE PARK

412 South Boundry Road (SR 107 west), **Ontonagon** 49953

❑   Phone: (906) 885-5275
     Web: www.michigandnr.com/parksandtrails/parklist.asp
❑   Admission: $6.00-$8.00 per vehicle.
❑   Miscellaneous: Lookout for black bears and black flies - they
     both love your food. Follow ranger's posted instructions to
     prevent unwanted visitors.

Hiking will be most to your liking here especially along the shore
of Lake of the Clouds or Mirror Lake. Stop in at the wilderness
Visitor Center (open late-May to mid-October, 10:00am - 6:00pm)
for a dramatic multi-image program, shown throughout the day.
The show takes visitors on a tour of the geologic events that
created the Porcupine Mountains, carries them through the
magnificent old-growth forests and considers the values of
Michigan's wilderness heritage. Camping is rough (even in cabins)
but auto campers are permitted at some sites. There's also beaches,
boating, fishing, swimming, and winter sports offered.

## OLD VICTORIA

Victoria Dam (4 miles southwest of town), **Rockland** 49960

❑   Phone: (906) 886-2617
❑   Hours: Daily, 9:00am-6:00pm. (Memorial Day-mid-October)
❑   Admissions: Donations.
❑   Miscellaneous: Picnic areas and hiking trails.

A restored settlement company town that thrived in the late 1800's.
Miners from England came to work the copper mines and built
many small homes, clubs and a barn for living. By the 1920's,
Upper Peninsula mining sharply declined due to low copper prices
and competition from out West. Guided tours explain the history of
the village and its decline.

## TWIN LAKES STATE PARK

**Toivola** - *(M-26 South), 49965. Phone: (906) 288-3321.* ***Web:*** *www.michigandnr.com/parksandtrails/parklist.asp.* Camping/cabins, boating, fishing, swimming and winter sports.

## INDIANHEAD MOUNTAIN SKI AREA

**Wakefield** - *500 Indianhead Road, 49968. Phone: (800) 3-INDIAN.* ***Web: www.indianheadmtn.com.*** A favorite of many Michiganders (state's largest vertical drop of over 600 feet), this resort offers 22 runs, rentals, on-slope lodging, babysitting, and lessons. (mid-November to mid-April).

Chapter 9

# Seasonal & Special Events

# JANUARY

## *TIP-UP TOWN, USA*

**NE - Houghton Lake**. **www.houghtonlakemichigan.net/tip.html**. (800) 248-LAKE. Chilly festival. Ice fishing with tip-up rigs (hence, the name of the town), parade and games such as ice softball, snow mobile racing or snow eating contests. Admission. (last two weekends in January)

## *INTERNATIONAL ICE SCULPTURE SPECTACULAR*

**SE - Plymouth**, Downtown. (I-275 to Ann Arbor Road west to Main Street). **www.wattsupinc.com/piss/Info.html** or (734) 459-6969. Up to 500,000 people walk the streets of downtown Plymouth to gaze at hundreds of blocks of carved ice (each several hundred pounds). Probably more ice to see here than anywhere and they even have a section for kids' make-believe carvings of delightful characters. Cozy shops and restaurants line the streets, plus many food vendors are on hand. Admission. (mid-January week)

## *HUNTER ICE FESTIVAL*

**SW – Niles**. (269) 687-4332. The country's best carvers slide into town to cut 400+ lb. ice blocks into cool sculptures. Face-painting and carnival games, too. FREE. (mid-January weekend)

# JANUARY / FEBRUARY

## *WINTER CARNIVALS/ FESTIVALS*

Things like polar bear dips, skating, snowmen building contests, ice bowling, broomball hockey, sleigh rides, cardboard tobogganing, sled dog races, snow mobile races and plenty of warm food and drink. (late January / early February)

- ❑ **NE – Mackinaw City**. (888) 455-8100. Winterfest. (third weekend)
- ❑ **UE – St. Ignace**. (800) 666-0160. Mackinaw Mush Sled Dog Race, Mackinaw City 300 Snowmobile Race and Battle of the Straits Gumbo Cook-off.
- ❑ **UW – Houghton**. (906) 487-2818. Michigan Tech campus. Early February for 4 days.

*For updates & travel games, visit:* **www.KidsLoveTravel.com**

# FEBRUARY

## *PERCHVILLE USA*

**NE - East Tawas.** (800) 55-TAWAS. Ice and shorelines. Ice fishing contests for all ages, ice demolition derby, all-you-can-eat perch dinners, and the annual Polar Bear Swim where adults cut a giant hole in the frozen bay, jump in and swim. Children's ice/snow games. Admission. (first or second weekend of February)

## *MAGICAL ICE CARVING WEEKEND*

**SW - St. Joseph.** Enjoy magic, entertainment and Ice Carvings throughout town, especially outside cafes around town. (third weekend in February)

## *INTERNATIONAL 500 SNOWMOBILE RACE*

**UE – Sault Ste. Marie.** (906) 635-1500 or **www.i-500.com.** Admission. (first weekend in February)

## *UP 200 SLED-DOG CHAMPIONSHIP*

**UW - Marquette** to **Escanaba** (finish in Mattson Park). (800) 544-4321. Mushers race their teams across 200 miles of the Winter Upper Peninsula. Visitors can race through steaming stacks of pancakes and syrup served throughout the day. (mid-February)

# MARCH

## *MAPLE SUGARING WEEKENDS*

❑   **CE - Midland,** Chippewa Nature Center. (989) 631-0830. With a naturalist along, tour the 1000 acre center, looking for maple sap. Learn how the sap is turned into syrup in the Sugar Shack. Donation admission. (weekends in March)

❑   **CW - Grand Rapids,** Blandford Nature Center, 1715 Hillburn NW, 49504. (616) 453-6192. Observe maple sap being gathered, taken inside the Sugar House, and boiled into maple syrup. Finally it is bottled and available for sampling and purchase. (weekends in March)

❑   **NE – Shepherd.** (989) 828-6486.

Maple Sugaring Weekends (*cont.*)

❑ **SE - Jackson**, Ella Sharp Museum. (517) 787-2320 or **www.ellasharp.org**. Maple tree tapping at a turn-of-the-century farm. Watch sap being processed and help make maple sugar candy. Sheep-shearing demos. (fourth Saturday in March)

❑ **SE – Lansing**, Fenner Nature Center, 2020E Mount Hope. (517) 483-4224. Walk into the woods and watch maple syrup being made. FREE. (mid-March weekend)

❑ **SW – Kalamazoo**, Nature Center. (269) 381-1574 or **www.naturecenter.org**. Visit Maple Grove and old-time sugar house. Pancake brunch. Hike trails to visit pioneer sugar shack. (weekends in March)

### *CLARE IRISH FESTIVAL*

**CW - Clare**. (888) AT-CLARE. Admission charged to some events. Everyone's Irish. Parade, leprechaun contest, Irish stew, music and dancing. (second weekend in March)

### *ST. PATRICK'S DAY PARADES*

❑ **CW - Grand Rapids**, Downtown. (616) 631-6953. Parade with marching bands, clowns, pipers and floats presented by the Ancient Order of Hiberians. (March)

❑ **NW – Manistee**, First Street. (231) 362-3480.

❑ **SE - Ypsilanti**. Travels from the Water Tower to Historic Depot Town. (734) 483-4444. An annual tradition, the parade features authentic costumes and antique autos. (Begins 2:00pm, March 13$^{th}$)

### *POW WOW*

**SE - Ann Arbor**. U of M, Crisler Arena. (734) 647-6999 or **www.umich.edu/~powwow/**. For several decades now, more than 1000 champion Native American singers, dancers, artisans and drummers gather for competitions. Nearly 12,000 people attend this event. Admission charged (last weekend in March)

# APRIL

### *COTTONTAIL EXPRESS*

Bring the family for a fun-filled ride, including treats and children's activities. Admission. (near Easter weekend, usually April)

- ❑  **CW – Coopersville**. Coopersville and Marne Railroad. **www.coopersvilleandmarne.org**.
- ❑  **SE – Walled Lake**. Coe Rail Scenic Train. (248) 960-9440.

### *EASTER EGG HUNTS*

- ❑  **SE - Ann Arbor**, Domino's Farms, (US-23 at Ann Arbor-Plymouth Road east). (734) 930-5032. Come Easter, it's the annual egg hunt when youngsters scour the grounds for plastic eggs that contain candy, stickers, or coupons redeemable for prizes. The Easter Bunny "pops" in and there's also face-painting, hayrides, clowns, and entertainment. (Easter weekend, usually April)
- ❑  **SE – Lansing**, City Parks. (517) 483-4293. Some are at dark by flashlight. Admission.
- ❑  **SW – St. Joseph**, Lake Bluff Park. Egg hunt, Bunny Walk & games.

### *BLOSSOMTIME*

**SW - Benton Harbor & St. Joseph**. **www.blossomtimefestival.org**. (269) 925-6301. 20 plus neighboring Southwest Michigan communities celebrate Michigan's fruit-growing country making pilgrimages into the countryside to see the orchards in bloom. Carnival, youth parade, and the finale Grand Floral Parade with its 100-plus flowered floats and their queens. (last Sunday in April for one week)

### *MAPLE SYRUP FESTIVAL*

**SW - Vermontville**. (517) 726-0394. Michigan's oldest maple-syrup festival. Parade, petting zoo, carnival and maple-sugar treats sold. (last weekend in April)

# MAY

## *ALMA HIGHLAND FESTIVAL AND GAMES*

CE - **Alma**, Alma College, downtown. (989) 463-8979. **www.almahighlandfestival.com**. More than 600 costumed bagpipers and drummers march onto the athletic field for performances and competitions. Dancers perform the sailor's hornpipe and Highland fling. Highland shortbread and briddies (pastries stuffed with ground meat). Competitions include border collie sheep-herding and tossing capers. Admission age 6+. (Memorial Day weekend)

## *FEAST OF THE SAINTE CLAIRE*

CE – **Port Huron**, Pine Grove Park. **www.phmuseum.org**. (810) 982-0891. I-94/I-64 Business Loop into downtown. This feast recreates and demonstrates the four periods of early MI history in the blue Water area. Staying in their historic, time period camps, these re-enactors provide an example of the daily life style of the 18th and 19th century. Lots to look at as you observe the ongoing demos of early American living, cooking, crafts and activities like: Tomahawk Throw, Fife & Drum Show, Colonial Wrestling, Frying Pan toss, Battles, Celtic Dancers, Dulcimer concerts and Highland Games. Feast on authentic colonial style foods like: black pot bean soup in a bread bowl, celtic turkey legs, bread pudding, old-time root beer and corn on the cob. Admission. (Memorial Day Weekend)

## *GREAT LAKES SPORT KITE CHAMPIONSHIPS*

CW - **Grand Haven**, Grand Haven State Park Beach. (800) 303-4097 or **www.mackinawkiteco.com/glskc.htm**. Sponsored by the Mackinaw Kite Company, this event fills the air with brightly colored, high-flying kites everywhere. One of the largest kite festivals in the Nation, you'll find up to 40,000 spectators, pilots flying kites (some craft up to 40 foot long), kite ballet events and lessons for beginners. (3rd long weekend in May)

### TULIP TIME

**CW - Holland**. (800) 822-2770. **www.tuliptime.org**. 8 miles of tulips (6 million red, yellow and pink blooms), Klompen Dancers, fireworks and top entertainment. To start the festival, the town crier bellows "the streets are dirty" and youngsters begin cleaning with brooms and pails. Volksparade is next with the Kinder Parade of 5000 children dressed in costume. There are Dutch treats like pigs in blankets and pastries galore (the Queens Inn Restaurant is open), a Muziekparade and Kinderplasts - music, clowns, puppets, petting zoo, arts & crafts for kids. Admission charged to some events. (begins week before Mother's Day in May)

### GREEKTOWN ARTS FESTIVAL

**SE - Detroit**, Greektown, (Monroe and Beaubien Streets). (877) GREEK-TOWN. Contemporary craftspeople demonstrations offer the public a chance to learn about the artists' ideas, techniques and materials. Also Greektown's famous food. (third weekend in May)

### EAST LANSING ART FESTIVAL

**SE - East Lansing**, Downtown between Abbott and Mac Streets, 48823. **www.ci.east-lansing.mi.us**. (517) 337-1731. Especially for kids are the performing dancers, storytellers, clowns and jugglers. Creative art project areas for kids include face painting and making a contribution to the Chalk Art Mural. Shuttles available from many parking sites nearby. (third weekend in May)

### MICHIGAN PARADE/MICHIGAN WEEK

**SE – Lansing**, downtown. (517) 323-2000. Celebrates events and people from Michigan's rich traditions in agriculture, industry, recreation, education, athletics and government. FREE. (third Saturday in May)

### MAYFAIRE

**SW – Marshall**, Wilder Creek Conservation Club. (269) 382-6120 or **www.mayfaireren.com**. Mayfaire comes complete with its own stone castle. Mayfaire takes place when the weather is similar to that experienced in Olde England. When there was a need for petticoats and all of the lavish garb that lends a truly magical feeling to an event such as this. Laurie's Fault provides excellent music and song and is touted as the "funniest and most amazing show in the past 500 years." Watch as Otto the Sword Swallower makes good on his name. There will also be a Royal Tourney, with one task held each day of the faire. Admission. (last two weekends in May)

# JUNE

### FREE FISHING WEEKEND

**STATEWIDE** - Inland and Great Lakes Waters. (800) 548-2555. All weekend long, all fishing license fees will be waived for resident and nonresident anglers. All fishing regulations will still apply. (second weekend in June)

### MICHIGAN LOG CABIN DAY

**CE – Port Huron** & **Statewide**. Log House at Port Huron Museum. (810) 982-0891, **www.phmuseum.org**. Celebrate with old-fashioned house party & square dance. FREE. (last Sunday in June)

### MICHIGAN SUGAR FESTIVAL

**CE – Sebewaing**. **www.sebewaing.org/SugarFestival.htm**. (800) 35-THUMB. How sweet it is…visit the sugar beet capital of the state for a parade, fireworks, sweet foods and the crowning of the sugar queen. (mid-June)

### LILAC FESTIVAL

**NE - Mackinac Island**. (800) 4-LILACS. Lilacs were first planted by French missionaries a couple of hundred years ago and the bushes still bloom full of white and purple flowers each year. Dancers, famous fudge, Grand Lilac Parade (100+ horses pulling lilac-theme floats with clowns and marching bands. (June)

### NORTHWOOD RENAISSANCE FESTIVAL

**NW – Traverse City**, Interlochen Eagles Arena on US-31/Honor Highway. (231) 885-1540 or **www.northwoodrenfest.com**. Thrill to the unique family entertainment found in Lochenshire, a recreated 16th century village and marketplace. Knights will be jousting and engaging in active games. Unusual wares will be sold. Delicious foods will be served and consumed. Lively music will fill the air as gloriously costumed lords and ladies walk about, interacting and conversing with guests. (three weekends in June)

## NATIONAL STRAWBERRY FESTIVAL

**SE - Belleville**, Wayne County Fairgrounds and downtown, (I-94 Belleville Road exit south into town). (734) 697-3137 or **www.nationalstrawberryfest.com**. If they're ripe, local farms can be visited heading in or out of town (Rowe's or Potter's). The festival draws 100,000 berry lovers, mostly families. A family circus, kids carnival and games, pony rides, and a parade Saturday. (Father's Day Weekend in June)

## INTERNATIONAL FREEDOM FESTIVAL

**SE - Detroit/Windsor**, Detroit Waterfront & Downtown Museums /Windsor Downtown Waterfront. Take the kids over the bridge or through the tunnel to Canada for the carnival rides, Canada's largest parade (July 1), or the Great Bed Race. On the U.S. side you'll find a children's carnival, food fair, tugboat race, international tug-of-war with Windsor, and finally fireworks on July 4th (said to be the largest pyrotechnic show in North America). **www.theparade.org/freedomfest/index.shtml**. (mid-June through July 4th)

## ANNUAL YANKEE DOODLE DAYS

**SE - Grand Ledge**. 517-627-2383 or **www.grandledgemi.com**. Festivities include children's carnival rides, boat cruises on the Princess Laura Riverboat, pig roast, entertainment tent, canoe races, dunk tank, tug of rope contest, duck race, fishing contest, garden club tour, fashion show and battle of the bands. The Yankee Doodle Days parade will be Friday night, Saturday morning and night. Favorite patriotic music and a freedom finale. (last full long weekend in June)

June (*cont.*)

### *MICHIGAN CHALLENGE BALLOONFEST*

**SE - Howell**, Howell High School area, (I-96 exit 133). **www.michiganchallenge.com**. 60,000 or more folks will share space with you watching skydiving, stunt kites, music, fireworks, and spectacular balloon launch flight competitions. There's also a carnival for the kids and bright balloon glows in the evening. Admission by carload ($10.00) or by entire weekend per person (slightly more). (third or fourth weekend in June)

### *CEREAL FEST*

**SW - Battle Creek**, Downtown along Michigan Avenue, (I-94 exit 98B). (800) 397-2240 or (269) 962-2240 or **www.cerealfest.com**. Hours: Thursday parade @ 6:00 pm. Children's activities Saturday 8:00am - Noon (games, FREE samples / literature). Farmers Market, Festival Park. The World's Longest Breakfast Table began in 1956 (celebration was set up for 7,000 people – 14,000 showed up!). They could see it was a hit and so competitors Kellogg's, Post, and Ralston Foods team up each year to serve over 60,000 people. Over 600 volunteers serve complimentary cereals, milk, Tang, Pop Tarts, donuts and Dole bananas on more than 300 tables lining one street. It's really a treat for the whole family and very well organized. We were pleasantly and promptly served within minutes and the variety of food choices was abundant. If you haven't already, be sure to stop by Kellogg's Cereal City USA, just a block away. (second week of June)

# JULY

### *4TH OF JULY CELEBRATIONS*

Independence Day is celebrated with parades, carnivals, entertainment, food and fireworks.

- ❑ **CE - Bay City**. Bay City Fireworks Festival. 888-BAY-TOWN. Three days around the 4th.
- ❑ **CE - Bridgeport**. Valley of Flags, Junction Valley Railroad. (989) 777-3480. Rides through display of flags. Five days around the 4th. **www.jvrailroad.com**.

- ❑  **CE - Flint**. Crossroads Village and Huckleberry Railroad. (800) 648-PARK. Parade through park and American flags everywhere.
- ❑  **CW - Grand Haven** Area. (800) 250-WAVE.
- ❑  **NE - Mackinaw City**, A Frontier Fourth, Historic Mill Creek. (231) 436-4100. 1820's style Independence Day with games, music, sawmill demonstrations, patriotic speeches and reading of the Declaration of Independence.
- ❑  **NE - Mackinac Island**, A Star Spangled Fourth, Fort Mackinac. (231) 436-4100. 1880's celebrations include cannon firings. Admission to Fort.
- ❑  **NE - Mackinac Island**, Old Fashioned Mackinac, Grand Hotel. (800) 33-GRAND.
- ❑  **NW – Boyne City**, Veterans Park. (231) 582-6222.
- ❑  **NW – Cadillac**. (800) 369-3836.
- ❑  **SE - Detroit**. International Freedom Fest. (313) 923-7400. Late June-early July. More than 100 festivals.
- ❑  **SE – Lansing**, Riverfront Park. (517) 483-4277.
- ❑  **SE - Jackson**, Cascade Falls Park. (517) 788-4320.
- ❑  **SW – Hastings**. Charlton Park. Old fashioned 4th of July. **www.charletonpark.org**.
- ❑  **SW - Marshall**, 4th of July Celebration. Cornwell's Turkeyville USA and downtown. (800) 877-5163.
- ❑  **SW - Saint Joseph** Pavilion. Patriotic Pops. (616) 934-7676.

## *RIVERDAYS FESTIVAL*

**CE - Midland**, Chippewassee Park and area surrounding the Tridge. (989) 839-9661. 17th and 18th century voyageurs reenactment, Valley Fife & Drum Corps music and pageantry. Paddlewheel cruises aboard the Princess Laura or get "hands-on" experience paddling the 32 foot canoe. Milk Jug Raft Race, Pancake Breakfast, Dinners, children's activities and concerts. (third weekend in July for 4 days)

July (*cont.*)

### PORT HURON TO MACKINAC RACE

**CE/NE – Port Huron** to **Mackinac**. (800) 852-4242 or **www.byc.com**. Parades, street vendors and the largest fresh water sailing event in the world. Race week starts officially with the International Day Parade on Wednesday. Family activities at the waterfront. (second or third week of July)

### NATIONAL BABY FOOD FESTIVAL

**CW - Fremont**, Downtown. (800) 592-BABY or **http://babyfoodfest.com/**. Five days of baby contests and people acting like baby contests. Try entering a Gerber (headquartered here) baby food eating contest (1st one to down 5 jars wins) or enter a baby in the baby crawl race (imagine what parents hold as prizes to get their babies to move towards the finish line!). A baby food cook-off, top live entertainment, a midway, and 2 downtown parades. (third long weekend in July)

### COAST GUARD FESTIVAL

**CW - Grand Haven**. (888) 207-2434 or **www.ghcgfest.org**. A Coast Guard tradition filled with family entertainment day and night leading up to the final Saturday. Saturday starts with the biggest and best parade in all of West Michigan, a carnival on Main Street, all leading up to the fantastic fireworks late at night. (begins last weekend in July for 10 days)

### MUSKEGON AIR FAIR

**CW - Muskegon**, Muskegon County Airport. (800) 250-WAVE or **www.muskegonairfair.com**. Solo aerobatics, barn-storming Red Baron Squadron and racing ground vehicles, and parachute teams. Michigan's largest Air Show. Admission. (third weekend in July)

### FREE ICE CREAM SOCIAL

**CW - New Era**. Country Dairy. **www.countrydairy.com**. (231) 861-4636. The small town of New Era, population 600, welcomes around 3000 people each year for its annual free ice cream social. The workers at Country Dairy devote the day to greeting their guests with good old-fashioned country hospitality. They offer free tours of their processing plant, hayrides and many children's activities. Of course the main attraction is always the free ice cream tent! Guests are encouraged to try all 17 flavors of premium ice cream that are produced right there on the farm, with milk from their own cows. (first Saturday in July)

## MICHIGAN BROWN TROUT FESTIVAL

**NE - Alpena**, Downtown and Alpena Mall. (800) 4-ALPENA or **www.oweb.com/upnorth/btrout/**. The Great Lakes' longest continuous fishing tournament. Anglers vie for top prizes and all can enjoy Art On the Bay, a Kid's Carnival, Fish Pond, and FREE concerts. (mid-to-end of July)

## ALPENFEST

**NE - Gaylord**, Downtown. (800) 345-8621. The featured activity is a Swiss tradition of the burning of the Boogg - where residents place all their troubles on slips of paper and throw them into a fire. Many parades and the world's largest coffee break. (third week in July)

## AU SABLE RIVER INTERNATIONAL CANOE MARATHON & RIVER FESTIVAL

**NE - Grayling** to **Oscoda**, Downtown and along Au Sable River. (800) 937-8837 or **www.ausablecanoemarathon.org**. Called the world's toughest spectator sport - why? Probably because it's tough to follow canoes by land and a good chunk of the race is through the night until daybreak. Because the kids might only be able to catch the beginning or end of this canoe race, downtown areas are prepared to fill the time with family activities like Youth Canoe Races, Children's Fishing Contest, a Festival Parade and Dance, and a tour of Camp Grayling - the nation's largest National Guard training facility. (last full weekend in July)

## AMON ORCHARDS

**NW – Acme**, 8066 US 31N. (231) 938-9160 or (800) 937-1644 or **www.amonorchards.com**. Cherry and fruit farm with motorized carriage rides through farm and area. (summer)

July (*cont.*)

### LITTLE RIVER BAND OF OTTAWA INDIANS POW-WOW

**NW – Manistee**, Little River Gathering Grounds (US 31 & M22). (231) 723-8288. 300+ tribes are together to display Native American singers, dancers, crafts and food. (first weekend in July)

### NATIONAL FOREST FESTIVAL

**NW - Manistee**, Downtown. **www.manistee.com/~edo/chamber**. (800) 288-2286. Visit the open houses of the Lymon Building and Water Works with local history artifacts, parades, dances, midway, boat parade and fireworks. ($4^{th}$ of July)

### NATIONAL CHERRY FESTIVAL

**NW - Traverse City**. (800) 968-3380 or **www.cherryfestival.org**. Cherry treats, three parades, two air shows, turtle races, band contests, mountain-bike rides, live performances and beach volleyball to begin with. There's also a Very Cherry Luncheon, Cherry Pie Eating Contest, cherry grove tours and fireworks above Grand Traverse Bay. (begins right before/after July $4^{th}$ for eight days)

### ANN ARBOR STREET ART FAIR

**SE - Ann Arbor**, Burton Carillon Tower on North University Ave. (734) 994-5260 or **www.artfair.org**. 1000+ artisans from across the nation set up booths. There are face-painting experts, beginner watercolor stations with try-it easels, Family art activity center, magicians, jugglers, and lots of American and ethnic food. (third long weekend in July)

### MICHIGAN TASTEFEST

**SE - Detroit**, New Center on West Grand Blvd., (between Woodard and the Lodge Freeway). **www.newcenter.com/tastefest/info.htm**. (313) 872-0188. World-wide flavored smorgasbord of food and entertainment, a Kid Zone, walking tours. FREE. (first week on July)

### HOT AIR JUBILEE

**SE - Jackson**, Reynolds Municipal Airport. Launches mornings & evenings, flight demo teams, stunt kites, Kids Kingdom, aircraft displays & carnival. **www.hotairjubilee.com**. (third weekend in July)

## *SALINE CELTIC FESTIVAL*

**SE - Saline**, Mill Pond Park. 48176. **www.salineceltic.org** or (734) 944-2810. A free shuttle to the park brings you Highland athletic competitions, children's activities, thematic reenactments, Celtic music and dancing and food. (second Saturday in July)

## *TEAM US NATIONALS BALLOON CHAMPIONSHIP AND AIR SHOW*

**SW - Battle Creek**. W.K. Kellogg Airport, (I-94 exit Helmer Road). (269) 962-0592 or **www.bcballoons.com**. 200 plus balloons (some shaped like Tony the Tiger, flowers, bears or fruit) take off in competitions, a top-level air show, fireworks choreographed to music, and many ground displays of aircraft. Parking fee. (eight days starting the Saturday before the 4th of July)

## *INTERNATIONAL CHERRY PIT SPITTING CHAMPIONSHIP*

**SW - Eau Claire**, Tree-Mendus Fruit Farm, (East on M-140 on Eureka Road). (612) 782-7101 or **www.treemendus-fruit.com**. The world record is almost 73 feet! Can you compete or do you just want to watch? Playground and petting corral too! (weekend before / after July 4th )

## *GOOD OLD DAYS & KNIGHTS AT THE SILVER LEAF RENAISSANCE FAIRE*

**SW – Kalamazoo**, River Oaks County Park (I-94 exit 85). **www.silverleafrenfaire.org**. Over 100 scheduled events each day, transporting you back to a medieval village, populated by ladies and their knights in shining armor, artisans, sword battles, Celtic tunes, live theatre, peasants, fairies, dragons, merchants, storytellers and peasant-powered rides. Admission. (last three weekends in July)

## *VENETIAN FESTIVAL*

**SW - St. Joseph**, St. Joseph River. **www.venetian.org**. (269) 983-7917. Two parades, one on land, and the other a lighted boat parade on the river. Live entertainment, fireworks, and food fair. (third long weekend in July)

# AUGUST

### SAWMILL DAY

**CE – Port Austin.** Huron City Museum. (on M-25). (989) 428-4123 or **http://huroncitymuseums.com**. Saw and shingle mills operating, music, llama, cart and pony rides, petting zoo, tractor display, food. Fee for activities. (third Saturday in August)

### ANTIQUE TRACTOR AND STEAM ENGINE SHOW

**NE - Alpena.** (800) 4-ALPENA. Return to yesteryear to see a hay press, sawmill, thresher motors, antique chain saws, stone crushers and a shingle mill. Food available. (second weekend in August)

### FOREST FEST

**NE - Grayling**, Hartwick Pines State Park, (I-75 & M-93). (989) 348-2537. Renaissance Forester performance of logging songs, visit by Smoky Bear, displays of DNR fire-fighting equipment, a tree giveaway, pine walks and Logging Museum (second Saturday in August)

### FLAT BELT FESTIVAL, (THE)

**NE - Grayling**, Wellington Farm Park, (I-75 to exit 251). (888) OLD-FARM. Park farmers demonstrate preparations for the upcoming harvest including threshing, blacksmithing, preping tractors, sawmill operations, and mill grinding grain to flour. (last weekend in August)

### IRONWORKERS FESTIVAL

**NE - Mackinaw City**, Mackinac Bridge. Ironworkers from around the world come here annually to test their skills in the column climbing, knot tying, rivot toss and spud throw. The prize is the coveted gold belt buckle. Also a celebration of the building of the Mackinac Bridge in 1957. (800) 666-0160. (second weekend in August)

### AFRICAN WORLD FESTIVAL

**SE - Detroit**, Wright Museum. (313) 494-5800. Sponsored by the Museum of African American History, this outdoor festival features cultural and educational programs, music, global cuisine, and storytellers at the Children's Village. FREE. (third long weekend of August)

## MICHIGAN STATE FAIR

**SE - Detroit**, State Fairgrounds, (Woodward and Eight Mile Road). (313) 369-8250 or **www.michigan.gov/mistatefair**. Open 10:00am - 10:00pm, this fair has a midway, baby animal birthing areas, champion animal contests, fair food, and free concerts daily by nationally famous artists. DNR Pocket Park (world's largest stove), pig races and children's theatre productions. Admission. (last 10 days of August)

## GREAT LAKES FOLK FESTIVAL

**SE – East Lansing**. **www.greatlakesfolkfest.net**. (517) 432-GLFF. Celebrating traditional visual and performing arts with musicians, dancers, craftspeople, storytellers, parades and lots of ethnic food. FREE. (mid-August weekend)

## MICHIGAN RENAISSANCE FESTIVAL

**SE - Holly**, Festival grounds near Mount Holly, (I-75 north exit 106). **www.renaissance-faire.com**. (800) 601-4848. Beginning in mid-August and running for seven weeks, the "Robinhood-ish" woods of Holly take you back to the sixteenth century. See knights in shining armor, strolling minstrels or Henry VIII characters. If you like, your family can dress as a lord or lady. Don't dress the kids too fancy though, all the food served is eaten with only your hands and fingers (ex. Giant turkey legs, cream soups served in bread bowls). Watch a mock jousting tourney, run from the friendly dragon, see jugglers and jesters, listen to storytellers, and best of all, ride on human-powered fair rides (it's hilarious). Admission $6.00-15.00 depending on age. Discount coupons available at area supermarkets. (mid-August weekend for seven weekends through September)

## KALAMAZOO SCOTTISH FESTIVAL

**SW – Kalamazoo**, County Fairgrounds. Ceud Mile Failte – "A Hundred Thousand Welcomes". Ceilidh contests, Celtic fold entertainment all afternoon, a history tent, expanded activities for younger Scots, and an informal pipe band competition. Admission. **www.kalamazooscottishfestival.org/ksf/**. (last Saturday in August)

August (*cont.*)

### NATIONAL BLUEBERRY FESTIVAL

**SW - South Haven**, Lake Michigan shores. (616) 637-5171 or **www.blueberryfestival.com**. Visit the "World's Highbush Blueberry Capital" with every blueberry food concoction, sand-sculpting contests and beach volleyball. (second long weekend in August)

### UPPER PENINSULA STATE FAIR

**UE - Escanaba**, (Fairground - east side of Escanaba – US-2), 49829. (906) 786-4011. All the usual fun is here from tractor pulls, motorcycle racing, live entertainment, great food, and rides for the whole family. Can't you just smell the barbecue? Admission. (mid-August)

# SEPTEMBER / OCTOBER

### GRANDPARENT'S DAY TRAIN

**CE - Bridgeport**, Junction Valley Railroad. (989) 777-3480. **www.jvrailroad.com**. Grandparents Day (Sunday) in September. When accompanied by paying grandchildren, grandparents are given a discount rate. Bring young and old to ride on the largest quarter size railroad in the world. (September)

### DEPNER FARMS CORN MAZE

**CE – Caseville.** (989) 856-4688 or **www.DepnerFarms.com**. The Depner Farms have their corn maze opened each fall on 6 acres. They also have a mini maze for the youngsters. Admission. (Labor Day weekend thru the first weekend in November)

### COUNTRY CORN MAZE

**CE – Corunna**, Country Corn Maze. 450 N. Vernon Road. (989) 743-6899. Three professionally designed and cut mazes to challenge all skill levels. Seasonal produce and pumpkin patch. Admission. (Thursday-Sunday, end of August thru early November)

## BALLOON FEST

**CE - Midland**, Midland County Fairgrounds. (989) 832-0090 or **www.remax-midland-mi.com/balloonfest.cfm**. Third weekend in September, Friday - Sunday. "Lift-off" to the United Way campaign with daily morning launches of 50 or so balloons. "After Glows" both Friday and Saturday nights. Skydiver shows. FREE admission. (mid-September)

## UNCLE JOHN'S CIDER MILL

**CE - St. Johns**, 8614 North US-27. **www.ujcidermill.com**. (989) 224-3686. Apples in September, pumpkins in October. Walk along the nature trail, take a tractor ride tour through the orchards, play in the fun house or check out the petting zoo and train rides. Small admission per activity. Farm store open daily 9:00am-dark, May-December. (Weekends in September and October)

## RED FLANNEL FESTIVAL

**CW - Cedar Springs**, Main Street and Morley Park, downtown, (US-131 exit 104). (616) 696-2662 or (800) 763-3273 Shoppe. **http://redflannelfestival.org/** Lumberjacks and clowns wore them - the original trapdoor red flannels made in this town since the early 1900's. They're still made here (purchase some at Cedar Specialties Store). An historical museum in Morley Park is usually open and features the history of red flannels (ex. Why the trapdoor?). A warning to visitors: be sure to wear red flannel (pajamas, long johns, shirts) as you walk the downtown streets or else the Keystone Cops might arrest you! Lumberjack food served. Parade. There's plenty of red flannel (many still with trapdoors) for yourself or your teddy bear to purchase. They're so adorable on our teddy! On your way up US131, stop for a meal at an authentic diner...Rosie's (M57, exit 101 east, www.rosiesdiner.com). (end of September or beginning of October)

## HONORING OUR ELDERS POW-WOW

**CW – Hart**, Fairgrounds. (800) 870-9786. Traders, dancers, drums and "Entering the Circle" spiritual ceremony. (Labor Day weekend)

September / October (*cont.*)

## FALL FESTIVAL

**CW – Rothbury**, Double JJ Ranch. **www.doublejj.com**. Old-fashioned hayride, pumpkin patch, corn maze, petting farm, Wild West Stunt Shows, cider and craft barn. Admission. (weekends end of September thru October)

## MACKINAW FUDGE FESTIVAL

**NE - Mackinaw City**, Downtown. (800) 666-0160. "Fudgies" from this state and neighboring states and countries come to taste and judge the area's famous fudge. Numerous "fudge-related" events include eating contests (got milk?). (last long weekend in September)

## KNAEBE'S MMMUNCHY KRUNCHY APPLE FARM

**NE - Rogers City**, 2622 Karsten Road, 49779. (989) 734-2567. Saturdays. Watch them press cider, then slurp some along with homemade donuts, apple pies or caramel apples. In October, they have goat and pony rides for kids. (September / October)

## LABOR DAY BRIDGE WALK

**NE - St. Ignace** to **Mackinaw City**. This annual crossing draws an average of 50,000 participant walkers. Starting in St. Ignace, the walkers head south across the Mackinac Bridge to the other side in Mackinaw City. This is the only time civilians are allowed to walk over the bridge. If you complete the 5 mile walk, you'll receive a Bridge Walk Certificate and enjoy a celebration in town. Labor Day. (800) 666-0160. (Labor Day - September)

## PARKER MILL

**SE - Ann Arbor**, 4650 Geddes, (east of US-23). (734) 971-6337. Weekends. FREE admission. This restored 1800's gristmill is one of the country's few remaining completely functional mill and log cabin. Picnicking is recommended. (September / October)

## FESTIVAL OF THE ARTS

SE - **Detroit**, University Cultural Center. (313) 577-5088 or **www.detroitfestival.com**. International arts festival held in a 20-block area and has a gigantic children's fair, street performances and great varieties of food. Admission. (long weekend in mid-September)

## APPLEFEST

SE - **Fenton**, Spicer Orchards, (US-23 to Clyde Road exit). (810) 632-7692 or **www.spicerorchards.com**. Take a hayride out to the orchards for apple picking, pony rides, Victorian Carriage House (storage for 10,000 bushels, a sorting machine, cider mill and shops) highlight this free event (weekends in September and October)

## RIVERFEST

SE - **Lansing**, Riverfront Park. (517) 483-4499. Highlights are the Electric Float Parade, live music performances, children's activities and a great carnival. (Labor Day Weekend)

## APPLE CHARLIE'S ORCHARD AND MILL

SE - **New Boston**, 38035 South Huron Road. (734) 753-9380. Open mid-August to January. Call for seasonal hours. Apples, cider press, petting farm, hayrides and a country store with farm gifts and freshly-made donuts. (September / October)

## PLYMOUTH ORCHARDS AND CIDER MILL

SE - **Plymouth**, 10865 Warren Road, (Ford Road west to Ridge Road, follow signs). **www.plymouthorchards.com**. (734) 455-2290. Petting farm, hayrides to orchards to pick apples, lots of fresh squeezed cider or cinnamon-sugar donuts or caramel apples available to eat there or take home. (September)

## RUBY CIDER MILL AND TREE FARM

SE - **Ruby**, 6567 Imlay City Road, (I-69 west exit 96). (810) 324-2662 or **www.rubyfarmsofmi.com**. A cider mill, carnival rides, wax museum (presidential), a Christmas gift shop, pony & wagon rides, and a petting zoo await you. (Weekends September through October)

September / October (*cont.*)

## ERWIN ORCHARDS & CIDER MILL

**SE – South Lyon**, (888) 824-3377. Wagon rides go to the U-Pick apple orchard, fresh red and yellow raspberry patch, and pumpkin patch. Free hay maze for kids, Nigerian dwarf goats to pet and feed, children's play area, daytime haunted barn and black hole. (daily, daytime September thru early November)

## COUNTRY FAIR WEEKENDS

**SE - Ypsilanti**, Wiard's Orchards, 5565 Merritt Road, (I-94 exit 183 south to Stony Creek south, follow signs. (734) 482-7744. www.wiards.com  Apple orchards, cider mill, fire engine rides, pony rides, wagon rides out to the apple-picking or pumpkin patch areas, face-painting and live entertainment. (September / October)

## JOLLAY ORCHARDS

**SW - Coloma**, 1850 Friday Road, (I-94 exit 39). (269) 468-3075 or **www.jollayorchards.com**. Hayrides through enchanted/ decorated orchards to u-pick apples. Make your own warm caramel apples and bakery with pies baked in a brown paper bag. (September/October weekends)

## FOUR FLAGS AREA APPLE FESTIVAL

**SW – Niles**. (269) 683-8870. Southern Michigan's apple-growing region showcases its harvest with apple-peeling and apple-baking contests. Lots of apple pie, dumplings and doughnuts. Parade, carnival, fireworks and entertainment. (last weekend of September)

## BARBOTT FARMS CORN MAZE

**SW – Stevensville**. (269) 422-2378 or **www.barbott.com**. Come and enjoy the ultimate Corn Maze with animals, hayrides and pumpkin patches along with the corn maze that will delight everyone. Pumpkinville - There you can climb the hay fort, walk the stone labyrinth, take a pit stop at the picnic tables, and pick a pumpkin. Admission. (Labor Day weekend – first week of November)

## MICHINEMACKINONG POW WOW

**UE – St. Ignace**, Hiawatha National Forest / Carp River campground. The Ojibwa people host gathering songs, dances and crafts demos. (800) 338-6660. Admission. (Labor Day Weekend)

# OCTOBER

## FALL HARVEST FESTIVALS

Join the rural farm environments at these locations as you help perform the tasks of harvest and the celebration of bounty. Old-fashioned foods, living history dramas and music. Pumpkins and crafts.

- ❑ **CE – Midland**, Chippewa Nature Center. **www.chippewanaturecenter.com.** (third weekend in September)
- ❑ **CE – Millington**, Parker Orchard. (989) 871-3031 (first weekend in October)
- ❑ **CW – Coopersville**, Farm Museum. (616) 997-8555. Kids crafts, scarecrow decorating, pig roast. Small fee. (first Saturday in October)
- ❑ **CW – Grand Rapids**, Blandford Nature Center. (616) 453-6192. Wagon rides. Fee. (first weekend in October)
- ❑ **CW – Middleville**, Historic Bowen Mills/Pioneer Park. (269) 795-7530. (weekends in September/October)
- ❑ **NE - Alpena**, Jesse Besser Museum. (989) 356-2202. (first Saturday in October)
- ❑ **NE – Levering**, Romanik's Ranch. Re-enactors, corn maze, pumpkin patch. (third long weekend in October)
- ❑ **SE - Dearborn**, Henry Ford Museum & Greenfield Village, 20900 Oakwood Blvd. (313) 271-1620.
- ❑ **SE - Jackson**, Ella Sharp Museum, 3225 Fourth Street. (517) 787-2320. (first Sunday in October)
- ❑ **SW – Berrien Springs**. Historic Courthouse Complex. (269) 471-1202. Admission. (first Saturday in October)
- ❑ **SW – St. Joseph**, downtown. (269) 982-0032. Pumpkin patch, petting zoo, face paint, sawdust scramble and sing-alongs. (second Saturday in October)

October (*cont.*)

### ANDY T'S FARMS

**CE - St. Johns**, 3131 South US-27. (989) 224-7674. Open, daily 9:00am - 8:00pm (April-December). Family fun farm with fresh veggies and fruit (esp. apples and pumpkins), U-pick tours, hayrides, a petting barn, holiday decorations and bakery. (October)

### HILTON'S APPLE ACRES

**CW – Caledonia**, 2893 108th Street. (616) 891-8019. Apple and pumpkin products, u-pick, play barn, hayrides, fall crafts. (weekends in October)

### PUMPKIN TRAIN

**CW - Coopersville**, Coopersville & Marne Railway. (616) 997-7000. Twice a day in the afternoon. Take a train with the Great Pumpkin. On board entertainment and refreshments. Pick your own pumpkin from the giant pile. Admission. (Weekends in October)

### KLACKLE ORCHARDS

**CW – Greenville**, 11466 W. Carson City Road (M59). (616) 754-8632 or **www.klackleorchards.com**. Corn maze, labyrinth, wagon pumpkin rides, elephant rides, inflatable play, u-pick apples/pumpkins, hayrides, pony rides, petting zoo, straw barn fort, kids crafts and music. (weekends in October)

### ORCHARD HILL FARM

**CW – Lowell**, 9896 Cascade Road SE. (616) 868-7229. Pumpkin & apples, play barn, hayrides, fall crafts and u-pick. (weekends in October)

### PUMPKINFEST

**CW - Remus**, 5100 Pierce Road, (south of M-20), 49340. (989) 967-8422. A Centennial Farm with plenty of animals and harvest crops. Country Store with cider, donuts, etc. Swinging Hay ropes, tractors, hayrides to pumpkin field. (Month long in October)

## *GREAT LAKES LIGHTHOUSE FESTIVAL*

**NE - Alpena**, Old and New Presque Isle Lighthouses. (800) 4-ALPENA. Plan to make it annually to tour and climb the famous short & spooky Old Presque Isle Lighthouse or the three times as tall - New Lighthouse. Keeper's quarters are open too. U.S. Coast Guard exhibits recall tales of disasters and valiant rescues. Some Admissions. (mid-October)

## *PUMPKINFEST*

**NE - Grayling**, Wellington Farm Park, (I-75 to exit 251). (888) OLD-FARM or **www.wellingtonfarmpark.org**. Visit the pumpkin patch, watch cider-making,   corn-husking, wood-carving, milling and blacksmithing demos. Punkin Chunkin – catapult pumpkins, corn maze, hayrides. Admission. (weekends in October)

## *APPLE BUTTER FESTIVAL*

**SE – Lansing**, Fenner Nature Center. (517) 483-4224. Tempt your taste buds with fresh cider and apple butter being made right before your eyes. Nature walks. (second or third weekend in October)

## *MICHIGAN PUMPKIN CARRYING CONTEST*

**SW – Charlotte**, Country Mill's Pumpkin Patch. (517) 543-1019 or **www.countrymill.com**. Michigan's only Pumpkin Carrying Contest. Come see how many pumpkins you can carry and earn the title of Pumpkin King or Queen. Load up the contestant and watch them walk 10 feet with as many pumpkins as they can carry in their arms. Keep all the pumpkins you carry. Prizes for highest carrier of the day. Admission for contest entry. (first Sunday in October)

## *THE MAIZE & GOOSE FESTIVAL*

**SW – Fennville**, Crane Farm, 6054 124th Avenue. (269) 561-8651 or **www.cranespiepantry.com**. You're invited to witness the annual migration of Canada Geese. Some 300,000 geese pass through the palate of fall colors in this area. Grand parade, music, games and food, corn maze, hayrides, u-pick. (mid-October long weekend – Festival. September/October - Maize)

# NOVEMBER

### *AMERICA'S THANKSGIVING DAY PARADE*

**SE - Detroit**. (along Woodward Avenue from the Cultural Center to downtown). (313) 923-7400 or **www.theparade.org**. Buy a ticket for a grandstand seat ($15) or rent a room downtown along Woodward or get there early (6:00am) for free space streetside. Signaling the traditional kickoff to the holidays, you'll see floats, marching bands, giant balloon characters, and finally, at the finale, Santa and his sleigh. The parade starts at approximately 9:15am. Hob Nobble Gobble® includes entertainment, thrilling games and magnificent food as the celebration of a "Journey to a New Land!" moves the location of Hob Nobble Gobble® from Cobo Center to The Wintergarden at the Renaissance Center. Also spine-tingling experiences in Adventureland, Boogieland, Playland, Starland, Glamland, Paradeland and all the other lands of Hob Nobble Gobble® (day before Thanksgiving) -(Parade -Thanksgiving Day)

### *AUTUMN HARVEST INDIAN FESTIVAL*

**SE – Detroit (Southfield)**. (248) 398-3400. Families are invited to be part of the Native American customs (music and dance) during this annual event. Feast on buffalo burgers, Indian tacos, fry bread, corn soup and other treats. (second weekend in November) ·

### *SILVER BELLS IN THE CITY*

**SE – Lansing**, downtown. (517) 372-4636. FREE family entertainment featuring an electric light parade, musical entertainment, ice sculptures, horse-drawn wagon rides, performances, admission to downtown cultural institutions and the lighting of Michigan's official holiday tree with fireworks. (third Friday in November)

# NOVEMBER / DECEMBER

## *CHRISTMAS PARADES*

- ❑ **CE – Saginaw**, downtown. (989) 753-9168. (fourth or fifth Saturday in November)
- ❑ **CW – Grand Rapids**, Santa Claus Parade. (616) 954-9409.
- ❑ **NW – Manistee**. (800) 288-2286. Sleighbell Parade with horse-drawn entries. (first weekend in December)
- ❑ **NW – Petoskey**, downtown. (231) 347-4150.
- ❑ **SE – Lansing**, downtown. (517) 372-4636. (Thursday evening before thanksgiving)
- ❑ **SW – Dowagiac**. (269) 782-8212. Horse-drawn carriage, Santa, dancers, music. (first Friday in December)
- ❑ **SW – St. Joseph**, Reindog Holiday Parade. Costumed pets, Santa, carolers and horse-drawn trolley rides. (first Saturday in December)
- ❑ **UW – Sault Ste. Marie**. (800) MI-SAULT. Parade of Lights.

## *CHRISTMAS FANTASYLAND TRAIN RIDE*

**CE - Bridgeport**. Junction Valley Railroad, 7065 Dixie Highway, 48722. (989) 777-3480. 2 mile evening rides through land aglow with 100,000 lights. Travel through Candlestick Trail, Candy Cane Pass, Santa Claus Lane, Soldier Alley, Valley Station Lit Highway, and Railway to Heaven. Elves will guide you to Santa and kids get to decorate their own ornament as a keepsake of their visit. Admission. (weekend evenings after Thanksgiving through the third weekend of December)

## *CHRISTMAS AT CROSSROADS*

**CE - Flint**, Crossroads Village. (800) 648-7275. Over 400,000 lights light up Crossroads Village and trackside displays. (Drive-thru viewing Monday nights in December). Craft demos, train rides, live entertainment in the Opera House, and festive traditional buffets (Sundays). **www.geneseecountyparks.org/crossroadsvillage.htm**. Discounted admission. (Tuesday-Sunday evenings beginning Friday after Thanksgiving)

November / December (*cont.*)

## HOLIDAYS AT THE ZOO

**CE – Saginaw**, Children's Zoo and Celebration Square. (989) 752-6338 or **www.saginawzoo.com**. See Santa and his reindeer along with wolves, bobcat and eagles. Ride the carousel. Lights. Refreshments. Admission. (Friday & Saturday evenings beginning day after Thanksgiving until weekend before Christmas)

## NITE LITES

**CW – Grand Rapids**, Fifth Third Ballpark. Follow the light as you drive through the Whitecaps stadium parking lot. The Great Awakening has lighted trees, reindeer, nativity scene, decorated tunnels and trees. Admission. (week of Thanksgiving until early January for six weeks)

## WAYNE COUNTY LIGHTFEST

**SE – Detroit (Westland)**. Hines and Merriman, (I-96 exit Merriman). (734) 261-1990. Nearly one million lights of arcs and tree-lined straights billed as the Midwest's largest holiday light show. More than 35 displays and a refreshment shelter, gifts, and visits with Santa. Admission $5.00 per car. Runs between (mid-November & January 1 - closed Christmas night).

## WONDERLAND OF LIGHTS

**SE - Lansing**. Potter Park Zoo. **www.potterparkzoo.org**. (517) 702-4730. Thousands of lights create a "Wildlife Wonderland" of unique zoo animal displays. Evenings beginning at dark. Admission. (Thanksgiving through December)

## NITE LITES

**SE - Jackson**, 200 West Ganson Street, Jackson County Fairgrounds, (I-94 exit 139). (800) 245-5282. A one-mile drive with 100,000 lights of "Candyland" (a candy cane treat is included with admission). They even have a drive up animated manger scene. Admission per vehicle ~ $5.00. (Wednesday - Sunday weekly beginning the week of Thanksgiving through Christmas)

# DECEMBER

## *CHRISTMAS OPEN HOUSES*

Museum homes are decorated for the holidays, mostly with Victorian themes. Visits from old Saint Nick, cookies and milk, and teas are offered for kids and parents. A great way to see local history with the focus on old-fashioned toys and festivities instead of, sometimes boring to kids, old artifacts.

- ❑ **CE – Frankenmuth** Historical Museum. (989) 652-9701. (long weekend after Thanksgiving)
- ❑ **CE – Midland**, Dow Gardens. **www.dowgardens.org**. FREE. (first weekend)
- ❑ **CE – Saginaw**, Children's Zoo. **www.saginawzoo.com**. FREE.
- ❑ **CW – Grand Rapids**, Frederik Meijer Gardens. (616) 957-1580.
- ❑ **CW – Grand Rapids**, Public Museum of Grand Rapids. (616) 456-3977. (weekends in December)
- ❑ **CW – Holland**, Cappon House, 228 W. 9th St. (888) 200-9123. (week after Christmas)
- ❑ **SE – Dearborn**, Greenfield Village. **www.thehenryford.org**. (first three weekends in December)
- ❑ **SE – Detroit (Grosse Pointe Shores)**. Edsel & Eleanor Ford House. (313) 884-4222 or **www.fordhouse.org**.
- ❑ **SE – Detroit (Rochester)**, MeadowBrook Hall, 280 South Adams, Oakland University campus. (248) 370-3140. Admission for some activities. (all month-long)
- ❑ **SE - Jackson**, Ella Sharp Museum, 3225 Fourth Street. (517) 787-2320. Admission includes meal.
- ❑ **SW – Berrien Springs**, Courthouse Complex. (269) 471-1202 or **www.berrienhistory.org**. FREE. (second Sunday in December)
- ❑ **SW – Hastings**, Charleton Village. (989) 945-3775. (second weekend in December)

December (*cont.*)

## *HOLIDAY MUSICALS*

Admission charged.

- ❑  **CE – Flint**. The Nutcracker. The Whiting. (888) 8-CENTER.
- ❑  **CW – Grand Rapids**. The Nutcracker. Grand Rapids Ballet, DeVos Hall. (616) 454-4771.
- ❑  **SE – Ann Arbor**. Ann Arbor Symphony Holiday Concert. Michigan Theatre. (734) 994-4801. Holiday music and a family sing-along.
- ❑  **SE – Detroit**. The Nutcracker Ballet - Detroit Opera House. (313) 576-5111. Music supplied by the Detroit Symphony Orchestra.
- ❑  **SE – Detroit (Rochester Hills)**. A Christmas Carol, MeadowBrook Theatre. (248) 370-4902.
- ❑  **SW – Marshall**. A Cornwell Christmas, **www.turkeyville.com**.
- ❑  **SW - Saugatuck**. "A Christmas Carol". (269) 857-1701. After the show, climb aboard a ride in a horse-drawn buggy thru town.

## *LONGWAY PLANETARIUM HOLIDAY SHOWS*

**CE - Flint**. (810) 237-3400 or **www.longway.org**. Friday evenings at 7:30pm, Saturday afternoon and evening, Sunday afternoon throughout December. Night sky shows with traditional and contemporary themes. Admission. (December)

## *SANTA EXPRESS TRAIN RIDES*

Santa and his helpers ride along and play games and sing songs to get everyone in the holiday spirit. Admission.

- ❑  **CW - Coopersville**, Coopersville & Marne Railway. (616) 997-7000. (Saturday mornings, the first three weekends in December)
- ❑  **SE – Walled Lake**, Coe Rail Family Train, 840 N. Pontiac Trail. (248) 960-9440. (departures twice an afternoon on second and third Saturday of December)

## *MUSICAL FOUNTAIN NATIVITY*

**CW - Grand Haven**, Grandstand at Harbor and Washington Streets on the riverfront. (800) 303-4096. A 40 foot nativity scene on Dewey Hill offers evening performances focused on the "spirit" of the holiday. Donations. (Evening performances in December, parade is first Saturday)

### NEW YEAR'S EARLY EVE

**CW – Grand Rapids**, Children's Museum. **www.grcm.org**. Take fun pictures, do a craft, face painting, snacks and juice, dress up and play. Entertainment and a balloon drop at 7:30pm. Admission. (New Years Eve 6:00-8:00pm)

### SANTA PARADE & FLAT RIVER ICE SCULPTURE CHALLENGE

**CW – Lowell**, downtown and fairgrounds. Breakfast with Santa, Parade, Ice Sculpture Contest, entertainment, warm food, and chainsaw sculpture.

### JINGLE BELL JUBILEE & CHRISTMAS VILLAGE

**CW – Rothbury**, Double JJ Resort. (800) 368-2535 or **www.doublejj.com**. Carolers, Holiday lights, sleigh rides, crafts and Santa's workshop. New Year's Eve Parties – Family Snow Tubing or Sundance Adult Party. Admission. (weekend evenings in December)

### KWAANZA

**SE - Detroit**, Museum of African American History, 315 East Warren Avenue. (313) 494-5800. Weeklong during Kwaanza. Kwaanza (first fruits) is an African celebration of the harvest and the fruits of the community's labor. Each day has a special focus: unity, self-determination, collective work and responsibility, cooperative economics, purpose, creativity and faith. (December)

### FIRST NIGHT

First Night is an alcohol-free festival of arts for children and adults. Many booths have kids crafts, storytelling, musical entertainment and dancing, kid-friendly food and a big Midnight celebration. Admission. (December 31 - Beginning mid-day New Year's Eve)

- ❑  **SE - Detroit**, Birmingham Principal Shopping District. (248) 258-9075 or **www.technomasters.com/firstnight**.
- ❑  **SE – Port Huron**. **www.firstnightph.org**
- ❑  **NW – Cadillac**. (231) 775-0654. High School and Middle School.

December (*cont.*)

## *NEW YEAR JUBILEE*

**SE - Ypsilanti**, Depot Town. **www.newyearjubilee.com**. (734) 480-1636. Alcohol-free evening of entertainment and fun for families. More than 45 performances in town churches and buildings. (December - Begins mid-day on New Year's Eve)

## *HOLIDAY BALLOON FEST*

**SW - Battle Creek**, Kellogg's Cereal City USA. Come experience the Holiday Balloon Fest at Kellogg's Cereal City USA with two evening Glittering Balloon glows and four Frosty balloon flights. This is a free family event, dress warm and bring your friends. **www.holidayballoonfest.com**. (first weekend in December)

## *MIDNIGHT AT THE CREEK*

**SW - Battle Creek**, Downtown. (800) 397-2240. Ring in the New Year with a family-oriented evening of activities, storytellers, kid-friendly food and beverage, and musical performances of all different types. (December 31)

## *CHRISTMAS PICKLE FESTIVAL*

**SW - Berrien Springs**, Downtown, I-94 to US-31 south. (616) 471-3116. Do you know about a German tradition at Christmas? The first child to find a glass pickle hidden in the tree gets an extra present! This is the town's inspiration for a holiday parade, street lighting, and pickle tastings. Pickle and non-pickle foods and gifts. Admission. (first week of December)

Master Index

# Activity Index

PROUDLY

MADE IN THE USA

# Travel Journal & Notes:

# GROUP DISCOUNTS &
# FUNDRAISING OPPORTUNITIES!

We're excited to introduce our books to your group! These guides for parents, grandparents, teachers and visitors are great tools to help you discover hundreds of fun places to visit. Our titles are great resources for all the wonderful places to travel either locally or across the region.

We are two parents who have researched, written and published these books. We have spent thousands of hours collecting information and *personally traveled over 250,000 miles* visiting all of the most unique places listed in our guides. The books are kid-tested and the descriptions include great hints on what kids like best!

Please consider the following Group Purchase options: *For the latest information, visit our website:* **www.KidsLoveTravel.com**

❑ **Group Discount/Fundraising** – Purchase books at the discount price of $2.95 off the suggested retail price for members/friends. Minimum order is ten books. You may mix titles to reach the minimum order. Greater discounts (~35%) are available for fundraisers. Minimum order is thirty books. Call for details.

❑ **Available for Interview/Speaking** – The authors have a treasure bag full of souvenirs from favorite places. We'd love to share ideas on planning fun trips to take children while exploring your home state. The authors are available, by appointment, *(based on availability)* at (614) 792-6451 or **michele@kidslovetravel.com**. A modest honorarium or minimum group sale purchase will apply. Call or visit our website for details.

Call us soon at (614) 792-6451 to make arrangements!
*Happy Exploring!*

- **KIDS LOVE GEORGIA** - Explore hidden islands, humbling habitats, and historic gold mines. See playful puppets, dancing dolphins, and comical kangaroos. "Watch out" for cowboys, Indians, and swamp creatures. Over 500 listings in one book about Georgia travel. 6 geographical zones, 272 pages.

- **KIDS LOVE ILLINOIS** – Explore places from Deere to Dinos, discover Giant Cities and the Mighty Mississippi, or cross the prairie to the Lands of Lincoln and Superman . Over 600 listings in one book about Illinois travel. 7 geographical zones, 288 pages.

- **KIDS LOVE INDIANA** - Discover places where you can "co-star" in a cartoon or climb a giant sand dune. Over 500 listings in one book about Indiana travel. 8 geographical zones, 280 pages.

- **KIDS LOVE KENTUCKY** - Discover places from Boone to Burgoo, from Caves to Corvettes, and from Lincoln to the Lands of Horses. Nearly 500 listings in one book about Kentucky travel. 5 geographic zones. 186 pages.

- **KIDS LOVE MICHIGAN** - Discover places where you can "race" over giant sand dunes, climb aboard a lighthouse "ship", eat at the world's largest breakfast table, or watch yummy foods being made. Almost 600 listings in one book about Michigan travel. 8 geographical zones, 264 pages.

- **KIDS LOVE NORTH CAROLINA** - Explore places where you can "discover" gold and pirate history, explore castles and strange houses, or learn of the "lost colony" and Mayberry. Over 500 listings in one book about travel. 6 geographical zones, 288 pages.

- **KIDS LOVE OHIO** - Discover places like hidden castles and caves, puppet and whistle factories, and laboratories of great inventors. Nearly 800 listings in one book about Ohio travel. 8 geographical zones, 288 pages.

- **KIDS LOVE PENNSYLVANIA** - Explore places where you can "discover" oil and coal, meet Ben Franklin, or watch your favorite toys and delicious, fresh snacks being made. Over 900 listings in one book about Pennsylvania travel. 9 geographical zones, 268 pages.

- **KIDS LOVE TENNESSEE** – Explore places where you can "discover" pearls, ride the rails, "meet" Three Kings (of Rights, Rock & Soul). Be inspired to sing listening to the rich traditions of Country music fame. Over 500 listings in one book about Tennessee travel. 6 geographical zones, 235 pages.

- **KIDS LOVE VIRGINIA** – Discover where ponies swim and dolphins dance, dig into archaeology and living history, or be dazzled by natural bridges and tunnels. Over 700 listings in one book about Virginia travel. 5 geographical zones. Includes Washington DC activities. 288 pages.

- **KIDS LOVE FLORIDA** - coming in late 2006. See website for details!

# ORDER FORM

## KIDS LOVE PUBLICATIONS

1985 Dina Court, Powell, Ohio  43065, (614) 792-6451
*For the latest titles, visit our website:* **www.KidsLoveTravel.com**

| # | Title | | Price | Total |
|---|-------|---|-------|-------|
| | Kids Love Georgia | | $14.95 | |
| | Kids Love Illinois | | $14.95 | |
| | Kids Love Indiana | | $14.95 | |
| | Kids Love Kentucky | | $14.95 | |
| | Kids Love Michigan | | $14.95 | |
| | Kids Love North Carolina | | $14.95 | |
| | Kids Love Ohio | | $14.95 | |
| | Kids Love Pennsylvania | | $14.95 | |
| | Kids Love Tennessee | | $14.95 | |
| | Kids Love Virginia | | $14.95 | |
| | Kids Love Travel Memories! | | $14.95 | |
| | **Combo Discount Pricing** | | | |
| | **Combo #2 - Any 2 Books** | | $28.95 | |
| | **Combo #3 - Any 3 Books** | | $37.95 | |
| | **Combo #4 - Any 4 Books** | | $47.95 | |
| | | | **Subtotal** | |

*(Please make check or money order payable to: KIDS LOVE PUBLICATIONS)*

(Ohio Residents Only – Your local rate) **Local/State Sales Tax**

☐ Master Card
☐ Visa

*$2.00 first book $1.00 each additional* **Shipping**

**TOTAL**

Account Number ☐☐☐☐-☐☐☐☐-☐☐☐☐-☐☐☐☐

Exp Date: ☐☐/☐☐ (Month/Year)

Cardholder's Name _____

Signature *(required)* _____

Name: _____

Address: _____

City: _____ State: _____

Zip: _____ Telephone: _____

All orders are generally shipped within 2 business days of receipt by US Mail. If you wish to have your books autographed, please include a legible note with the message you'd like written in your book. Your satisfaction is 100% guaranteed or simply return your order for a prompt refund. Thanks for your order. Happy Exploring!

"Where to go?, What to do?, and How much will it cost?", are all questions that they have heard throughout the years from friends and family. These questions became the inspiration that motivated them to research, write and publish the "Kids Love" travel series.

This adventure of writing and publishing family travel books has taken them on a journey of experiences that they never could have imagined. They have appeared as guests on hundreds of radio and television shows, had featured articles in statewide newspapers and magazines, spoken to thousands of people at schools and conventions, and write monthly columns in many publications talking about "family friendly" places to travel.

George Zavatsky and Michele (Darrall) Zavatsky were raised in the Midwest and have lived in many different cities. They currently reside in a suburb of Columbus, Ohio. They feel very blessed to be able to create their own career that allows them to research, write and publish a series of best-selling kids' travel books. Besides the wonderful adventure of marriage, they place great importance on being loving parents to Jenny & Daniel.